Novels
The Terrible Threes
Reckless Eyeballing
The Terrible Twos
Flight to Canada
The Last Days of Louisiana Red
Mumbo Jumbo
Yellow Back Radio Broke Down
The Free-lance Pall Bearers

Essays
Writin' Is Fightin'
God Made Alaska for the Indians
Shrovetide in Old New Orleans

Poetry
New and Collected Poems (*1988*)
Points of View (*1988*)
A Secretary to the Spirits (*1978*)
Chattanooga (*1974*)
Conjure (*1972*)
Catechism of D Neoamerican Hoodoo Church (*1970*)

Plays
Mother Hubbard, formerly Hell Hath No Fury
The Ace Boons
Savage Wilds

Anthologies
Calafia
19 Necromancers from Now

New and Collected Poems

ISHMAEL REED

New and Collected Poems

ATHENEUM   *New York*   1988

This book includes poems from three previously published collections by Ishmael Reed: *Conjure, Chattanooga,* and *A Secretary to the Spirits.* Many of these poems have appeared in journals and anthologies, and acknowledgment is gratefully made to the editors of *The Berkeley Fiction Review, River Styx, California Living, The Buffalo Evening News, Up Late: American Poetry since 1970, Wind Row, New Letters, Lips, The Berkeley Poetry Review, Black World, Mark in Time, Yardbird Reader, Umbra, Black World, Liberator, Essence, Ikon, Scholastic, For Now, In a Time of Revolution, Where's Vietnam?, Poets of Today, The Poetry of the Negro, 1745–1970, The New Black Poetry, Soulscript, The L.A. Free Press, The Black Poets, Dices,* and *The Norton Anthology of Poetry.*

Some of the material in this book, set to music by leading jazz composers, can be heard on two albums released by Pangaea records: Conjure I and Conjure II (available in LP, cassette and compact disc).

Atheneum
Macmillan Publishing Company
866 Third Avenue, New York, N.Y. 10022

                    Library of Congress Cataloging-in-Publication Data
Reed, Ishmael, 1938–
  [Poems]
  New and collected poems / Ishmael Reed.
    p. cm.
    ISBN 0-689-12003-6
  I. Title
PS3568.E365N49   1988   88-19024
811'.54—dc9   CIP

Macmillan books are available at special discounts for bulk purchases for sales promotions, premiums, fund-raising, or educational use. For details, contact:

                    Special Sales Director
                    Macmillan Publishing Company
                    866 Third Avenue
                    New York, N.Y. 10022

10 9 8 7 6 5 4 3 2 1

Printed in the United States of America

To Carla

I Don't Want To Set the World on Fire;
I Just Want To Light a Flame in Your Heart

Contents

CONJURE

CHATTANOOGA

A SECRETARY TO THE SPIRITS

POINTS OF VIEW

Conjure

The Ghost in Birmingham

The only Holy Ghost in Birmingham is Denmark Vesey's Holy Ghost, brooding, moving in and out of things. No one notices the figure in antique cloak of the last century, haunting the pool games, talking of the weather with a passerby, attending mass meetings, standing guard, coming up behind each wave of protest, reloading a pistol. No one notices the antique figure in shabby clothing, moving in and out of things—rallies of moonshine gatherings—who usurps a pulpit and preaches a fire sermon, plucking the plumage of a furious hawk, a sparrow having passively died, moving in and out of chicken markets, watching sparrow habits become hawk habits, through bar stools and greenless parks, beauty salons, floating games, going somewhere, haranguing the crowds, his sleeves rolled up like a steelworker's, hurling epithets at the pharoah's club-wielding brigade, under orders to hunt down the firstborn of each low lit hearth.

There are no bulls in America in the sense of great symbols, which preside over resuscitation of godheads, that shake the dead land green. Only the "bull" of Birmingham, papier mâché, ten dollars down monthly terms, carbon copy mock heroic American variety of bullhood, who told a crowded room of flashbulbs that there was an outsider moving in and out of things that night, a spectre who flashed through the night like Pentecost.

He's right, there was.

Not the spook of the Judaic mystery, the universal immersed in the particular. Not the outsider from unpopular mysteries, a monstrous dialectic waddling through the corridors of his brain, but the nebulous presence hidden by flashbulbing events in Birmingham, Metempsychosis stroking the air.

Pragma the bitch has a knight errant called Abbadon, in the old texts the advocate of dreadful policies. The whore, her abominations spilling over, her stinking afterbirths sliming their way towards a bay of pigs, has a bland and well-groomed knight errant who said that "if we hand down a few more decisions, pile up paper, snap a few more pictures by Bachrach of famous people before grand rhetorical columns of the doric order, perhaps they will stop coming out into the streets in Raleigh, Greensboro, Jackson and Atlanta (sometimes called the Athens of the south).

Pragma's well-groomed and bland procurer is on long distance
    manufacturing heroes,
Heroes who bray in sirens screaming in from Idlewild, winging in
    from points south,
Their utterances cast into bronze by press-card-carrying harpies,
    those creatures of distorted reality.

O ebony-limbed Osiris, what clown folk singer or acrobat shall I
    place the tin wreath upon?
When will Osiris be scattered over 100 ghettos?

Heroes are ferried in by motorcycle escorts, their faces cast into by
    Pointillism, by Artzybasheff,
Sculptor of Henry Luce's America.

Introducing the King of Birmingham, sometimes called the
    anointed one,
And receives the tin wreath across Americana banquet rooms,
His hands dripping with blood like a fanatical monk as rebellion
    squirms on the stake.

Introducing the Black Caligula, who performs a strip tease of the
    psyche,
Between Tiffany ads and Vat 69, giving up a little pussy for a well-
    groomed and bland knight errant.

O ebony-limbed Osiris, what knight club tap dancing charlatan
    shall I place the tin wreath upon?
All things are flowing said the poet when gods ambushed gods:
    Khan follows Confucius
    Light follows darkness
Tin wreathed heroes are followed by the figure in antique clothes,
    obscured by the flashbulbing events in Birmingham.
Metempsychosis in the air.

The Jackal-Headed Cowboy

We were—clinging to our arboreal—rustled
by a poplin dude so fast that even now
we mistake big mack trucks flying
confederate crossbones for rampaging
steer, leaping into their sandpaper hides
and lassoing their stubble faced drivers as they roar into
corn flaked greasy spoons.

We span the spic and spanned cesspools
nerves rankling like hot headed guerrillas
bayoneting artery routes and crawling through
our bowels with blades in their teeth.

Our mohair suits, our watches, our horn
rimmed glasses and several telephones
petition us to slow down as we forget
whose soupcan we swim.

We stand at Brooklyn Bridge like
mayakovsky before, deafened by the nuts
and bolts and clogged in the comings and
goings of goings of Usura

We are homesick weary travelers in the
jungian sense and miss the brew of the
long night's pipe.

Our dreams point like bushy mavericks to
hawking game and scattering ripple falls.
We will swing from giant cables as if
they were hemp, hacking away at sky
scrapers till they tumble into christmas
crowds.

We will raid chock full O nuts untying
apron strings crouching stealthily in the streets
breaking up conference rooms sweeping away
forms memo pads, ransoming bank presidents
shoving dollar bills through their mahogany
jaws.

We will sit on Empire Sofas listening to
Gabrieli's fortissimo trumpets blare for
stewed and staggering Popes as Tom Tom mallets
beat the base of our brains.
We will leap tall couplets in a single bound
and chant chant Chant until our pudgy swollen
lips go on strike.
Our daughters will shake rattle roll and slop
snapping their fingers until grandfather
clocks' knees buckle and Tudor mansions free
their cobwebs.
Our mothers will sing shout swing and foam
making gothic spires get happy clapping the
night like blown up Zeppelin.

We will sizzle burn crackle and fry like combs
snapping the naps of Henri Christophe's daughters.
and We will scramble breasts bleating like
some tribe run amuck up and down desecrating
cosmotological graveyard factories.
and We will mash stock exchange bugs till
their sticky brown insides spill out like
reams of ticker tape.
and We will drag off yelling pinching bawling
shouting pep pills, detergents, acne powders,
clean rooms untampered maiden heads finger bowls
napkins renaissance glassware time subscriptions
reducing formulas
—please call before visiting—
—very happy to make your acquaintanceship i'm sure—
and boil down one big vat of unanimal stew
topped with kegs and kegs of whipped dynamite
and cheery smithereens.
and then We will rush like crazed antelopes

with our bastard babies number books mojo goofer
dusting razor blades chicken thighs spooky ha'nts
daddygracing fatherdivining jack legged preaching
bojangles sugar raying mamas into one scorching
burning lake and have a jigging hoedown with the
Quadrilling Sun.
and the panting moneygrabbing landlord
leeching redneck judges will scuffle
the embankment and drag the lipstick sky outside.
and their fuzzy patriarchs from Katzenjammer orphic
will offer hogmaws and the thunder bird and their overseers
will offer elixir bottles of pre punch cards
and the protocol hollering thunder will announce
our main man who'll bathe us and swathe us.
and Our man's spur jingles'll cause the clouds to
kick the dust in flight.
And his gutbucketing rompity bump will
cause sweaty limp flags to furl retreat
and the Jackal-headed cowboy will ride reins
whiplashing his brass legs and knobby hips.
And fast draw Anubis with his crank letters from Ra
will Gallop Gallop Gallop

our mummified profiled trail boss
as our swashbuckling storm fucking mob rides shot
gun for the moon and the whole sieged stage coach
of the world will heave and rock as we
bang stomp shuffle stampede cartwheel and cakewalk our
way into Limbo.

The Gangster's Death

how did he die/ O if i told you,
you would slap your hand
                              against your forehead
and say good grief/ if I gripped you
by the lapel and told how they dumped
        thalidomide hand grenades
into his blood stream and/
                              how they injected
a cyst into his spirit the size of an egg
which grew and grew until floating
        gangrene encircled the globe
and/ how guerrillas dropped from trees like
mean pythons
                              and squeezed out his life
so that jungle birds fled their perches/
so that hand clapping monkeys   tumbled
        from branches and/
how twelve year olds snatched B-52's
        from the skies with their bare hands and/
how betty grable couldn't open a hershey bar
        without the wrapper exploding and/
how thin bent women wrapped bicycle chains
        around their knuckles saying
        we will fight until the last bra or/
        give us bread or shoot us/ and/
how killing him became child's play
in Danang in Mekong in Santo Domingo

                  and how rigor mortis was sprinkled
in boston soups
                        giving rum running families
stiff back aches

so that they were no longer able to sit
at the elbows of the president
with turkey muskets   or/ sit
on their behinds watching the boat races
off Massachusetts through field glasses but/
how they found their duck pants
      pulled off in the get-back-in-the-alleys
      of the world and/
how they were routed by the people
      spitting into their palms
      just waiting to use those lobster pinchers
      or smash that martini glass and/
how they warned him
                        and gave him a chance
      with no behind the back dillinger
      killing by flat headed dicks but/
how they held megaphones
                        in their fists
      saying   come out with your hands up and/
how refusing to believe the jig was up
      he accused them
                        of apocalyptic barking
      saying out of the corner of his mouth
      come in and get me and/
how they snagged at his khaki legs
      until their mouths were full
      of ankles and calves and/
how they sank their teeth into his swanky jugular
      getting the sweet taste of max factor
      on their tongues and/
how his screams were so loud
      that the skins of eardrums blew off
      and blood trickled
                        down the edges of mouths

and people got hip to his aliases/
                        i mean/
democracy and freedom began bouncing
all over the world
            like bad checks
as people began scratching their heads

and stroking their chins
as his rhetoric stuck in his fat throat
      while he quoted
men with frills on their wrists
and fake moles on their cheeks
and swans on their snuff boxes
    who sit in Gilbert Stuart's portraits
    talking like baroque clocks/
    who sit talking turkey talk
  to people who say   we don't want
                to hear it
as they lean over their plows reading Mao
wringing the necks of turkeys
    and making turkey talk gobble
    in upon itself
in Mekong and Danang and Santo Domingo
and

Che Guevara made personal appearances everywhere

Che Guevara in Macy's putting incendiary flowers
on marked down hats   and women
scratching out each other's eyes over ambulances
Che Guevara in Congress putting TNT shavings
in the ink wells   and politicians
tripped over their jowls trying to get away
Che Guevara in small towns and hamlets
where cans jump from the hands of stock clerks
    in flaming super markets/
where skyrocketing devil's food cakes
    contain the teeth of republican bankers/
where the steer of gentleman farmers
    shoot over the moon like beefy missiles
             while undeveloped people
stand in road shoulders saying
fly Che fly bop   a few for us
    put cement on his feet
    and take him for a ride

O Walt Whitman
visionary of leaking faucets
great grand daddy of drips
   you said I hear america singing
but/ how can you sing when your throat is slit
and O/ how can you see when your head bobs
   in a sewer
in Danang and Mekong and Santo Domingo

and look at them weep for a stiff/
                              i mean
a limp dead hood
Bishops humping their backsides/
folding their hands in front of their noses
forming a human carpet for a zombie
men and women looking like sick dust mops/
   running their busted thumbs
   across whiskey headed guitars/
weeping into the evil smelling carnations
   of Baby Face McNamara
   and Killer Rusk
whose arms are loaded with hijacked rest
in peace wreaths and/
look at them hump this stiff in harlem/
sticking out their lower lips/
and because he two timed them/
      midget manicheans shaking their fists
      in bullet proof telephone booths/
      dialing legbar on long distance
      receiving extra terrestrial sorry
                              wrong number
seeing big nosed black people land in space ships/
seeing swamp gas/
shoving inauthentic fireballs down their throats/
bursting their lungs on existentialist rope skipping/
      look at them mourn/
drop dead egalitarians and CIA polyglots
   crying into their bill folds
   we must love one another or die
while little boys wipe out whole regiments with bamboo sticks
while wrinkled face mandarins store 17 megatons in Haiku

for people have been holding his death birds
on their wrists and his death birds
make their arms sag with their filthy nests
and his death birds at their baby's testicles
and they got sick and fed up
with those goddamn birds
and they brought their wrists together and blew/
                                        i mean/

puffed their jaws and blew and shooed
    these death birds his way
and he is mourned by
drop dead egalitarians and CIA polyglots and
midget manicheans and Brooks Brothers Black People
    throwing valentines at crackers
    for a few spoons by Kirk's old Maryland engraved/
    for a look at Lassie's purple tongue/
    for a lock of roy rogers' hair/
    for a Lawrence Welk champagne bubble

as for me/ like the man said
i'm always glad when the chickens come home to roost

The Feral Pioneers

FOR DANCER

I rise at 2 a.m. these mornings, to
polish my horns; to see if the killing
has stopped. It is still snowing outside;
it comes down in screaming white
clots.

We sleep on the floor. I popped over
the dog last night & we ate it with
roots & berries.

The night before, lights of a
wounded coyote I found in
the pass.
(The horse froze weeks ago)

Our covered wagons be trapped
in strange caverns of the world.
Our journey, an entry in the thirty-
year old Missourian's '49 Diary.
   'All along the desert road from the
   very start, even the wayside was strewed
   with dead bodies of oxen, mules & horses
   & the stench was horrible.'

America, the mirage of a
naked prospector, with sand
in the throat, crawls thru
the stink.
Will never reach the Seven Cities.
Will lie in ruins of
once great steer.

I return to the cabin's
warmest room; Pope Joan is
still asleep. I lie down, my hands
supporting my head.

In the window, an apparition,
Charles Ives:
tears have pressed white hair
to face.

Instructions to a Princess

FOR TIM

it is like the plot of an ol
novel. yr mother comes down
from the attic at midnite & tries
on weird hats. i sit in my study
the secret inside me. i deal it
choice pieces of my heart. down
in the village they gossip abt
the new bride.
i have been saving all this
love for you my dear. if my
house burns down, open my face
& you will be amazed.

There's a Whale in my Thigh

There's a whale in my thigh. at
nite he swims the 7 seas. on
cold days i can feel him sleeping.
i went to the dr to see abt myself.
'do you feel this?' the dr asked,
a harpoon in my flesh. i nodded
yes in a clinic room of frozen
poetry.
'then there's no whale in yr thigh.'

there's a whale in my mind. i
feed him arrogant prophets.

I am a Cowboy in the Boat of Ra

*'The devil must be forced to reveal any such physical evil
(potions, charms, fetishes, etc.) still outside the body
and these must be burned.'* (Rituale Romanum, *published
1947, endorsed by the coat-of-arms and introductory
letter from Francis cardinal Spellman)*

I am a cowboy in the boat of Ra,
sidewinders in the saloons of fools
bit my forehead   like   O
the untrustworthiness of Egyptologists
who do not know their trips. Who was that
dog-faced man? they asked, the day I rode
from town.

School marms with halitosis cannot see
the Nefertiti fake chipped on the run by slick
germans, the hawk behind Sonny Rollins' head or
the ritual beard of his axe; a longhorn winding
its bells thru the Field of Reeds.

I am a cowboy in the boat of Ra. I bedded
down with Isis, Lady of the Boogaloo, dove
down deep in her horny, stuck up her Wells-Far-ago
in daring midday getaway. 'Start grabbing the
blue,' I said from top of my double crown.

I am a cowboy in the boat of Ra. Ezzard Charles
of the Chisholm Trail. Took up the bass but they
blew off my thumb. Alchemist in ringmanship but a
sucker for the right cross.

I am a cowboy in the boat of Ra. Vamoosed from
the temple i bide my time. The price on the wanted

poster was a-going down, outlaw alias copped my stance
and moody greenhorns were making me dance;
   while my mouth's
shooting iron got its chambers jammed.

I am a cowboy in the boat of Ra. Boning-up in
the ol West i bide my time. You should see
me pick off these tin cans whippersnappers. I
write the motown long plays for the comeback of
Osiris. Make them up when stars stare at sleeping
steer out here near the campfire. Women arrive
on the backs of goats and throw themselves on
my Bowie.

I am a cowboy in the boat of Ra. Lord of the lash,
the Loup Garou Kid. Half breed son of Pisces and
Aquarius. I hold the souls of men in my pot. I do
the dirty boogie with scorpions. I make the bulls
keep still and was the first swinger to grape the taste.

I am a cowboy in his boat. Pope Joan of the
Ptah Ra. C/mere a minute willya doll?
Be a good girl and
bring me my Buffalo horn of black powder
bring me my headdress of black feathers
bring me my bones of Ju-Ju snake
go get my eyelids of red paint.
Hand me my shadow

I'm going into town after Set

I am a cowboy in the boat of Ra

look out Set   here i come Set
to get Set   to sunset Set
to unseat Set   to Set down Set

          usurper of the Royal couch
          —imposter RAdio of Moses' bush
          party pooper O hater of dance
          vampire outlaw of the milky way

Black Power Poem

A spectre is haunting america—the spectre of neo-hoodooism. all the powers of old america have entered into a holy alli ance to exorcise this spectre: allen ginsberg timothy leary richard nixon edward teller billy graham time magazine the new york review of books and the underground press.

may the best church win. shake hands now and come out conjuring

Neo-HooDoo Manifesto

Neo-HooDoo is a "Lost American Church" updated. Neo-HooDoo is the music of James Brown without the lyrics and ads for Black Capitalism. Neo-HooDoo is the 8 basic dances of 19th-century New Orleans' *Place Congo*—the Calinda the Bamboula the Chacta the Babouille the Conjaille the Juba the Congo and the VooDoo—modernized into the Philly Dog, the Hully Gully, the Funky Chicken, the Popcorn, the Boogaloo and the dance of great American choreographer Buddy Bradley.

Neo-HooDoos would rather "shake that thing" than be stiff and erect. (There were more people performing a Neo-HooDoo sacred dance, the Boogaloo, at Woodstock than chanting Hare Krishna . . . Hare Hare!) All so-called "Store Front Churches" and "Rock Festivals" receive their matrix in the HooDoo rites of Marie Laveau conducted at New Orleans' Lake Pontchartrain, and Bayou St. John in the 1880s. The power of HooDoo challenged the stability of civil authority in New Orleans and was driven underground where to this day it flourishes in the Black ghettos throughout the country. Thats why in Ralph Ellison's modern novel *Invisible Man* New Orleans is described as "The Home of Mystery." "Everybody from New Orleans got that thing," Louis Armstrong said once.

HooDoo is the strange and beautiful "fits" the Black slave Tituba gave the children of Salem. (Notice the arm waving ecstatic females seemingly possessed at the "Pentecostal," "Baptist," and "Rock Festivals," [all fronts for Neo-HooDoo]). The reason that HooDoo isn't given the credit it deserves in influencing American Culture is because the students of that culture both "overground" and "underground" are uptight closet Jeho-vah revisionists. They would assert the American and East Indian and Chinese thing before they would the Black thing. Their spiritual leaders Ezra Pound and T. S. Eliot hated Africa and "Darkies." In Theodore Roszak's book—*The Making of a Counter Culture*—there is barely any mention of the Black influence on this culture even though its members dress like Blacks talk like Blacks walk like Blacks, gesture like Blacks wear Afros and indulge in Black music and dance (Neo-HooDoo).

Neo-HooDoo is sexual, sensual and digs the old "heathen" good good loving. An early American HooDoo song says:

> Now lady I ain't no mill man
> Just the mill man's son
> But I can do your grinding
> till the mill man comes

Which doesn't mean that women are treated as "sexual toys" in Neo-HooDoo or as one slick Jeho-vah Revisionist recently said, "victims of a raging hormone imbalance." Neo-HooDoo claims many women philosophers and theoreticians which is more than ugh religions Christianity and its offspring Islam can claim. When our theoretician Zora Neale Hurston asked a *Mambo* (a female priestess in the Haitian VooDoo) a definition of VooDoo the Mambo lifted her skirts and exhibited her Erzulie Seal, her Isis seal. Neo-HooDoo identifies with Julia Jackson who stripped HooDoo of its oppressive Catholic layer—Julia Jackson said when asked the origin of the amulets and talismans in her studio, "I make all my own stuff. It saves money and it's as good. People who has to buy their stuff ain't using their heads."

Neo-HooDoo is not a church for egotripping—it takes its "organization" from Haitian VooDoo of which Milo Rigaud wrote:

Unlike other established religions, there is no hierarchy of bishops, archbishops, cardinals, or a pope in VooDoo. Each oum'phor is a law unto itself, following the traditions of Voo-Doo but modifying and changing the ceremonies and rituals in various ways. Secrets of VooDoo.

Neo-HooDoo believes that every man is an artist and every artist a priest. You can bring your own creative ideas to Neo-HooDoo. Charlie "Yardbird (Thoth)" Parker is an example of the Neo-HooDoo artist as an innovator and improvisor.

Neo-HooDoo, Christ the landlord deity ("render unto Caesar") is on probation. This includes "The Black Christ" and "The Hippie Christ." Neo-HooDoo tells Christ to get lost. (Judas Iscariot holds an honorary degree from Neo-HooDoo.)

Whereas at the center of Christianity lies the graveyard the organ-drone and the cross, the center of Neo-HooDoo is the drum the anhk and the Dance. So Fine, Barefootin, Heard it Through The Grapevine, are all Neo-HooDoos.

Neo-HooDoo has "seen a lot of things in this old world."

Neo-HooDoo borrows from Ancient Egyptians (ritual accessories of Ancient Egypt are still sold in the House of Candles and Talismans on Stanton Street in New York, the Botanical Gardens in East Harlem, and Min and Mom on Haight Street in San Francisco, examples of underground centers found in ghettos throughout America).

Neo-HooDoo borrows from Haiti Africa and South America. Neo-HooDoo comes in all styles and moods.

Louis Jordon Nellie Lutcher John Lee Hooker Ma Rainey Dinah Washington the Temptations Ike and Tina Turner Aretha Franklin Muddy Waters Otis Redding Sly and the Family Stone B.B. King Junior Wells Bessie Smith Jelly Roll Morton Ray Charles Jimi Hendrix Buddy Miles the 5th Dimension the Chambers Brothers Etta James and acolytes Creedance Clearwater Revival the Flaming Embers Procol Harum are all Neo-HooDoos. Neo-HooDoo never turns down pork. In fact Neo-HooDoo is the Bar-B-Cue of Amerika. The Neo-HooDoo cuisine is Geechee Gree Gree Verta Mae's *Vibration Cooking*. (Ortiz Walton's Neo-HooDoo Jass Band performs at the Native Son Restaurant in Berkeley, California. Joe Overstreet's Neo-HooDoo exhibit will happen at the Berkeley Gallery Sept. 1, 1970 in Berkeley.)

Neo-HooDoo ain't Negritude. Neo-HooDoo never been to France. Neo-HooDoo is "your Mama" as Larry Neal said. Neo-HooDoos Little Richard and Chuck Berry nearly succeeded in converting the Beatles. When the Beatles said they were more popular than Christ they seemed astonished at the resulting outcry. This is because although they could feebly through amplification and technological sham "mimic" (as if Little Richard and Chuck Berry were Loa [Spirits] practicing ventriloquism on their "Horses") the Beatles failed to realize that they were conjuring the music and ritual (although imitation) of a Forgotten Faith, a traditional enemy of Christianity which Christianity the Cop Religion has had to drive underground each time they meet. Neo-HooDoo now demands a rematch, the referees were bribed and the adversary had resin on his gloves.

The Vatican Forbids Jazz Masses in Italy
Rome, Aug. 6 (UPI)—The Vatican today barred jazz and popular music from masses in Italian churches and forbade young Roman Catholics to change prayers or readings used on Sundays and holy days.

It said such changes in worship were "eccentric and arbitrary."

A Vatican document distributed to all Italian bishops did not refer to similar experimental masses elsewhere in the world, although Pope Paul VI and other high-ranking churchmen are known to dislike the growing tendency to deviate from the accepted form of the mass.

Some Italian churches have permitted jazz masses played by combos while youthful worshipers sang such songs as "We Shall Overcome."

Church leaders two years ago rebuked priests who permitted such experiments. The New York Times, August 7, 1970.

Africa is the home of the loa (Spirits) of Neo-HooDoo although we are building our own American "pantheon." Thousands of "Spirits" (Ka) who would laugh at Jeho-vah's fury concerning "false idols" (translated everybody else's religion) or "fetishes." Moses, Jeho-vah's messenger and zombie swiped the secrets of VooDoo from old Jethro but nevertheless ended up with a curse. (Warning, many White "Black delineators" who practiced HooDoo VooDoo for gain and did not "feed" the Black Spirits of HooDoo ended up tragically. Bix Beiderbecke and Irene Castle (who exploited Black Dance in the 1920s and relished in dressing up as a Nun) are examples of this tragic tendency.

Moses had a near heart attack when he saw his sons dancing nude before the Black Bull God Apis. They were dancing to a "heathen sound" that Moses had "heard before in Egypt" (probably a mixture of Sun Ra and Jimmy Reed played in the nightclub district of ancient Egypt's "The Domain of Osiris"—named after the god who enjoyed the fancy footwork of the pigmies).

The continuing war between Moses and his "Sons" was recently acted out in Chicago in the guise of an American "trial."

I have called Jeho-vah (most likely Set the Egyptian Sat-on [a pun on the fiend's penalty] Satan) somewhere "a party-pooper and hater of dance." Neo-HooDoos are detectives of the metaphysical about to make a pinch. We have issued warrants for a god arrest. If Jeho-vah reveals his real name he will be released on his own recognizance dehorned and put out to pasture.

A dangerous paranoid pain-in-the-neck a CopGod from the git-go, Jeho-vah was the successful law and order candidate in the mythological relay of the 4th century A.D. Jeho-vah is the God of punishment. The H-Bomb is a typical Jeho-vah "miracle." Jeho-vah is why we are in Vietnam. He told Moses to go out and "subdue" the world.

There has never been in history another such culture as the Western civilization—a culture which has practiced the belief that the physical and social environment of man is subject to rational manipulation and that history is subject to the will and action of man; whereas central to the traditional cultures of the rivals of Western civilization, those of Africa and Asia, is a belief that it is environment that dominates man. The Politics of Hysteria, *Edmund Stillman and William Pfaff.*

"Political leaders" are merely altar boys from Jeho-vah. While the targets of some "revolutionaries" are Laundromats and candy stores, Neo-HooDoo targets are TV the museums the symphony halls and churches art music and literature departments in Christianizing (education I think they call it!) universities which propagate the Art of Jeho-vah—much Byzantine Middle Ages Renaissance painting of Jeho-vah's "500 years of civilization" as Nixon put it are Jeho-vah propaganda. Many White revolutionaries can only get together with 3rd world people on the most mundane "political" level because they are of Jeho-vah's party and don't know it. How much Black music do so-called revolutionary underground radio stations play. On the other hand how much Bach?

Neo-HooDoos are Black Red (Black Hawk an American Indian was an early philosopher of the HooDoo Church) and occasionally White (Madamemoiselle Charlotte is a Haitian Loa [Spirit]).

> Neo-HooDoo is a litany seeking its text
> Neo-HooDoo is a Dance and Music closing in on its words
> Neo-HooDoo is a Church finding its lyrics
> Cecil Brown Al Young Calvin Hernton
> David Henderson Steve Cannon Quincy Troupe

Ted Joans Victor Cruz N. H. Pritchard Ishmael Reed
Lennox Raphael Sarah Fabio Ron Welburn are Neo-
HooDoo's "Manhattan Project" of writing . . .

A Neo-HooDoo celebration will involve the dance music
and poetry of Neo-HooDoo and whatever ideas the
participating artists might add. A Neo-HooDoo seal
is the Face of an Old American Train.
Neo-HooDoo signs are everywhere!
Neo-HooDoo is the Now Locomotive swinging
up the Tracks of the American Soul.

Almost 100 years ago HooDoo was forced to say
Goodbye to America. Now HooDoo is
back as Neo-HooDoo
You can't keep a good church down!

The Neo-HooDoo Aesthetic

Gombo Févi

A whole chicken—if chicken cannot be
had, veal will serve instead; a little ham;
crabs, or shrimps, or both, according to the
taste of the consumer; okra according to the
quantity of soup needed; onions, garlic, parsley,
red pepper, etc. Thicken with plenty of rice.
(Don't forget to cut up the gombo or okra.)

Gombo Filé

Same as above except the okra is
pul-verised and oysters are used

Why do I call it "The Neo-HooDoo
Aesthetic"?

*The proportions of ingredients used depend
upon the cook!*

Sermonette

a poet was busted by a topless judge
his friends went to morristwn nj & put
black powder on his honah's doorstep
black powder into his honah's car
black powder on his honah's briefs
tiny dolls into his honah's mind

by nightfall his honah could a go go no mo
his dog went crazy & ran into a crocodile
his widow fell from a wall &
hanged herself
his daughter was run over by a black man
cming home for the wakes the two boys
skidded into mourning
all the next of kin's teeth fell out

gimmie dat ol time
     religion

it's good enough
   for me!

Mojo Queen of the Feathery Plumes

Why do you want me to slap you
before I make love to you, then
wonder why I do you like I do?

*Dark Lady at Koptos, strange lady
at Koptos, Mojo Queen of the
Feathery Plumes*

Crawling, pleading and being
kittenish are no habits of the
world's rare cat; shut up in
the mind's dark cage; prowling
in a garden of persimmon, mangoes
and the long black python

*Dark Lady at Koptos, strange lady
at Koptos, Mojo Queen of the
Feathery Plumes*

When the hunter comes his gleaming
blue coat will galvanize him; his
pearls of sabre teeth will electrify
him; his avocado-green claws will
expose his guts

*Dark Lady at Koptos, strange lady
at Koptos, Mojo Queen of the
Feathery Plumes*

The scout will run back thru
the forest; 4 Thieves Vinegar
on his tail; the whole safari
not far behind his trail; the dolls
left behind will bare your face;
and the cloth on the bush will be
your lace; you are the jeweler's Ruby
that has fled its case

Dark Lady at Koptos, strange lady
at Koptos, Mojo Queen of the Feathery
Plumes

The cat was dying to meet you
in the flesh but you never came
he wanted you wild but you wanted
him tame, why is your highness afraid
of the night?

Dark Lady at Koptos, strange lady at Koptos
Mojo Queen of the Feathery Plumes

The Black Cock

FOR JIM HENDRIX, HOODOO FROM HIS
NATURAL BORN

He frightens all the witches and the dragons in their lair
He cues the clear blue daylight and He gives the night its dare
He flaps His wings for warning and He struts atop a mare
for when He crows they quiver and when He comes they flee

In His coal black plumage and His bright red crown
and His golden beaked fury and His calculated frown
in His webbed footed glory He sends Jehovah down
for when He crows they quiver and when He comes they flee

O they dance around the fire and they boil the gall of wolves
and they sing their strange crude melodies and play their
weirder tunes and the villagers close their windows and the grave-
yard starts to heave and the cross wont help their victims and
the screaming fills the night and the young girls die with
open eyes and the skies are lavender light
but when He crows they quiver and when He comes they flee

Well the sheriff is getting desperate as they go their nature's way
killing cattle smothering infants slaughtering those who block their
     way
and the countryside swarms with numbness as their magic circle
     grows
but when He crows they tremble and when He comes they flee

Posting hex-signs on their wagons simple worried farmers pray
passing laws and faking justice only feed the witches brew
violet stones are rendered helpless drunken priests are helpless too
but when He crows they quiver and when He comes they flee

We have seen them in their ritual we have catalogued their crimes
we are weary of their torture but we cannot bring them down
their ancient hoodoo enemy who does the work, the trick,
strikes peril in their dead fiend's hearts and pecks their flesh to
    quick
love Him feed Him He will never let you down
for when He crows they quiver and when He comes they frown

Betty's Ball Blues

Betty took the ring
from her fabled Jellyroll
Betty took the ring
from her fabled Jellyroll
She gave it all to Dupree
and eased it on his soul

She climbed his ancient redwood
and sang out from his peak
She climbed his ancient redwood
and sang out from his peak
She thrilled his natural forest
and made his demon creep

She shook the constellations
and dazzled them cross his eyes
She shook the constellations
and dazzled them cross his eyes
She showered his head with quasars
and made his Taurus cry

China China China
Come blow my China horn
China China China
Come blow my China horn
Telegraph my indigo skyship
and make its voyage long

Betty touched his organ
made his cathedral rock
Betty touched his organ
made his cathedral rock
His worshippers moaned
and shouted, His
stained glass windows cracked

One night she dressed
in scarlet and threw
her man a Ball
One night she dressed
in scarlet and threw
her man a Ball
The Butlers came as
zombies, the
guests walked thru
the walls

Dupree he shot the
jeweler, She had him
under a spell,
Dupree he shot the
jeweler, She had him
under a spell

The calmest man in
Sing-Sing is happy
in his cell

The Wardrobe Master of Paradise

He pins the hems of Angels and
He dresses them to kill
He has no time for fashion
No money's in His till
You wont see Him in Paris
or in a New York store
He's the wardrobe master
of Paradise; He keeps right
on His toes

He works from ancient patterns
He doesn't mind they bore
His models have no measurements
His buyers never roar
He never cares to gossip
He works right on the floor
He's the wardrobe master
of Paradise; He keeps right
on His toes

The evil cities burn to
a crisp, from where His
clients go; their eyes
are blood red carnage, their
purpose never fluffed,
His customers total seven
they have no time to pose
He's the wardrobe master
of Paradise; He keeps right
on His toes

He does not sweat the phony
trends, or fashions dumb
decree; His style is always
chic and in, He never takes
a fee
In Vogue or Glamour or Harper's
Bazaar; He's never written up
He's the wardrobe master
of Paradise; He keeps right
on His toes

The ups and downs of Commerce
His shop will not effect:
the whims of a fickle market
the trifles of jet-sets
The society editor would
rather die than ask Him for
a tip; He sews uninterrupted
He isn't one for quips
His light burns in the pit-black night
I've never seen Him doze
He's the wardrobe master
of Paradise; He keeps right
on His toes

Catechism of d Neoamerican Hoodoo Church

a little red wagon for d black bureaucrat
who in d winter of 1967 when i refused to
deform d works of ellison & wright—his betters—
to accommodate a viewpoint this clerk thot irresistible,
did not hire me for d teaching job
which he invitd me to take
in d first place.

this is for u insect w/ no antennae, goofy
papers piling on yr desk—for u & others. where
do u fugitives frm d file cabinet of death get
off in yr attempt to control d artist?
keep yr programming to those computers u love so
much, for he who meddles w/ nigro-mancers
courts his demise!

i
our pens are free
do not move by decree. accept no memos
frm jackbootd demogs who wd exile our minds.
dare tell d artist his role. issue demands on
cultural revolution. 2 words frm china where an
ol woman sends bold painters to pick grasshoppers
at 3 in d a.m. w/ no tea, no cigarettes & no
beer. cause ol women like landscapes or portraits
of their husbands face. done 50 yrs ago. standing
on a hill. a god, a majesty, d first chairman.
o, we who hv no dreams permit us to say yr name
all day. we are junk beneath yr feet,
mosquito noises to yr ears, we crawl on our
bellies & roll over 3 times for u. u are
definitely sho nuff d 1 my man.

ii

is this how artists shd greet u?
isnt yr apartment by d river enough? d
trees in d park? palisades by moonlight is
choice i hear. arent u satisfid? do u
want to be a minister of culture? (minister, a
jive title frm a dead church!) dressd in a
business suit w/ medals on yr chest? hving
painters fetch yr short, writers doing yr taxes,
musicians entertaining yr mistresses, sculptors
polishing yr silverware. do u desire 4 names
instead of 2?

iii

    i do not write solictd
    manuscripts—oswald spengler said
    to joseph goebbels when askd to make a
    lie taste like sweet milk.

because they wrote d way they saw it, said
their prayers wrong, forgot to put on their number in d
a.m., got tore dwn in d streets & cut d fool:
men changd their names to islam & hung up d phone on them.
meatheaded philosophers left rank tongues of ugly mouth on
their tables. only new/ark kept us warm that summer. but
now they will pick up d tab. those dear dead beats who put
our souls to d wall. tried us in absentia before
some grand karate who hd no style. plumes on garveys hat
he was.

iv

word of my mysteries is getting around. do not cm
said d dean / invite cancelld to speak in our chapel
at delaware state. we hv checkd yr background. u make
d crucifixes melt. d governor cant replace them.
stop   stop   outlandish customer.

v

i am becoming spooky & afar you all. I
stir in my humfo, taking notes. a black cat
superstars on my shoulder. a johnny root dwells

in my purse. on d one wall: bobs picture
of marie laveaus tomb in st louis #2. it is
all washd out w/x . . . s, & dead flowers &
fuck wallace signs. on d other wall:
d pastd scarab on grandpops chest, he was
a nigro-mancer frm chattanooga. so i got it
honest. i floor them w/ my gris gris. what
more do i want ask d flatfoots who patrol d beat
of my time. d whole pie? o no u small fry
spirits. d chefs hat, d kitchen, d right
to help make a menu that will end 2 thousand yrs
of bad news.

vi
muhammed? a rewrite man for d wrong daily
news. messenger for cons of d pharaohs court.
perry mason to moses d murderer & thief. pr man
for d prophets of SET. as for poets? chapt
26 my friends—check it out. it is all there in
icewater clear.

ghandi? middleclass lawyer stuck on himself.
freed d brahmins so they cd sip tea & hate cows.
lenins pants didnt fit too good,
people couldnt smoke in front of him, on d
train to petrograd he gv them passes to go
to d head.

d new houngans are to d left of buck rogers,
ok buck up w/yr hands. where did u stash
our galaxies?

vii
bulletin

       to d one who put our
art on a line. now odd shapes will nibble u.
its our turn to put u thru changes. to drop
dour walter winchells on u like, i predict
that tomorrow yr hands will be stiff. to d
one who gaggd a poet. hants will eat yr

cornflakes. golfballs will swell in yr jaws at noon.
horrid masks will gape thru yr window at dusk. it will
be an all day spectacular. look out now,
it is already beginning. to d one who strongarmd
a painter. hear d noise climbing yr steps? u will
be its horse. how does that grab u? how come u
pull d sheets over yr head? & last & least o cactus
for brains. u muggd a playwright, berkeley cal.
spring 68. We hv yr photos. lots of them. what
was that u just spat/up
a lizard or a spider?

viii
spelling out my business i hv gone
indoors. raking d coals over my liver,
listening to my stories w/ yng widow
brown, talking up a trash in bars (if
i feel up to it). doing all those things put down
in that odor of hog doodoo printd as
a poem in black fire. i caught d whiff of yr
stink thou sow w/ mud for thots. d next
round is on me. black halloween on d rocks.
straight no chaser.

down d hatch d spooks will fly/ some
will thrive & some will die/ by these
rattles in our hands/ mighty spirits
will shake d land.

so excuse me while i do d sooner toomer.
jean that is. im gone schooner to a meta
physical country. behind d eyes. im gone be.
a rootarmd ravenheaded longbeard im gone be.
a zigaboo jazzer teaching mountain
lions of passion how to truck.

ix
goodhomefolks gave me ishmael. how
did they know he was d'afflictd one'?
carrying a gag in his breast pocket. giving
a scene a scent of snowd under w/ bedevilment.

i am d mad mad scientist in love w/ d dark.
d villagers dont understand me. here they come
with their torches. there goes a rock
thru d window. i hv time for a few more hobbies:
making d cab drivers dream of wotan
cutting out pictures of paper murderers

like d ol woman w/ d yng face
or is it d yng woman w/ d ol face?
take yr pick. put it to my chest.
watch it bend. its all a big punchline
i share w/ u. to keep u in stitches.
& ull be so wise when their showstopper
comes:
      this is how yr ears shd feel
      this is what u shd eat
      this is who u shd sleep w/
      this is how u shd talk
      this is how u shd write
      this is how u shd paint
      these dances are d best
      these films are d best
      this is how u shd groom yrself
      these are d new gods we made for u
u are a bucket of feces before them.
we know what is best for u. bend down
& kiss some wood.
make love to leather, if u
dont u will be offd

x
& d cannd laughter will fade &
d dirty chickens will fly his coop
for he was just a geek u see.
o houngans of america—post this on yr
temples.

DO YR ART D WAY U WANT
ANYWAY U WANT
ANY WANGOL U WANT
ITS UP TO U/ WHAT WILL WORK
FOR U.

so sez d neoarmerican hoodoo
church of free spirits who
need no
monarch
no gunghoguru
no busybody ray frm d heddahopper planet
of wide black hats & stickpins. he was
just a 666* frm a late late show &
only d clucks threw pennies

*false prophet of the apocalypse

Why I Often Allude to Osiris

ikhnaton looked like
prophet jones, who brick
by brick broke up a
french chateau & set it
down in detroit. he was
'elongated' like prophet
jones & had a hairdresser's
taste.
ikhnaton moved cities for
his mother-in-law &
each finger of his hands
bore rings.

ikhnaton brought re
ligious fascism to egypt.

where once man animals
plants & stars freely
roamed thru each other's
rooms, ikhnaton came up
with the door.

(a lot of people in new york
 go for him—museum curators
 politicians & tragic mulattoes)

i'll take osiris any
time.
prefiguring JB he
funky chickened into
ethiopia & everybody had
a good time. osiris in
vented the popcorn, the
slow drag & the lindy hop.

he'd rather dance than rule.

My Thing Abt Cats

In berkeley whenever
black cats saw dancer &
me they crossed over to
the other side. alan &
carol's cat jumped over
my feet. someone else's
cat pressed its paw against
my leg, in seattle it's
green eyes all the way.
"they cry all the time when
ever you go out, but when
you return they stop," dancer
said of the 3 cats in the back
yard on st mark's place, there
is a woman downstairs who makes
their sounds when she feeds them.
we don't get along.

Man or Butterfly

it is like lao tse's dream, my
strange affair with cities.
sometimes i can't tell whether
i am a writer writing abt cities
or a city with cities writing
abt me.
a city in peril. everything that
makes me tick is on the bum. all
of my goods and services are wearing
down. nothing resides in me anymore.
i am becoming a ghost town with not
even an occasional riot to perk me
up

> they are setting up a
> commission to find out what
> is wrong with me. i
> am the lead off witness

Hoodoo Poem in Transient

1nce a year marie laveau
        rises frm her workshop
        in st louis #2, boards
        a bus & rides dwn to
        the lake. she threw
        parties there 100 years
        ago.
        some
        lake

Monsters From The Ozarks

The Gollygog
The Bingbuffer
The Moogie
The Fillyloo
The Behemoth
The Snawfus
The Gowrow
The Spiro
The Agnew

Beware: Do Not Read This Poem

tonite, *thriller* was
abt an ol woman, so vain she
surrounded her self w/
   many mirrors

It got so bad that finally she
locked herself indoors & her
whole life became the
   mirrors

one day the villagers broke
into her house, but she was too
swift for them. she disappeared
    into a mirror
each tenant who bought the house
after that, lost a loved one to
    the ol woman in the mirror:
    first a little girl
    then a young woman
    then the young woman/s husband

the hunger of this poem is legendary
it has taken in many victims
back off from this poem
it has drawn in yr feet
back off from this poem
it has drawn in yr legs
back off from this poem
it is a greedy mirror
you are into this poem. from
   the waist down
nobody can hear you can they?

this poem has had you up to here
        belch
this poem aint got no manners
you cant call out frm this poem
relax now & go w/ this poem
move & roll on to this poem

        do not resist this poem
        this poem has yr eyes
        this poem has his head
        this poem has his arms
        this poem has his fingers
        this poem has his fingertips

this poem is the reader & the
        reader this poem

statistic: the us bureau of missing persons reports
        that in 1968 over 100,000 people disappeared
        leaving no solid clues
                nor trace   only
    a space   in the lives of their friends

Dualism

I am outside of
history. i wish
i had some peanuts, it
looks hungry there in
its cage

i am inside of
history. its
hungrier than i
thot

Guilty, the New York Philharmonic
Signs Up a Whale

Today the New York
Philharmonic signed up
a whale.
Ortiz Walton Is black
& better than Casals.
Well Ortiz, I guess you'll
have to swim the Atlantic

If my Enemy is a Clown, a Natural Born Clown

i tore down my thoughts
roped in my nightmares
remembered a thousand curses
made blasphemous vows to demons
choked on the blood of hosts
        ate my hat
threw fits in the street
got up bitchy each day
told off the mailman
lost many friends
left parties in a huff
dry fucked a dozen juke boxes
made anarchist speeches in brad
the falcon's 55 (but was never
thrown out)
drank 10 martinis a minute
until 1 day the book was finished

my unspeakable terror between the
covers, on you i said to the
enemies of the souls

well lorca, pushkin i tried
but in this place they assassinate
you with pussy or pats on
the back, lemon chiffon between
the cheeks or 2 weeks on a mile
long beach.

i have been the only negro
on the plane 10 times this year
and its only the 2nd month

i am removing my blindfold and
leaving the dock. the judge
giggles constantly and the prosecutor
invited me to dinner

no forwarding address please

i called it pin the tail on the devil
they called it avant garde
they just can't be serious
these big turkeys

The Piping Down of God

god is above grammar
a monk once said. i
want to sit on the window
god told the ticket clerk. you
mean next to the window the
clerk corrected. no, on
the window god insisted. the
clouds have a right to
cheer their boss.

the clerk apologized
& god piped down.

Anon. Poster:

poor sam presents at

<small>ESTHER'S ORBIT ROOM</small>

1753–7th Street Oakland California
Reunion of Soul
with the Sensational Team of
Vernon & Jewel
(back together again)
music by
the Young Lyons

American Airlines Sutra

put yr cup on my tray
the stewardess said 40,000
feet up. (well i've
never done it that way. what
have i got to lose.)

i climb into a cab & the
woman driver is singing
along with Frank Sinatra
"how was your flight coming in?"

(another one. these americans,
only one thing on their
minds).

The Inside Track

a longshot if he cracks up in
doors, but 2 to 1 he
flips out on tv. every
time nixon goes before the
cameras, 80,000 bookies
hold their breaths

For Cardinal Spellman
Who Hated Voo Doo

sick
black grass will
grow on his plot and
the goats will eat
& choke on it

and the keeper of the children's
cries
will terrify his neighbors
& gravediggers
will ask for two weeks
off

when will the next one's
brain explode
or turn from meat to
rock

tomorrow
a week
a month from someday
or the next three turns
of the
moon

Dragon's Blood

just because you
cant see d stones dont
mean im not building.
you aint no mason. how
d fuck would you know.

Columbia

a dumb
figure
skater per
forming to
strauss'
*also spake
zarathustra*.

she stumbled
during the spin.

i saw this today
on wide wide
world of
sports.

no lie.

Treatment for Dance W/ Trick Ending

one cop enters a store
a 2nd cop pulls a cat frm a tree
a 3rd cop helps an ol woman across
      the street
a 4th cop slaps a prisoner

the cop who pulled the cat frm the
tree leaves the store with a package
& whistling walks dwn the street
the prisoner is put into a box away frm
his fellows
the ol woman files a complaint

one nite in 1965 at 3 in the AM i
stumble down second ave.
8 cadillacs pull up in front
of ratner's. it is a shift of
the 9th precinct. coming on duty
the next morning the cobbler
awakes to find his shoes ruined

Back to Back: 3rd Eye

FOR D.H.

Who are you? Napoleon or something? Fresh from Elba, liberating the countryside? You wonder why cheering throngs don't turn out to greet you, in Oakland, in Richmond, in El Cerrito, behind the county courthouse on the telephone book. New York will follow you like a Westside meatpacking house that barters your heart for free ice. They keep to themselves out here.

> Marlon Brando's silver hair sells
> Up-America cakes on the weekends.

STOP!

Western Union for Zora Neale Hurston:
> *Moscow has fallen! Please wire Erzulie for triumphant
> march into the art!*

Off d Pig

background:
        a reckoning has left
some minds hard hit. they blow,
crying for help, out to sea like
dead trees & receding housetops. i
can sympathize. i mean, all of us
have had our dreams broken over some
body's head. those scratched phono
graph records of d soul.
we

                all have been zombed along
d way of a thousand eyes glowing at midnite.
                our pupils have been vacant
                our hands have been icey &
                we have walked with d tell tale
                lurch
all of us have had this crisis of consciousness
which didnt do nobody no good
or a search for identity
which didnt make no never mind neither

at those times we got down on our knees & call
ed up the last resort. seldom do we bother him
for he is doing heavy duty for d universe. only
once has he been disturbed & this was to
        put some color into a woman's blues
he came like a black fire engine spun & sped
by khepera
he is very pressed for time &
do nots play

he apologises for being late
he rolls up his sleeves & rests his bird
he starts to say a few words to d crowd.
he sees d priests are out to lunch so he
just goes on head with what he got to do

out of d night blazing from ceciltaylorpianos
    Thoth sets down his fine black self
d first black scribe
d one who fixes up their art
d one who draws d circle with his pen
d man who beats around d bush
d smeller outer of d fiend

        jehovah-apep jumps up bad on d set
        but squeals as spears bring him down

a curfew is lifted on soul
friendly crowds greet one another in d streets
Osiris struts his stuff & dos d thang to words
    hidden beneath d desert

chorus—just like a legendary train that
        one has heard of but never seen
        broke all records in its prime
        takes you where you want to go right fast

        i hears you woo woo o neo american hoo doo church
        i hears you woo woo o neo american hoo doo church
        i hears you woo woo o neo american hoo doo church
        i hears you woo woo o neo american hoo doo church
        amen-ra   a-men ra   a-man ra

General Science

things in motion
hv a tendency to
stay in motion. the
most intelligent
ghosts are those
who do not know
they are dead:

something just
crossed my
hands

Report of the Reed Commission

I conclude that for
the first time in
history the practical
man is the loon and the
loon the practical man

a man on the radio just
said that air pollution
is caused by jelly fish.

What You Mean I Can't Irony?

A high-yellow lawyer woman
told me I ought to go to
Europe to "broaden your per
spective." This happened at
a black black cocktail party
an oil portrait, Andrew Carnegie,
smiling down

White Hope

jack johnson licked
one pug so, d man
retired to a farm.
never again opened
his mouth save to
talk abt peachtrees
sow & last year's
almanac;

and whenever somebody
say jack johnson,

he'd get that far away
look.

Untitled I

friday in berkeley. the crippled
ship has just returned frm
behind the moon. fools wave
flags on destroyers in the pacific
i am worried abt this dog
lying in the street. he wants
to get some sun. the old man
across the street trims his
rosebush while just 4 blocks
away there is a war. people
are being arraigned
fingerprinted
hauled away to st rita
made to lie on the floor
the newspapers will lie
abt all this. abt these
12 year olds throwing
stones at the cops, they
wanted to get at some sun
no matter what heavy
traffic was coming down
on them

Untitled II

that house has
a pall of bad
luck hovering over
head
i told you
not to go there
anymore. see
what you get?

Untitled III

everybody in columbia
heights speaks french
ever go to a party there?
bore you to tears.

Untitled IV

the difference between
my heart & your
intellect, my un
disciplined way of
doing
things (i failed
the written driver's
test for example)
& your science, is
the difference between
the earth &
the snow.

the earth wears its
colors well. builds them
loves them & sticks with
them

the snow needs no one.
it lies there all cold
like. it greases behind
wolftracks & wingless
dead birds.
it is a hardship on the poor

thinking is its downfall

Gangster Goes Legit

One day he became six eyes.
The tommy gun on the desk,
as many.
he went into the tommy gun
business

This Poetry Anthology I'm Reading

this poetry anthology
i'm reading reminds me
of washington d.c.
every page some marbled
trash. old adjectives stand
next to flagcovered coffins.
murderers mumbling in
their sleep.

in the rose garden the
madman strolls alone. the
grin on his face just
won't quit

Dress Rehearsal Paranoia #2

In san francisco they are
taking up a collection. if
the earthquake won't come
they'll send for it.

Paul Laurence Dunbar in The Tenderloin

Even at 26, the hush when
you unexpectedly walked
into a theatre. One year
after *The History of Cakewalk.*

Desiring not to cause
a fuss, you sit alone
in the rear, watching a re
hearsal.
The actors are impressed. Wel
don Johnson, so super at des
cription, jots it all down.

I dont blame you for
disliking Whitman, Paul.
He lacked your style, like
your highcollared mandalaed
portrait in hayden's
Kaleidoscope; unobserved,
Death, the uncouth critic
does a first draft on your
    breath.

Badman of the Guest Professor

FOR JOE OVERSTREET, DAVID HENDERSON,
ALBERT AYLER & D MYSTERIOUS
'H' WHO CUT UP D REMBRANDTS

i
u worry me whoever u are
i know u didnt want me to
come here but here i am just
d same; hi-jacking yr stagecoach,
hauling in yr pocket watches & mak
ing u hoof it all d way to
town. black bard, a robber w/ an
art: i left some curses in d cash
box so ull know its me

listen man, i cant help it if
yr thing is over, kaput,
   finis
no matter how u slice it dick
u are done. a dead duck all out
of quacks. d nagging hiccup dat
goes on & on w/out a simple glass
   of water for relief

ii
uve been teaching shakespeare for
20 years only to find d joke
   on u
d eavesdropping rascal who got it
in d shins because he didnt know
enough to keep his feet behind d cur
tains: a sad-sacked head served on a

platter in titus andronicus or falstaff
  too fat to make a go of it
  anymore

iii
its not my fault dat yr tradition
was knocked off wop style & left in
d alley w/ pricks in its mouth. i
read abt it in d papers but it was no
  skin off my nose
wasnt me who opened d gates & allowed
d rustlers to slip thru unnoticed. u
ought to do something abt yr security or
  mend yr fences partner
dont look at me if all dese niggers
are ripping it up like deadwood dick;
doing art d way its never been done. mak
ing wurlitzer sorry he made d piano dat
will drive mozart to d tennis
  courts
making smith-corona feel like d red
faced university dat has just delivered china
  some 50 e-leben h bomb experts

i didnt deliver d blow dat drove d
abstract expressionists to my ladies
linoleum where dey sleep beneath tons of
wax & dogshit & d muddy feet of children or
because some badassed blackpainter done sent
french impressionism to d walls of highrise
  lobbies where dey belong is not my fault
martha graham will never do d jerk
shes a sweet ol soul but her hips
cant roll; as stiff as d greek
statues she loves so much

iv
dese are d reasons u did me nasty
j alfred prufrock, d trick u pull
d in d bookstore today; stand in d
corner no peaches for a week, u lemon

u must blame me because yr wife is
ugly. 86-d by a thousand discriminating
saunas. dats why u did dat sneaky thing
i wont tell d townsfolk because u hv
to live here and im just passing thru

v

u got one thing right tho. i did say
dat everytime i read william faulkner i
go to sleep.

fitzgerald wdnt hv known a gangster if one
had snatched zelda & made her a moll tho
    she wd hv been grateful i bet

bonnie of clyde wrote d saga of suicide
sal just as d feds were closing in. it is
worth more than d collected works of ts
elliot a trembling anglican whose address
is now d hell dat thrilld him so
last word from down there he was open
ing a publishing co dat will bore d
devil back to paradise

vi

& by d way did u hear abt grammar?
cut to ribbons in a photo finish by
stevie wonder, a blindboy who dances
on a heel. he just came out of d slang
& broke it down before millions.
    it was bloody murder

vii

to make a long poem shorter—3 things
    moleheaded lame w/4 or 5 eyes

1) yr world is riding off into d sunset
2) d chips are down & nobody will chance yr i.o.u.s.
3) d last wish was a fluke so now u hv to re
turn to being a fish
p.s. d enchantment has worn off

dats why u didnt like my reading list—right?
it didnt include anyone on it dat u cd in
vite to a cocktail party & shoot a lot of
        bull—right?
so u want to take it out on my hide—right?
well i got news for u professor nothing—i
am my own brand while u must be d fantasy of
        a japanese cartoonist

a strangekind of dinosaurmouse
i can see it all now. d leaves
are running low. its d eve of
extinction & dere are no holes to
accept yr behind. u wander abt yr
long neck probing a tree. u think
its a tree but its really a trap. a
cry of victory goes up in d kitchen of
d world. a pest is dead. a prehis
toric pest at dat. a really funnytime
prehistoric pest whom we will lug into
a museum to show everyone how really funny
u are
        yr fate wd make a good
scenario but d plot is between u &
charles darwin.

as i said, im passing thru, just sing
ing my song. get along little doggie &
jazz like dat. word has it dat a big gold
shipment is coming to californy. i hv to
ride all night if im to meet my pardners
dey want me to help score d ambush

From the Files of Agent 22

a black banana
can make you high
bad apples can get
you wasted
the wrong kind of
grapes tore up
for days
and a rancid orange
plastered

know your spirits
before entering
strange orchards

Introducing a New Loa

as i conclude this Work, a great hydrogen cloud, twenty seven million miles long leisurely passes thru this solar system at 40,000 miles per hr. "The biggest thing yet seen in space." No one knows where it came from. Another galaxy? This solar system?

it took the small halo of another planet, out to make a rep for itself, to squeal on it. I claim it as my floating orphan. When i walked past the FM antenna just now, it called out my name. I respond to it. I call it the invisible train for which this Work has been but a modest schedule. A time-table subject to change. Greetings from the swinging HooDoo cloud; way up there, the softest touch in Everything; doing a dance they call

"The Our Turn"

Chattanooga

Chattanooga

1

Some say that Chattanooga is the
Old name for Lookout Mountain
To others it is an uncouth name
Used only by the uncivilised
Our a-historical period sees it
As merely a town in Tennessee
To old timers of the Volunteer State
Chattanooga is "The Pittsburgh of
The South"
According to the Cherokee
Chattanooga is a rock that
Comes to a point

They're all right
Chattanooga is something you
Can have anyway you want it
The summit of what you are
I've paid my fare on that
Mountain Incline #2, Chattanooga
I want my ride up
I want Chattanooga

2

Like Nickajack a plucky Blood
I've escaped my battle near
Clover Bottom, braved the
Jolly Roger raising pirates
Had my near miss at Moccasin Bend
To reach your summit so
Give into me Chattanooga
I've dodged the Grey Confederate sharpshooters

Escaped my brother's tomahawks with only
Some minor burns
Traversed a Chickamauga of my own
Making, so
You belong to me Chattanooga

3
I take your East Ninth Street to my
Heart, pay court on your Market
Street of rubboard players and organ
Grinders of Haitian colors rioting
And old Zip Coon Dancers
I want to hear Bessie Smith belt out
I'm wild about that thing in
Your Ivory Theatre
Chattanooga
Coca-Cola's homebase
City on my mind

4
My 6th grade teacher asked me to
Name the highest mountain in the world
I didn't even hesitate, "Lookout Mountain"
I shouted. They laughed
Eastern nitpickers, putting on the
Ritz laughed at my Chattanooga ways
Which means you're always up to it

To get to Chattanooga you must
Have your Tennessee
"She has as many lives as a
cat. As to killing her, even
the floods have failed
you may knock the breath out of
her that's all. She will re-
fill her lungs and draw
a longer breath than ever"
From a Knoxville editorial—
1870s

5

Chattanooga is a woman to me too
I want to run my hands through her
Hair of New Jersey tea and redroot
Aint no harm in that
Be caressed and showered in
Her Ruby Falls
That's only natural
Heal myself in her
Minnehaha Springs
58 degrees F. all year
Around. Climb all over her
Ridges and hills
I wear a sign on my chest
"Chattanooga or bust"

6

"HOLD CHATTANOOGA AT ALL HAZARDS"—Grant
   to Thomas

When I tasted your big juicy
Black berries ignoring the rattle-
Snakes they said came to Cameron
Hill after the rain, I knew I
Had to have you Chattanooga
When I swam in Lincoln Park
Listening to Fats Domino sing
I found my thrill on Blueberry
Hill on the loudspeaker
I knew you were mine Chattanooga
Chattanooga whose Howard Negro
School taught my mother Latin
Tennyson and Dunbar
Whose Miller Bros. Department
Store cheated my Uncle out of
What was coming to him
A pension, he only had 6
Months to go
Chattanooooooooooooooooooooooga
Chattanooooooooooooooooooooooga
"WE WILL HOLD THE TOWN TILL WE STARVE"—
   Thomas to Grant

7

To get to Chattanooga you must
Go through your Tennessee
I've taken all the scotsboros
One state can dish out
Made Dr. Shockley's "Monkey Trials"
The laughing stock of the Nation
Capt. Marvel Dr. Sylvanias shazam
Scientists running from light-
ning, so
Open your borders. Tennessee
Hide your TVA
DeSota determined, this
Serpent handler is coming
Through

Are you ready Lookout Mountain?

"Give all of my Generals what he's
drinking," Lincoln said, when the
Potomac crowd called Grant a lush

8

I'm going to strut all over your
Point like Old Sam Grant did
My belly full of good Tennessee
Whiskey, puffing on
A.05 cigar
The campaign for Chattanooga
Behind me
Breathing a spell
Ponying up for
Appomattox!

Railroad Bill, A Conjure Man

A HOODOO SUITE

Railroad Bill, a conjure man
Could change hisself to a tree
He could change hisself to a
Lake, a ram, he could be
What he wanted to be

When a man-hunt came he became
An old slave shouting boss
He went thataway. A toothless
Old slave standing next to a
Hog that laughed as they
Galloped away.
Would laugh as they galloped
Away

Railroad Bill was a conjure man
He could change hisself to a bird
He could change hisself to a brook
A hill he could be what he wanted
To be

One time old Bill changed hisself
To a dog and led a pack on his
Trail. He led the hounds around
And around. And laughed a-wagging
His tail. And laughed
A-wagging his tail

Morris Slater was from Escambia
County, he went to town a-toting
A rifle. When he left that

Day he was bounty.
Morris Slater was Railroad Bill
Morris Slater was Railroad Bill

Railroad Bill was an electrical
Man he could change hisself into
Watts. He could up his voltage
Whenever he pleased
He could, you bet he could
He could, you bet he could

Now look here boy hand over that
Gun, hand over it now not later
I needs my gun said Morris Slater
The man who was Railroad Bill
I'll shoot you dead you SOB
let me be whatever I please
The policeman persisted he just
Wouldn't listen and was buried the
Following eve. Was buried the
Following eve. Many dignitaries
Lots of speech-making.

Railroad Bill was a hunting man
Never had no trouble fetching game
He hid in the forest for those
Few years and lived like a natural
King. Whenever old Bill would
Need a new coat he'd sound out his
Friend the Panther. When Bill got
Tired of living off plants the
Farmers would give him some hens.
In swine-killing time the leavings of
Slaughter. They'd give Bill the
Leavings of slaughter. When he
needed love their fine Corinas
They'd lend old Bill their daughters

Railroad Bill was a conjure man he
Could change hisself to a song. He
Could change hisself to some blues

Some reds he could be what he wanted
To be

E. S. McMillan said he'd get old
Bill or turn in his silver star
Bill told the Sheriff you best
Leave me be said the outlaw from
Tombigbee. Leave me be warned
Bill in 1893

Down in Yellowhammer land
By the humming Chattahoochee
Where the cajun banjo pickers
Strum. In Keego, Volina, and
Astoreth they sing the song of
How come

Bill killed McMillan but wasn't
Willin rather reason than shoot
A villain. Rather reason than
Shoot McMillan

"Railroad Bill was the worst old coon
Killed McMillan by the light of the
Moon
Was lookin for Railroad Bill
Was lookin for Railroad Bill"

Railroad Bill was a gris-gris man
He could change hisself to a mask
A Ziba, a Zulu
A Zambia mask. A Zaramo
Doll as well
One with a necklace on it
A Zaramo doll made of wood

I'm bad, I'm bad said Leonard
McGowin. He'll be in hell and dead he
        Said in 1896
Shot old Bill at Tidmore's store
This was near Atmore that Bill was
        Killed in 1896.

He was buying candy for some children
Procuring sweets for the farmers' kids

Leonard McGowin and R. C. John as
Cowardly as they come. Sneaked up
On Bill while he wasn't lookin.
Ambushed old Railroad Bill
Ambushed the conjure man. Shot him
In the back. Blew his head off.

Well, lawmen came from miles around
All smiles the lawmen came.
They'd finally got rid of
Railroad Bill who could be what
He wanted to be

Wasn't so the old folks claimed
From their shacks in the Wawbeek
Wood. That aint our Bill in that
old coffin, that aint our man
You killed. Our Bill is in the
Dogwood flower and in the grain
We eat
See that livestock grazing there
That Bull is Railroad Bill
The mean one over there near the
Fence, that one is Railroad Bill

Now Hollywood they's doing old
Bill they hired a teacher from
Yale. To treat and script and
Strip old Bill, this classics
Professor from Yale.
He'll take old Bill the conjure
Man and give him a-na-ly-sis. He'll
Put old Bill on a leather couch
And find out why he did it.
Why he stole the caboose and
Avoided nooses why Bill raised so
Much sand.

He'll say Bill had a complex
He'll say it was all due to Bill's
Mother. He'll be playing the
Dozens on Bill, this
Professor from Yale

They'll make old Bill a neurotic
Case these tycoons of the silver
Screen. They'll take their cue
From the teacher from Yale they
Gave the pile of green
A bicycle-riding dude from Yale
Who set Bill for the screen
Who set Bill for the screen

They'll shoot Bill zoom Bill and
Pan old Bill until he looks plain
Sick. Just like they did old Nat
The fox and tried to do Malik
Just like they did Jack Johnson
Just like they did Jack Johnson

But it wont work what these hacks
Will do, these manicured hacks from
Malibu cause the people will see
That aint our Bill but a haint of
The silver screen. A disembodied
Wish of a Yalie's dream

Our Bill is where the camellia
Grows and by the waterfalls. He's
Sleeping in a hundred trees and in
A hundred skies. That cumulus
That just went by that's Bill's
Old smiling face. He's having a joke
On Hollywood
He's on the varmint's case.

Railroad Bill was a wizard. And
His final trick was tame. Wasn't
Nothing to become some celluloid
And do in all the frames.

And how did he manage technology
And how did Bill get so modern?
He changed hisself to a production
Assistant and went to work with
The scissors.
While nobody looked he scissored
Old Bill he used the scissors.

Railroad Bill was a conjure man
He could change hisself to the end.
He could outwit the chase and throw
Off the scent he didn't care what
They sent. He didn't give a damn what
They sent.
Railroad Bill was a conjure man
Railroad Bill was a star he could change
Hisself to the sun, the moon
Railroad Bill was free
Railroad Bill was free

The Kardek Method

No son, I dont wanta draw
I hung up my *Petro* in the Spring
of '68. Had got done with pick
ing notches; and what with the wing
ing and all, I ask you, was it
worth it?
So uncock your rod friend. Have
a sitdown.
While I stand back about 15 feet
think about some positive things. The
gals at the Road to Ruin Cabaret at the
end of the trail. The ranch in
Arizona you have your heart set
on.
Dont fret the blue rays emanating from
my fingers. They aint gonna cut you.
A-ha. Just as I thought. Your outside
aura looks a little grey. Your particles
cry the dull murmur of dying. I detect
a little green and red inside your
protecting sheet. You are here but
your ghost running cross a desert in a
greyhound. It bought a ticket to
No Place In Particular.
Swoooooooooooooooooooosh!!
Yonder went the Combined Hand Pass
    Feel Better?

Haitians

1

Fell the leader and
Confuse the pack
Nature's way, this
Shaggy, limping buffalo
Is downed by
Fanged schemers with plenty
Of time, a dry, crawling,
Beach fooled a Chief Whale into
Thinking it was a sea

2

We too are taken in like
Fishbelly, Mississippi in
Paris, no sooner had he
Arrived but here they come
The jackals
Camping about his favorite
Cafés
Mooching off of him, the Blackamoors
Bearing tales about him on
A greenback pillow to the
Crew-cutted sheik
Remember?
The Island of Hallucinations

3

The prospect of Bird going
Tenor made saxophones leap
Like it was a Wall Street crash
Many hornmen were wiped out

4

You know, I used to be a
Hyena, many grins ago
Before my cabin door, this
Morning, the naked rooster
In the Georgia Sea Islands our
Brothers and Sisters have a
Cure for this mess. They
Let the sun infuse the print
    Me too

Skirt Dance

i am to my honey what marijuana is
to tiajuana. the acapulco gold of her
secret harvest. up her lush coasts i
glide at midnite bringing a full boat.
(that's all the spanish i know.)

Kali's Galaxy

My 200 inch eyes are trained
on you, my love spectroscope
Breaking down your wavelengths
With my oscillating ear
I have painted your
Portrait: ermine curled about
Yonder's glistening neck

They say you are light-years
Away, but they understand so
Little

You are so near to me
We collide
Our stars erupt into supernovae
An ecstatic cataclysm that
Amazes astronomers

I enter your Milky Way
Seeking out your suns
Absorbing your heat
Circumventing your orbs
Radiating your nights

Once inside your heavens
I hop from world to world
Until I can go no longer
And Z out in your dust
Your new constellation
Known for my shining process
And fish-tailed chariot

Poison Light

FOR J. OVERSTREET

Last night
I played Kirk Douglas to
Your Burt Lancaster. Reflecting
20 years of tough guys I
Saw at the Plaza Theatre in
Buffalo, New York. I can
Roll an L like Bogart
You swagger like Wayne

Ours was a bad performance
The audience, our friends
Panned it. The box office
Hocked the producers

We must stop behaving like
The poison light we grew on

Ancient loas are stranded
They want artfare home
Our friends watch us. They
Want to hear what we say

Let's face it
My eye has come a long way
So has your tongue
They belong on a pyramid wall
Not in a slum
("Dead End"; 1937)

The Decade that Screamed

       the sun came up
the people yawned and stretched
in rat traps whipping mildewed cats,
pomaded and braced in gold bathrooms of
baroque toilet boxes,
from chairs with paws,
from snuff cases,
from the puzzlement of round square rooms
they poured into the streets,
yelling down phantom taxi cabs,
jostling old men
blowing their noses with tired flags

some came in steel rickshaws
some in buicks
some on weird pack animals
talking extinct words
(linguists bought them kool aid)
some popped gum
some were carried
some grumbled
some fondled pistols
others in trench coats jotted down names
for the state   took photos

babies set up tents
and auctioned off errant mothers
jive oatmeal was flung at finger-wagging humanists
who drew up their hind legs and split for the cafés
covering their faces with *Les Temps Moderne*
with grapefruit and cherries

a famous editor was hanged on the spot for quoting
jefferson with almost no deliberation his credit cards
stamps line gauge correspondence and grey pages
slid towards the sewer

some sprinted
some bopped
some leaned on shaky lamp posts
others sat down
crossed their legs
and marveled
as the old men
talked of what was
talked of what is
talked of what is to come
talked crazy talk
toyed with their whiskers
threw difficult finger exercises at each other
(white lightning)

jumped like birds
jumped like lions
(yellow thunder)

a girl above   on a ledge toes over the edge
knees knocking teeth chattering

       JUMP JUMP JUMP (millions of hands megaphoning
          razored lips)

some danced
some sang
some vomited
stained themselves
pared fingernails

the moon came sick with old testament hang ups
people fought over exits
rain rain on the splintered girl
rain rain on deserted rickshaws, buicks

in certain rooms we ball our fists
"today in Cyprus, gunbattling"
in certain rooms we say   how awful
"today in Detroit, sniper fire"
rain rain on the splintered girl
rain rain on the baby auctioneers

The Katskills Kiss Romance Goodbye

1

After twenty years of nods
He enters the new regime
The machine guns have been
Removed from the block
The women don't wear anything
You can see everything

2

Hendrick Hudson's Tavern
Has slipped beneath the
Freeway where holiday drivers
Rush as if they've seen the
Hessian Trooper seeking his
Head

3

They get their goosebumps at
The drive-in nowadays, where
The Lady in White at Raven
Rock is Bette Davis and
Burton apes Major André
Hanging before the Haunted
Bridge

4

A New England historian has
Proof that King George wasn't
So bad.
Gave in to every demand
Donated tea to the American needy
Yankees are just naturally jumpy

5

Where once stood madmen
Buttonholing you
Gentlemen think of Martinis
On the train to Mount Vernon

6

R.I.P. old Rip
Cuddle up in your Romance
Your dog Wolf is dead
Your crazy galligaskins out
Of style
Your cabbages have been canned
Your firelock isn't registered
Your nagging wife became a
Scientist, you were keeping
Her down

7

Go back to the Boarded Up
Alley and catch some more winks
Dreaming is still on the house

Untitled

law isn't all
The drivers test
Says nothing about
dogs, but people
stop anyway

Antigone, This Is It

FOR FRED

Whatever your name, whatever
Your beef, I read you like I
Read a book
You would gut a nursery
To make the papers, like
Medea your Poster Queen
You murder children
With no father's consent

You map your treachery shrewdly,
A computer
Click clicking
As it tracks a ship
Headed for the Unknown
Making complex maneuvers
Before splashing down into
Mystery

Suppose everyone wanted it their
Way, traffic would be bottled up
The Horsemen couldn't come
There would be no beauty, no radio
No one could hear your monologues
Without drums or chorus
In which you are right
And others, shadows, snatching things

Fate, The Gods, A Jinx, The Ruling Class
Taboo, everything but you
All the while you so helpless
So charming, so innocent

Crossed your legs and the lawyer
Muttered, dropped your hankie
And the judges stuttered

You forgot one thing though, thief
Leaving a silver earring at the
Scene of a house you've pilfered
You will trip up somewhere
And the case will be closed

Standup Antigone,
The jury finds you guilty
Antigone, may the Eater
Of The Dead savor your heart
You wrong girl, you wrong
Antigone, you dead, wrong
Antigone, this is it

Your hair will turn white overnight

And the Devil Sent a Ford Pinto
Which She Also Routed

Sarah was banged &
Slammed & thrown &
Jostled, shook &
Shifted & ripped
& rumpled

D nex day she was on
D freeway

Tennesseeee women

    thoroughbreds

Cuckoo

A cuckoo is a funny bird
Ridiculously masked he will
Tickle your tummy with
His quill
He will look like you
And be your brother

He will cheep your old favorites
At the drop of your dime

A cuckoo is a silly thing
Until he eliminates your offspring
And splits your ears with
His origin

Rock Me, Baby

Turning Screw: In wave-guide
Technique an ad
Justing element in the form of
A rod whose depth of pene
Tration through the wall into
A wave-guide or cavity is ad-
Justable by rotating a screw

Mystery 1st Lady

franklin pierce's wife never
came downstairs.   she never
came upstairs either.

To a Daughter of Isaiah

I saw your drumming lover
On the tube last night
His wrists had been riveted
He made faces, like Jazz
Was a dentist
His gutbucket was
Straight from the Academy
That is, you couldn't
Grind to it
(Matthew Arnold, blowing
His nose)

He drummed, I summed
You up while helping white
Wine get better:
Your juicy Ethiopian art
Lips (my, my)
Your moans. What moans!
Even the ceiling over the bed
Got hard

This happened way back in a book
You were my daughter of Isaiah
I was your flail and crook

My Brothers

They come up here
Shit on my floor
Spill my liquor
Talk loud
Giggle about my books
Remove things from their
Natural places

They come up here
And crackle the snot-
Nosed sniggle about
My walk my ways my words

Signify about what is
Dear to me

My brothers
They come up here and
Hint at underhanded things
Look at me as if to
Invite me outside

My brothers
They come up here
And put me on the hot
Seat so I feel I am
Walking the last mile

My wrong, sorry, no
Manners brothers

I will invite them again
I must like it?

You tell me

Contest ends at midnight

The Vachel Lindsay Fault

All wines are
Not the same
Red, nor are
All Bloods

Nothing to
Brood about
But, nevertheless
A dud

Back to Africa

A Tartar Wolf
Spider
Spinning
From the ceiling

Instead of
Squashing
You look
It up

Swift, Tiny and Fine

He can climb vulgar
Like scooting up the
Side of a diamond
Discourse with a phoenix
Sail out to sea in a
Golden-brown doughnut
He can run a rodeo
With ants

    This man
Can make the M in Mc
Donald's a rainbow
Transpose a sonata from
Fiddle to trumpet
Run out to the back yard
Pick a plum, eat that
Plum, run back
Sit down, cross his
Legs, smile
Then hear that sonata
Before it's tooted

Good

What the heck
I'm sick of Roller Derby champeens

A hummingbird standing still in mid air,
Robert Hayden is The Great Aware

Crocodiles

A crocodile dont hunt
Him's victims
They hunts him
All he do is
Open he jaws

Al Capone in Alaska

or
hoodoo ecology vs the judeo-
christian tendency to *let em*
have it!

The Eskimo hunts
the whale & each year
the whale flowers for the
Eskimo.
This must be love baby!
One receiving with respect
from a Giver who has
plenty.
There is no hatred here.
There is One Big Happy
Family here.

American & Canadian Christians
submachine gun the whales.
They gallantly sail out &
shoot them as if the Pacific
were a Chicago garage on
St. Valentine's day

Visit to a Small College

you name your buildings after
john greenleaf whittier. you
left a great critic Nick Aaron
Ford waiting at the airport
for 3 hours. the room i
sleep in is scorching but
when i request an air
conditioner you think it
a joke.

"open the window," you chuckle.

you invited me here but
don't have my books on your
list, or in your
bookstore.

i landed in your town
at 12 midnite & sarah
pointed to the blood on the
moon.

that will teach me to
mark my omens. believing
in future ones and up
dating old ones.
let's see
the president dropped the first
baseball of the season last yr.
what does that portend?

The Atlantic Monthly, December 1970

THE LAST STANZA OF WHICH IS A RUSSELLIAN
STANZA NAMED FOR ITS BEST CRAFTSMAN—
NIPSEY RUSSELL

Many whiskey ads. More even than *The
New Yorker*. Not even the subtlety of
Coolidge, wearing Indian feathers but
Seagram's V.O. covers an entire page.
Does enamel prose drive its readers
to drink? Living in New York? Or
Commentary's exchange of letters be
tween Podhoretz and Kazin? Rapiers!
Stilettos! Letter knives used to open
linen envelopes, 19 stories above the
upper West Side.

Well what about us and our razors?
*The Rhythms, The Chicago Nation,
The Crescent Moons, The Pythons or
The Berkeley Boppers?* Man, we
Dukes and do we? Muhammad Ali rum
blers; Riders of the Purple Rage

Dear *Atlantic Monthly* Dec. 1970.
Is Augustus still the Emperor? Can
Rev. Billy Moyers dance on a dime?
Is that Ralph Ellison in Frank Sin-
atra's raincoat or Floyd Patterson
lifting several White Hopes from
the canvas? The album notes for
Strangers in the Night?

Well what did I expect? The multi
ple assassin theory of the *L.A.
Free Press*? *E.V.O.*'s hepatitis
yellow? The Dubious Achievements of
Esquire? The Schwarz is Beautiful
school teacher over at *Evergreen*
clinging to her English text?

You pays your dollar and you gets
Tabbed. Ah, that smooth velvet taste
We've come a long way from *Sneaky
Pete*, now hain't we? You know
we is

Confidentially though,
a young writer informed me that
this *Atlantic* issue made him
feel like Sugar Ray among the
Mormons. The black-as-Ham Utah
night when Sugar took off Gene
Fullmer's jaw. Never will for
get it. A left hook from out
of nowhere. And before his crafty
handlers could wise their boy to
the Sean O Casey shuffle and the
Mark Twain Possum, Fullmer had
done received his Baron Saturday
and was out cold on the floor.

"Why did they stop it? I'm not
hurt, the Kayoed Kid complain
ed. But it was too late, the sta
dium was empty, and Sugar was
on the train.

The Last Week in 30

FOR VICTOR CRUZ ON D MOON

5 before 2/22 i am
a magnified lizard in
a science fiction film. 1944
is when it was made; the
year ol men played volley
ball w/ children before add
ing them to the bones of
      europe

mother of dragons a swell
head said just as the ufo
carried him off. right
on time too; they signed his
happy papers d day befo. he
couldn/t keep his tongue
      still

i am spending my birthday in
a city built on junk left by
    a   glacier

a zoology professor/s wife jumped
off a bridge last week. that
fri he heard heavy breathing on
the other end of the line. the
news called it alienation

aint gon kill this cat. i
am moving into a new age. today
i broke the ice. my pulse begins to
move across a new world.

Loup Garou Means Change Into

If Loup Garou means change into
When will I banish mine?
I say, if Loup Garou means change
Into when will I shed mine?
This eager Beast inside of me
Seems never satisfied

I was driving on the Nimitz wasn't
Paying it no mind
I was driving on the Nimitz wasn't
Paying it no mind
Before you could say "Mr. 5 by 5"
I was doin 99

My Cherokee is crazy
Can't drink no more than 4
My Cherokee is crazy
Can't stand no more than 4
By the time I had my 15th one
I was whooping across the floor
I was talking whiskey talking
I was whooping across the floor

Well, I whistled at a Gypsy who was reading at my cards
She was looking at my glad hand when something came
Across the yard started wafting across the kitchen
Started drifting in the room, the black went out her
Eyeballs a cat sprung cross her tomb
I couldn't know what happened till I looked behind the door
Where I saw her cold pale husband
WHO'S BEEN DEAD SINCE 44

They say if you get your 30
You can get your 35
Folks say if you get to 30
You can make it to 35
The only stipulation is you
Leave your Beast outside

Loup Garou the violent one
When will you lay off me
Loup Garou the Evil one
Release my heart my seed
Your storm has come too many times
And yanked me to your sea

I said please Mr. Loup Garou
When will you drop my goat
I said mercy Mr. Loup Garou
Please give me victory
I put out the beans that evening
Next morning I was free

.05

If i had a nickel
For all the women who've
Rejected me in my life
I would be the head of the
World Bank with a flunkie
To hold my derby as i
Prepared to fly chartered
Jet to sign a check
Giving India a new lease
On life

If i had a nickel for
All the women who've loved
Me in my life i would be
The World Bank's assistant
Janitor and wouldn't need
To wear a derby
All i'd think about would
Be going home

The Author Reflects on His 35th Birthday

35? I have been looking forward
To you for many years now
So much so that
I feel you and I are old
Friends and so on this day, 35
I propose a toast to
Me and You
35? From this day on
I swear before the bountiful
Osiris that
If I ever
If I EVER
Try to bring out the
Best in folks again I
Want somebody to take me
Outside and kick me up and
Down the sidewalk or
Sit me in a corner with a
Funnel on my head

Make me as hard as a rock
35, like the fellow in
The story about the
Big one that got away
Let me laugh my head off
With Moby Dick as we reminisce
About them suckers who went
Down with the *Pequod*
35? I ain't been mean enough
Make me real real mean

Mean as old Marie rolling her eyes
Mean as the town Bessie sings about
"Where all the birds sing bass"

35? Make me Tennessee mean
Cobra mean
Cuckoo mean
Injun mean
Dracula mean
Beethovenian-brows mean
Miles Davis mean
Don't-offer-assistance-when
Quicksand-is-tugging-some-poor
Dope-under-mean
Pawnbroker mean
Pharaoh mean
That's it, 35
Make me Pharaoh mean
Mean as can be
Mean as the dickens
Meaner than mean

When I walk down the street
I want them to whisper
There goes Mr. Mean
"He's double mean
He even turned the skeletons
In his closet out into
The cold"

And 35?
Don't let me trust anybody
Over Reed but
Just in case
Put a tail on that
Negro too

                         February 22, 1973

Jacket Notes

Being a colored poet
Is like going over
Niagara Falls in a
Barrel

An 8 year old can do what
You do unaided

The barrel maker doesn't
Think you can cut it

The gawkers on the bridge
Hope you fall on your
Face

The tourist bus full of
Paying customers broke-down
Just out of Buffalo

Some would rather dig
The postcards than
Catch your act

A mile from the brink
It begins to storm

But what really hurts is
You're bigger than the
Barrel

A Secretary to
the Spirits

Pocadonia

You dragged me into your love pond
Pocadonia, your snapping turtle got the
best of me
You dragged me into your love pond
Pocadonia, your snapping turtle got
the best of me
It was raining down on Hang-over morning
my head was in a sag
I looked over at your pillow
A crease was where you used to be

For one whole year after you left
I wouldn't hardly touch my food
For one skinny year after you left
I wouldn't hardly touch my food
lived on wheat chex and peanut butter
lived on crusty bread and rice

Slept on a cold cold floor for a mattress
Dressed in salt water crocodile skin
Slept on a cold cold floor for a mattress
Dressed in salt water crocodile skin
People would point at me and murmur
Whenever I'd leave my den

Caught catfish with my barehands
And breaded it Cedar Rapids style
Caught catfish with my barehands
and fried it Cedar Rapids style
My only form of diversion
Was the hoot owls who were hooting outside

Used to go up on Indian Mountain
Watch the Gold Coast ships come in
Used to go up on Indian Mountain
Watch the Gold Coast ships come in
Wondering where was my red-eyed Pocadonia
Wondering where was my baby's been

I see by the Magnavox
where they burn candles for you
on the beaches of Rio
Images of you on the finest pottery
All the school girls wear the shampoo
you wear
Your face on the national stamps like
the King's
The drunk plays your song on the
Seabird till three
Pocadonia, Pocadonia why have you
forgotten me?

You up there on television
doing your standard trance dance
the thirty-foot Indian Python
the one I gave you resting on
your shoulders like white wings
They done made you Ms. Spirit World

Pocadonia Pocadonia
Do you remember me?
As you ride next to your new Obeah
Three finger Jack of the Bugaboo trade
In his 1971 white Eldorado, eyes behind shades
Wearer of imitation leopard skin suits
He's made you his slave
He has a franchise on wing-tipped shoes
He's done turned your eye again

His rhythm section sounds like beer cans
Rattling from the rear of a wedding hearse
You always like them loud Pocadonia
Your bent for plaid men with their lucky Roots

Rabbit's foot $300.00 leather-pants skin tight
They love to show out at ringside
During the Ali-Frazier fight
Pocadonia, you have gone red on me again

Pocadonia, my love do you remember me
When they duppy you again please don't
Call on me
I'm like a full-up motel with a fabulous view
My dreams, they say, No Vacancy to you
I'm like a full-up motel with a fabulous view
My dreams, they say, No Vacancy to you

Poem Delivered Before Assembly of Colored People Held at Glide Memorial Church, Oct. 4, 1973 and Called to Protest Recent Events in the Sovereign Republic of Chile

In the winter of 1966 Pablo Neruda
Lifted 195 lbs of ragged scrawls
That wanted to be a poet and put
Me in the picture where we stood
Laughing like school chums

No little man ever lifted me like that

Pablo Neruda was a big man
It is impossible for me to believe that
Cancer could waste him
He was filled with barrel-chested poetry
From stocky head to feet and
Had no need for mortal organs
The cancer wasn't inside of Pablo Neruda
Cancer won't go near poetry
The cancer was inside ITT
The Cancer God with the
Nose of President Waterbugger
The tight-Baptist lips of John Foster Dulles
And the fleshy Q Ball head of
Melvin Laird
Dick Tracy's last victim

The Cancer God with the body
Of the rat-sucking Indian Plague Flea
All creepy transparent and hunched up
Stalks the South American copper
Country with its pet anaconda
It breathes and hollers like

All thc Japanese sci fi monsters
Rolled into one: Hogzilla
Its excrescency supply the Portuguese
With napalm

The Cancer God is a bully who mooches up
Rational gentle and humanistic men
But when it picked a fight with the poet
It got all the cobalt-blue words it could use
And reels about holding in its insides

Do something about my wounded mother
Says President Waterbugger
Shambling across the San Clemente beach
Whose sand is skulls grinded
Do something about my wounded mother
Says the slobbering tacky thing
Pausing long enough from his hobby
Ripping-off the eggs of the world
Their albumen oozing down his American
Flag lapel, his bareassed elephant
Gyrating its dung-wings
Give her all of South America if shc wants it
And if she makes a mess
Get somebody to clean it up
Somebody dumb
A colonel who holds his inaugural address
Upside down and sports
Miss-matched socks

And if they can't stomach their
New leaders' uglysucker French
Angel faces then cover them up with
A uniform or hide its Most Disgusting
In a tank
Cover it up like they want to cover
Me up those pitiful eyes gazing from
The palm tree freeway of the Dead War

President Waterbugger your crimes
Will not leave office
No imperial plastic surgeon can
Remove them from your face
They enter the bedroom of your
Hacienda at night and rob you
Of your sleep
They call out your name

President Waterbugger
Next to you Hitler resembles
A kindergarten aide
Who only wanted to raise some geese
And cried when listening to
Dietrich Fischer-Dieskau
Everything you put your paws on
Becomes all crummy and yukky
In New Jersey the mob cries for Jumboburgers
In Florida the old people are stealing Vitamin E

President Waterbugger only your crimes
Want to be near you now
Your daughters have moved out of town
Your wife refuses to hold your hand
On the elevator
Inexplicably, Lincoln's picture
Just fell from the wall
Next time you kill a poet
You'd better read his poems first
Or they will rise up and surround you
Like 1945 fire cannons a few miles from
Berlin
And History will find no trace of
Your ashes in the bunker of your hell

A Secretary to the Spirits

The following minutes were
logged by this Secretary to
the Spirits during the last five
years which have occasionally been
like a devil woman on a heart

Sometimes I felt
only a beetle could inch up
from this situation
Y'awl know what I mean

I am no beetle
not even a bishop
got 90% wrong on the priest's
exam
Scared of snakes

Just a red baboon with the
hurricane's eye
got up sometimes in a Businessman's
three-piece
Mostly an errand boy for the spirits
It's honest Work
You can even come by promotions
I'll rise or
maybe grow up even

I hail from a long line of
risers
like Grand ma ma, old oak
off on a new path
she sculpts from the clay

Sather Tower Mystery

Seems there was this Professor
a member of what should be called
The Good German Department

Must have signed his name to
5,000 petitions in front of
the Co-Op on Cedar
and bought two tons of benefit
cookies
Blames Texas for the sorry
state of the oceans
Rode a Greyhound bus "Civil
Rights," Alabama, 1960
Found the long yellow war
"deplorable"
Believes John "Duke" Wayne's
values to be inferior to his

He said, "Ishmael, I'd
love to do the right thing
for as you know I'm all for
the right thing and against
the wrong thing, but
these plaster of paris busts
of deceased Europeans
Our secret ways
Our sacred fears

"These books, leather-bound
'copyright 1789'
All of these things, precious
to me, gleaming like the
stainless steel coffee urn in
the faculty club, an original
Maybeck, 1902

"I'd stand up for Camelot
by golly, even if it meant
shooting all the infidels in
the world," he said
reaching into his desk drawer

"Why, I might even have to
shoot you, Ishmael"

Staring down the cold
tunnel of a hard .38
I thought

*Most people are to the right
when it comes to where they must
eat and lay their heads!*

Foolology

Shaken by his bad press, the wolf
presses north, leaving caribou to
the fox,
Raven, the snow player gets his
before buzzards with bright red
collars move in to dine near the
bottom of a long scavenger line

This poem is about a skunk, no
rather about a man, who though
not of the skunk family uses
his round-eye the way skunks do

After he eats, his friends eat
He is a fool and his friends are
fools but sometimes it's hard to
tell who is the biggest fool this
fool or his fool friends

By the time they catch us
we're not there
We crows
Nobody's ever seen a dead crow
on the highway

First moral: Don't do business
with people for whom April first
is an important date
they will use your bank balance to
buy eight thousand pies, tunics,
ballet slippers with bells and
a mail order lake in the middle of
a desert for splash parties

Second moral: Before you can spot the
fools in others you must rid yourself
of the fool in you
You can tell a fool by his big mouth

The Return of Julian the Apostate to Rome

Julian
Come back
It can't be long
For the emperor

He sees plots everywhere
Has executed three postmen
Rants in print against his
Former allies
Imagines himself a
Yoruba god
Has asked the Bishops to
Deify him

Not only is he short
He's nuts

Julian come back
The people are crapping
In the temples
Barbarian professors
Are teaching one god
They are ripping the limbs
Off our fetishes
They are carving the sea
Monsters from our totems
They made a pile of our
Wood sculpture and set fire
To it

Julian
Come back
Rude hags
Have crashed the senate
And are spitting on the
Elders

Meanwhile, Julian
The perennial art major
Ponders in the right wing
Of the monastery museum

The Egyptian collection

Sputin

Like Venus
My spin is retrograde
A rebel in more ways than one

I click my heels
In seedy taverns
& pinch the barmaids
On the cheeks

Madeira drips from
My devilish beard
My eyes sparkle dart
Flicker & sear
Man, do I love to dance

Something tells me the
Tzar will summon me to
Save his imperial hide

I peeped his messenger
Speeding through the gates of
The Winter Palace

He's heading this way

Soon, my fellow peasants will
See me in the Gazette
Taking tea with the royal family

They'll say
That crazy bum?

Sky Diving

"It's a good way to live and
A good way to die"
From a Frankenheimer video about
Sky diving
The hero telling why he liked to

       The following noon he leaped
       But his parachute wasn't with him
       He spread out on the field like
       Scrambled eggs

Life is not always
Hi-lifing inside
Archibald Motley's
"Chicken Shack"
You in your derby
Your honey in her beret
Styling before a small vintage
Car

Like too many of us
I am a man who never had much
Use for a real father
And so when I'm heading
For a crash
No one will catch me but
Me

The year is only five days old
Already a comet has glittered out
Its glow sandbagged by
The jealous sun

Happens to the best of us
Our brilliance falling off
Like hair from Berkeley's roving
Dogs

Even on Rose Bowl day
An otherwise joyous occasion
A float veered into the crowd
Somebody got bruised over the incident
Like a love affair on second ave.

It's a good lesson to us all
In these downhill days of a
Hard-hearted decade
Jetting through the world
Our tails on fire

    You can't always count
    On things opening up for you
    Know when to let go
    Learn how to fall

Soul Proprietorship

I.

Billy Eckstine, now I
understand why you
went solo, even if it meant crooning
the Pastrami and Rye circuit from
Miami to Grossinger's
Maybe you got tired of babysitting
for other people's tubas, or
running out for reeds
Maybe you got tired of the
spitballs breaking the skin
of your neck while in the midst
of one of those ostentatious supper-
club bows
The bounced checks and half-empty
seats were hard on your dignity
and the bad publicity you received
from the black eye you gave your
agent, co-hort in a secret
deal with management
didn't help

II.

You always had to put ice packs
on the lead tenor's head in Chicago
when by late afternoon a concert
was scheduled for Detroit
And there was always the genius
He was avant garde
which meant he had trouble playing
in scales of five flats
he spurned your attempts to

teach him things and went out
to organize his own band
They called their bloopers "new
music" and drew "experimental"
customers

customers who never smiled
and owned high blood pressure
When you travel single you
can take time out to catch up
with the funnies
You no longer have to order
40 cups of coffee
10 black
5 with cream, and
12 regular
You no longer have to keep
tabs on the two guys who wanted
tea

III.

And when your only companion became
your thought
You came up with the Billy Eckstine
Shirt
With prints as beautiful as
the handle of an Islamic sword
and you made a million silver dollars
And you bought an old Spanish mansion
in California whose
wings could be seen from the sea
They look like two shining silver
collars, billowing, for lift off

Vamp

No wonder the vampire
Is dead
From the hem of his
Cloak to the roots of
His fangs he is one big
Dummy

    Doesn't he
Know that creeping
Through the open windows
Of people's lives can
Lead to his extinction?
Carrying off peoples'
Dear ones can get him stuck

    You can't even
Stake the stud without
Becoming caked in his
Blood

    There is a vampire
Who is cutting into
My orderly progression
In my profession
He shadows me about the
Country like an itinerant
Snake
Everything I do, It do

He converts my
Friends into his concoctions
And convinces peasants that
I am their devil
He is putting ignorant
Heat on me

A wicked trick is dying
For me to use it
I can't hold out much longer
Vampire
In my sleep I hear you screaming
Vamp

Wise up Blood Sucker
Or you will have the
Dawn you hate

Sixth Street Corporate War

Not all rats live in sewers
Some of them dwell in 100,000 dollar
rat's nests on the Alameda
and drive to work in a Mercedes
laboratory rat white
You wouldn't even know they were
rats
on the mailbox it says Mr. Rodent

As big as a coffee table book
(The only book in the house)
he spends his time nibbling ratboy
in a rathouse with its
cheesy rat kitchen or scampering
on a rat sofa or in a bed of
rats
Or you might find him at the Ratskeller
wetting his rat whiskers on
rat soup
"my favorite drink" said
This shareholder rat there he
go old bureaucratic rat investor
in rattraps where people live
like rats

As years went by he gained more
status until he became the esteemed
Doctor Rattus
Crashed a tomcat convention and
demanded to be put on the
banquet
This even woke up Scrounger

or Mr. All Claws,
the toastmaster tomcat
catnapping on the dais
after a night of pre-
convention howling
"whaddya say, boys"
said the thrice decorated
rat scrapper
"rat cocktail
rat of the day
rat a la carte
or rat mousse?"

The other cats being
democrats cast their
votes by secret ballot
gulp!

Poetry Makes Rhythm in Philosophy

Maybe it was the Bichot
Beaujolais, 1970
But in an a.m. upstairs on
Crescent Ave. I had a conversation
with K.C. Bird

    We were discussing
rhythm and I said
"Rhythm makes everything move
the seasons swing
it backs up the elements
Like walking Paul-Chamber's fingers"

    "My worthy constituent"
Bird said, "The Universe is a
spiralling Big Band in a
polka-dotted speakeasy,
effusively generating new light
every one-night stand"

We agreed that nature can't
do without rhythm but rhythm can
get along without nature

This rhythm, a stylized Spring
conducted by a blue-collared man
in Keds and denims
(His Williamsville swimming pool
shaped like a bass clef)
in Baird Hall
on Sunday afternoons
Admission Free!

All *harrumphs!* must be
checked in at
the door

I wanted to spin
Bennie Moten's
"It's Hard to Laugh or Smile"
but the reject wouldn't automate
and the changer refused to drop
"Progress," you know

Just as well
because Bird vanished

A steel band had
entered the room

Untitled

Today I feel bearish
I've just climbed out of
A stream with a jerking
Trout in my paw

Anyone who messes with
Me today will be hugged
And dispatched

The Reactionary Poet

If you are a revolutionary
Then I must be a reactionary
For if you stand for the future
I have no choice but to
Be with the past

Bring back suspenders!
Bring back Mom!
Homemade ice cream
Picnics in the park
Flagpole sitting
Straw hats
Rent parties
Corn liquor
The banjo
Georgia quilts
Krazy Kat
Restock

The syncopation of
Fletcher Henderson
The Kiplingesque lines
of James Weldon Johnson
Black Eagle
Mickey Mouse
The Bach Family
Sunday School
Even Mayor La Guardia
Who read the comics
Is more appealing than
Your version of
What Lies Ahead

In your world of
Tomorrow Humor
Will be locked up and
The key thrown away
The public address system
Will pound out headaches
All day
Everybody will wear the same
Funny caps
And the same funny jackets
Enchantment will be found
Expendable, charm, a
Luxury
Love and kisses
A crime against the state
Duke Ellington will be
Ordered to write more marches
"For the people," naturally

If you are what's coming
I must be what's going

Make it by steamboat
I likes to take it real slow

Rough Trade Slumlord Totem

Here's how you put your enemy
atop a totem where the scavengers
get at him

This is for you, dummy
who hoarded our writings in
your basement, four solid months
like your brother landlord of
Sitka, Alaska, who chopped-up
the Tlingit totems for bar-b-cue chairs

The Raven will get you sucker
The Raven will hunt you down
Gaaaaaa! Gaaaaaaa! sucker

The thunder will empty its
bladder on your face you
seal-cow man who wobbles on
his belly with common
law fish in his mouth

May seagulls litter your
Punch-and-Judy corked eyes
May the eagle mistake your
snout for a mouse and sink
its claws into it
May the paint used on your
head be slum lord paint bound
to peel in a short time

And when you crash I hope
your landing place be
a maggot's hunting party
And while the rest of the
totem journey's into mother
soil
your segment remains
your sideshow providing
Laughing Forest
with a belly full

Tea Dancer Turns Thirty-nine

They will swoon no more his
four o'clock afternoons,
He bids farewell to his taxi
dancing heart throbs
He donates his clicks to the
Boogie Hall of Fame
Roll on Mississippi Roll on

From Beyond, cognac-voiced
Bojangles sent him El Rito
strawberries covered with Jack
Frost sugar, big as peaches!

A gesture from a man who could
Essence so, God ringed Satan to
wish him Happy Birthday

       Not too far back
his silver medals danced in
the brightest hock windows of
Bret Harte Boardwalk.
Now, it's caviar omelettes at
number one Fifth Ave

What changed his luck?

The little lady he calls his
Tiger Balm, the one beneath a Coit
Tower, half way up from Half Moon
Bay?

He hurries to her
Her red dragon in his eyes
red as the red trees of Modesto
red as the red in the red bridge of
death
Moon Ocean red

Colorwheels light upon Filipino gazers
in the Palace of Old Tokyo town their
wriggling rumps rooting for Donald Byrd
and the Black Byrds while just across town
romance has been replaced by shrunken jeans
You look like a sack, he said, before she
hurled chocolate milk at his white
European double-breasted suit

An embarrassing situation for the Order
of the Golden Bear, on the other side
of the Bay Bridge, having to negotiate
with lucky Feet who tripped them up
like the accidental hero in the Bank Dick
He spilled ashes all over the Queen's
Thug rug
She could do nothing but smile her
Silver-Jubilee smile, an outrage
to the civilized world
Would your majesty jern me in a game
of chanct? he said, sweeping his big
hairy floor-length arms and flipping
drumsticks to the ceiling
Will crocodiles reach Kampala this
year, or the Taj Mahal yellow?

They laughed at his blue serge suit
Dobbs crumpled from being sat on
but when he fired a revolver into
the cushion, they knew he wasn't
kidding

And then there was the
Tea Dancer's march when the old ones
put the young set to shame with their
glides, kneebends, squats and
twirls

These days you have to have a Ph.D.
In the old days all you had to do was
dance

We mount our old days next to our stuffed
shoes and feed them wines only popes used
to drink

He's a spin around fool and his eyes are
kind of hazy but that don't mean he's lazy
if anything it means he's crazy
Give him a thousand dollars and he'll
sign off his professional frog's legs
(a minute of silence for Legs Diamond,
tea dancer, slain in Niagara Falls phone
booth—most people run out of steam—
tea dancers run out of dimes)

He doesn't know the difference between
his golden slippers and Stacey Adams
continued Fast Foods, the Boss
I ought to know, I run a factory full
of dead horses
when I'm not killing television

He thought of what Leslie Laguna said
in the Hotel Loretto up near Santa
Fe way, about why hares are heroines
in trickster tales
Because they're quick! she said
The Quick and the Dead

And so from the Papyrus Room
of the Pyramid Hotel
high above the River Nile of
his dream
Let's spin out some to
a crackling bundle
of Tennessee two-fisted
aqua-eyed fire
Born in grand old Oakland
on the day of six twos
Her smile spanned the delivery room

Finally, this item
today is the seventh
day of the seventh month
of the seventy-seventh year
of this century

Apples grow on trees!

Points of View

For Dancer

When lovers die they blossom
grapes
That's why there's so much
wine in love
That's why I'm still drunk
on you

Earthquake Blues

Well the cat started actin funny
and the dog howled all night long
I say the cat started actin very frightful
and the birds chirped all night long
The ground began to rumble
As the panic hit the town.

Mr. Earthquake Mr. Earthquake
you don't know good from bad
Mr. Earthquake Mr. Earthquake
you don't know good from bad
You kill the little child in its nursery
You burn up the widow's pad

The buildings started swaying
like a drunk man walking home
The buildings started swaying
like a drunk man walking home
The people they were running
and the hurt folks began to moan

Mr. Earthquake Mr. Earthquake
you don't know good from bad
Mr. Earthquake Mr. Earthquake
you don't know good from bad
You kill the little child in its nursery
You burn up the widow's pad

I got underneath my table
Had my head between my knees
I got underneath the table
Had my head between my knees
The dishes they were rattlin
and the house was rockin me

Mr. Earthquake Mr. Earthquake
you don't know good from bad
Mr. Earthquake Mr. Earthquake
you don't know good from bad
You kill the little child in its nursery
You burn up the widow's pad

I was worried about my baby
Was she safe or was she dead
I was worried about my baby
Was she safe or was she dead
When she phoned and said I'm
ok, Daddy. Then I went on back
to bed.

Mr. Earthquake Mr. Earthquake
you don't know good from bad
Mr. Earthquake Mr. Earthquake
you don't know good from bad
You kill the little child in its nursery
You burn up the widow's pad

Points of View

I

The pioneer stands in front of the
Old pioneer's home with his back-pack
walking stick and rifle
Wasn't me that Kisadi Frog-Klan
Indian was talking about when he
mentioned the horrors of Alaska
What horrors of Alaska?
Why Baranof was a swell fellow
Generous to the Indians, he was
known as far south as California
for his good deeds
Before we came the Indians were
making love to their children and
sacrificing their slaves, because
the Raven told them so, according
to them
"They couldn't even speak good
English and called the streams and
the mountains funny names
They were giving each other refrigerators
the potlatches had become so bad

We made them stop
They'd build a canoe abandon
it, then build another
We made them stop that, too
Now they have lawyers

They can have anything they want
If they want to go whaling
when we know they don't need to
go whaling
The lawyers see to it that they
go whaling
They're just like us
They buy frozen snow peas
just like we do
They're crazy about motorcycles
Just like we are

We brought them civilization
We brought them penicillin
We brought them Johnny Carson
Softball
We brought them trailer camps
They'd get married at fourteen
and die at 24
We brought them longevity

II
They brought us carbon dioxide
They brought us contractors
We told them not to dig there
They were clawed by two eagles
While uncovering the graves of
two medicine men

The white man has the mind of a
walrus's malignant left ball
We don't think the way they do
They arrive at the rate of one
thousand per month in cars
whose license plates read
texas oklahoma and mississippi
They built the Sheffield Hotel on
a herring bed
Everywhere are their dogs
Everywhere are their guns
Everywhere are their salmon-faced

women who get knocked up a lot
and sometimes enter the Chanel
restaurant wearing mysterious black
eyes, socked into their Viking-eyes
by men whose hair is plastered with
seal dung
It all began when
Chief Kowee of the Raven Klan showed
Joe Juneau the location of the gold
Now Mount Juneau is as empty as
a box of popcorn on the floor of
a picture show
When our people saw the first
Russian ship, we thought it was
the White Raven's return
Instead it was the Czarina's pirate
Dressed in Russian merchant's clothes
and a peacock's hat.
He shot Katlian in the back

The Ballad of Charlie James

I
Hunter's Point: Night
Papa Charlie James awakes
to see the 'Frisco police
at the foot of his bed
"Bring them hands from
underneath them sheets so's
we can see them. Let us see
what you got beneath those
sheets," they said, shooting
seventeen rounds of ammunition
into Charlie's bed

II
He survived the crazy rhythms
in his chest
his lungs whistling like
ghost winds, but he couldn't
survive the police
Hazardous to your health
if you are poor, Indian, or
Chicano, or if you're a sixty
year old black man asleep in
bed "Bring them hands from
underneath those sheets so's we can
see them, let us see what you got
beneath those sheets"

Like in Count Albuquerque's
town, where underneath the freeway
a lone woman wears "I Want Your Body"
on her t-shirt, a black man can get

shot for just horsing around
They use the redman for target
practice, they hang the Mexican
in jail.
O ain't it a shame what they did
to poor Charlie James. Have mercy
and ain't it a shame
"He just played dominoes
drank soda water, and looked
out the window" his neighbors said
Thinking of his poor wife in a
Georgia loony bin
she saw her children die
one by one
Thinking of his mother out
there in the backwater cemetery
her shroud faded
her eye sockets, windows for
spiders, "Bring them hands
from underneath those sheets so's
we can see them. Let us see what you
have beneath those sheets"
The sign on Charlie's door
"Making Love Is Good For You"
shot full of bulletholes

His brains liver and kidneys
gone up in smoke
"Making Love Is Good For You"
His stomach will hold no more
beans
no more bad coffee
his lips have seen their last
cigarette
O ain't it a shame what they did
To Charlie James. Have mercy ain't
it a shame.

They said his homicide was justified
the parrot D.A. "concurred"
The police were just doing their
duty, they said, and the
parrot D.A. "concurred, concurred"
O the parrot D.A. "concurred"
O ain't it a shame what they did
to poor Charlie James
"Making Love Is Good For You"
"Bring them hands from underneath
those sheets so's we can see them.
Let's see what you have beneath those
sheets."

Points of View

The pioneers and the indians
disagree about a lot of things
for example, the pioneer says that
when you meet a bear in the woods
you should yell at him and if that
doesn't work, you should fell him
The indians say that you should
whisper to him softly and call him by
loving nicknames
No one's bothered to ask the bear
what he thinks

Bitch

When's the last time you
saw a dog eat a dog

When men invented the term
Bitch
They were talking about
themselves

Datsun's Death

"Down in Puerto Rico, when
we didn't have no kerosene
we used the stuff to read by"
the stuff
he took his first drink
at twenty, and by the age of
40 had sauced up enough to fill
all the billboard bottles from
Lafitte's Galveston to Houston's
Texas
There's enough light in his belly
to fire all the gas lamps in
Cincinnati
He remembers getting burned in Cincinnati
his radiator was hot
his temperature was rising
like the white 68 Dodge grumbling
up Moeser Lane, as ferocious as a
pit-bull
The accident cop would later
say
It must have been built like a
tank
rammed into my piece of tail
a hit and run, you've been there
haven't you partner
haven't you?

It was A.T. and T. which reminded us
that the heaviest traffic occurs at
4:30 a.m.
All the phone circuits are busy

I loves you baby
You know i loves you baby!
Do you loves me baby?
I don't care what you women
say
Prometheus was a man
the X rays just came back
his liver looks terrible

For the ground crew
at the Kirksville
airport a sweetheart
is the otter jetstream
of Illinois Airlines
while the two-toned
Monte Carlo parked next
to the Robin breasted
cornfield is baby

For me heaven was
tooling around in the
driver's seat of my
280ZX
my honey of the midnight blue
my import car of the year
mutilated by the brazen chrome
of a snorting bull-car
hot and swerving under
the El Cerrito moon

Plymouth, Cadillac, Mercury
Montego, the automobile gods
rattled in their Richmond junkyards
Chrysler and Ford sales went down
30% the next day
And the shining new sacrifices on display
at banner-waving San Bruno
parking lots,
Wept from their windshields
Some used-up like my Datsun
Head mashed against the rhododendrons

On the Fourth of July in Sitka, 1982

On the fourth of July in Sitka
Filipinos sold shish-ka-bob from their
booths in the park
On the fourth of July in Sitka, the children
dressed in deerskin jackets
and coonskin caps
On the fourth of July in Sitka, you
could buy fishpie in the basement of St. Michael's
Church, where the vodka-drunken Russians used to
pray
But the red white and blue cake was not for sale

On the fourth of July in Sitka the people
kicked off shoes and ran through the
streets, pushing beds
On the fourth of July in Sitka, tour buses
with yellow snouts and square heads
delivered tourists to the Shee Atika lodge
where they stared at floats designed by
Sheldon Jackson College and
the Alaska Women in Timber
On the fourth of July in Sitka the
Gajaa Heen dancers performed, wearing their
Klan emblems of Beaver Wolf Killer Whale
Porpoise, and Dog Salmon

On the fourth of July in Sitka the Libertarian
Party announced the winners of its five dollar raffle
1st Prize, a Winchester .300 Magnum
2nd Prize, an Ithaca 12 gauge shotgun
3rd Prize, a Sportsman III knife

On the fourth of July in Sitka the
softball teams were honored at the American
Legion Club and the players drank champagne till dawn
On the fourth of July in Sitka, the night was
speckled with Japanese fireworks
sponsored by Alaska Lumber and Pulp

On the fifth of July in Sitka
a Canadian destroyer brought to Sitka
for the fourth of July in Sitka sailed
through Sitka Sound and out into the
Northern Pacific
All of the men on board stood at
attention, saluting their audience
three bald eagles, two ravens, and me
watching the whole show from Davidoff Hill
the fifth of July in Sitka

Petite Kid Everett

The bantamweight King of
Newark
He couldn't box
He couldn't dance
He just kept coming at
you, glass chin first
Taking five punches for
every one he connected with
you

Petite Kid Everett
He missed a lot
Slipped a lot and
By mid–life he'd
developed one heck
of a sorehead
Took to fighting in
the alley
Gave up wearing a mouthpiece
Beat up his trainers
Beat up the referee
Beat up his fans
Beat up everybody who was
in his corner
Even jumped on Houston Jr.
the lame pail boy
Who didn't have good sense

Petite Kid Everett
There's talk of a comeback
He's got new backers
He stands on one of the four
corners, near the Prudential Life
Building
Trading blows with ghosts
Don't it make you wanna cry?

Turning Pro

There are just so many years
you can play amateur baseball
without turning pro
All of a sudden you realize
you're ten years older than
everybody in the dugout
and that the shortstop could
be your son

The front office complains
about your slowness in making
the line-up
They send down memos about
your faulty bunts and point out
how the runners are always faking
you out
"His ability to steal bases
has faded" they say
They say they can't convince
the accountant that there's such
a thing as "Old Time's Sake"
But just as the scribes were
beginning to write you
off
as a has-been on his last leg
You pulled out that fateful
shut-out
and the whistles went off
and the fireworks scorched a
747
And your name lit up the scoreboard
and the fans carried you on their
shoulders right out of the stadium
and into the majors

Epistolary Monologue

My Dearest Michael:

My favorite lady-in-waiting is so loyal. She certainly can keep a secret. Every day at teatime she sneaks me three bottles of Beefeater. She knows that I can't stand tea. Today she brought me your note. This morning, she had to bring me two tablets of Myaatal. I still haven't recovered from my trip to America. Must have been the tacos and beans we ate at the Reagan's Ranch. That woman is so rude. You remember how she tried to upstage me during her trip to London? Wailing about town with her motorcycle escorts. Got up in that tacky red dress and those wide-brimmed hats that make her resemble a witch. I was speaking to her husband, and the poor man fell asleep. Still telling the same jokes.

But back to your note, my sweet. Michael, I was so touched, but how would it look if another scandal happened to the Windsors? They still haven't gotten over Uncle Edward. If I ran away with you, the public would take away our allowances and evict us from Buckingham Palace. How would we survive? On hotdogs and beans. Our only experience is shaking hands and smiling. And there doesn't seem to be an awful demand for people who know how to walk in processions.

Somebody has to keep a level head. Andrew carrying on with that tart. Diana locked up in her room starving herself, all because she found out Charles's secret. The secret we've kept from the public all these years. Her look-alike is threatening to reveal the whole sordid business if she doesn't receive more money. And Princess Anne. Granted that she is my daughter, but sometimes I think that she's so ugly she should be arrested for public ugliness. The poor young man she's living with is always talking about leaving her. He says that he has to put a bag over her head in order to get a good night's sleep. So please understand, my darling. I do love you. Queens have feelings too, but if I married you, a poor laborer, who would feed my horses and my dogs?

Well, it's 2:00 a.m. here in the Palace. As the Americans say, "I'm in my gin." I just turned off all of the lights. Everyone here is so wasteful. Philip and my bodyguards are in the next room watching videocassettes of "Dynasty" and squealing with delight. O, I wish I could be like that Krystle. Always taking chances, going where her heart leads. But I've grown accustomed to my duty, my position, and the grand tradition of which I am a symbol.

And so, don't be cross with me when my lady-in-waiting delivers this note to you. Goodbye, my darling. And please forgive me for having you arrested. But when we were lying in bed that morning, and you complained about what you would and wouldn't do, I had to put you in your place. Though we were lovers, I was still your sovereign, which meant that my wish was your command.

Love,
Lilibet

Monkey Island

To the monkeys on Monkey Island
the danger signal for man is the
same as that for an approaching
python
That's why the monkeys on Monkey
Island chatter their tails off
when we stand in front of their
cages
They know something that we
Zoo Keepers don't know
Haven't you thought of a person
and said to yourself
that snake

The Pope Replies to the Ayatollah Khomeini

My Dear Khomeini:

I read your fourteen thousand dollar
ad asking me why the Vatican waited
all of these years to send an envoy
to complain about conditions in Iran
You're right, we should have sent one
when the Shah was in power, look,
I'm in total agreement with you
Khomeini, that Christ, had he lived in
Iran under the Shah, would have led the
biggest damned revolt you ever saw

Believe me, Khomeini, I knew about
the Shah's decadence, his extravagance
his misdeeds, and how he lolled about
in luxury with Iran's loot
I knew about the trail of jewels which
led to his Dad's capture
but a fella has to eat and so when
David Rockefeller asked me to do something
how could I refuse?

You can afford to be holier than thou
What is it, 30 dollars per barrel these days?
You must be bathing in oil
While each day I suffer a new indignity

You know that rock record they made me
do? It's 300 on the Charts which is about
as low as you can get.
And I guess you read where I

had to call in all those Cardinals and
for the first time reveal the Vatican
budget?
I had to just about get down on my hands
and knees to get them to co-sign for a
loan
The Vatican jet has a mechanical problem
and the Rolls-Royce needs a new engine
The staff hasn't been paid in months
and the power company is threatening to
turn off the candles
To add to that, the building inspector
has listed us as having 30,000 code
violations
I'm telling you, Khomeini, that
so many people are leaving the church
I have this nightmare where I
wake up one day in Los Angeles and
I'm the only one left

Pretty soon we'll be one of those
cults you read about in the *San
Francisco Chronicle*
And so, Khomeini, I promise
you that when we pay off the
deficit, I won't send an envoy
I'll come visit you myself

I'd like to discuss this plan
that Patriarch Dimitrios, of
the Greek Orthodox Church, and I
just came up with

You know, we haven't spoken to
those fellows in 900 years but
when you are 20 million dollars
in the red
You'll talk to anybody

Inaugural Day, 1981

I feel like a Zulu
spying from a rock while
below, the settlers exchange
toasts on the grounds where
a massacre of the Zulus occurred
They are filthy rich
Their wives are dolled-up in
black mink
There is much hugging and
squealing
These people like
Glenn Miller a whole lot
    52 of their countrymen
have been freed by the barbarians
overseas
    "Just out of the trees. The
Only way I'm going back is in a
B-52," he said, putting some hair
on his chest, and passing around
a jug of whiskey
    The settlers shoot at stars
    The settlers jitterbug all
    night
On the Zulu grounds
I have nine children buried there
nine were all they could find

Mossy

If you want to save some money
Always stare a gift cat in the mouth
Especially if you bought him on
Russian Hill
He might have developed
A palate

Untitled

When California is split in two
The Northern part will be called
The Republic of Jambalaya
The Southern part will be called
Summer Camp

Grizzly

He always prided himself on
never being caught with his paws down
The flying grizzly left his bear
tracks at fifty thousand feet
his life, a daily peach blossom
He always managed to find some
hot honey to dip into
He was smiling all the time
Licking his lips, till Mrs.
Grizzly discovered him in the
bush with some outside trim of
a wonderful red cabbage and Mrs.
Grizzly grounded her
Teddy Bear
the rough rider under her fur coat
she was not taken in by his sweet
word-bees
Last trip back to the cave
he felt like he'd entered customs
after a return from an enemy city
What are these claw marks doing on your back?
Are those huckleberry stains on the front
of your pants?
Why do you have that fishy smell?
The divorce left him belly-up

He's somewhere right now
dressed in white and black
checkered pants
being led at the neck by a rope
While he bangs on a dirty
bass drum
a little monkey toots a whistle
and little dogs taunt him
and little children tug at
his ears

Judas

Funny about best friends
huh, Lord
Always up in your face
laughing and talking
leading the praise after
your miracles
That Judas, you had great
hopes for him
Good background
Good-looking, even in a
corduroy suit, made in
Poland, and thirty dollar
shoes
It was his quiet appeal that
kept the group in wine money

As soon as you turned your
back, he took your business
to the Goyim
Told them you going around
telling everybody you the
son-of-god
See how careful you have to
be about whom you go bar-
hopping with, Jesus

Now you're drowsy, Jesus
They've pricked you full of
Thorazine
They've given you electro-
convulsive therapy

You don't know where you
are
You have sores where the
straight-jacket doesn't fit
You're wringing wet from
where you've been sweatin
all night
You squirm on filthy straw

But stick it out, Jesus
where you're going
the drums don't stop
They serve Napa Valley
champagne at every meal
Everybody smokes big cigars
Sweet Angel hair be tingling
your back while you invent
proverbs in a hot tub

Where Judas is going
the people don't know how
to fix ribs
the biscuits taste like
baking soda
The wine is sweet and sticky
Flowers can't grow on this
landscape of jinxed hearts
the Field of Blood
to this day it's called
the Field of Blood

Dialog Outside the Lakeside Grocery

The grocery had provided him with
boxes of rotten lettuce
He was loading them onto a
yellow pick-up truck
He was a frail white man and
wore a plaid woolen shirt and
frayed dungarees
I was sitting in a gray chevrolet
rent-a-dent
"I have eight adult geese and
twenty-six ducks," he said
and i said
"I'll bet you have a big management
problem," and he said
"They're no trouble at all. My
wife raised two of them in the house.
When she goes near their pen
the geese waddle towards her
and nibble the lettuce out of her
hand"
"I'd never think of killing them"
he said
"They keep me out of the bars"

Invasion

Tough guy
He fondles the public
as though it were a
kissing baby
Playing giddyup with his
Stetson
His wife has this thing about
the color blue
Why is it that when the old
men have power the young men
fly home in star-spangled skins

Beats me
The liars on t.v.
They have turned me against the
head of hair, parted on the left side
Under the eyes of god, at night
They cry into sympathetic bourbon
Casper, the malevolent duppy
Doesn't crack a smile in his
hard pinched face
They bombed the mad house by
accident
A level headed pilot came back
Three times, the nurse testified
"I'll remember his grin for the
rest of my life."

The mad house is located on the
Island of Grenada
It is where they chain the crazy
people

Untitled

Alaska's rape
dismemberment
disassembled piece by piece
and shipped to the lower
forty-eight so that people
in Dallas may own whale-
sized cadillacs and lear
jets which cost Alaska an
arm and a leg just like
ravished Jamaica whose
stolen sugar built Mansfield
Park where idle gang rapers
discuss flower beds and
old furniture
Jamaica, Alaska, sisters
dragged into an alley
used and abandoned

Poem for Two Daughters

Everybody wants to know
Where's your oldest daughter
Her first sentence was
phenomenon
Sixteen years later she
stands before you, drawing
on a cigarette
She says she's found you
out
She has exactly eighty dollars
to her name
she thinks she grown
She says she wants her emancipation
You tell her to spell it
She calls you a nerd, a dork
and other words you hear on the
3:15 Arlington #7 Bus
The Yo-Yo special

We used to chide the sightseeing
middle aged in those days when
we stood on our heads outside the Dom
Now, we are the ones sitting on the
greyline
We cannot figure out what it is
we are staring at

Our stomachs hurt
We gaze from houses with un-
obstructed views of the Bay
thirty years ago we couldn't come
up here
Nowadays the neighbors bring pies

Our daughters are either standing up
for the first time or flying

The youngest one puts everything
into her mouth, pencils, your hair
graham crackers, the cat, the car keys
even the Sesame Street book covered
with blue-fuzzed creatures with
purple noses and egg-shaped eyes
She trounces the trampoline in
the kindergym but's too plump for
the Olympics
Her first sentence was: "I see"

The oldest one, as fast as
Clifford Brown on Cherokee
Of another system, impatient
with your inability to cope with
the basic concepts of her world
grinds you up with her mind
Intellectually shoves you about
like you the
wildest Turkey in the state of
Georgia, guiding the hunters to
your roost
You have to fall back on
"It's so because I say it's so"

The differences between the three
would be revealed if someone were to
ask each what they would do if
the world was offered to them on
a silver platter
The youngest one would say
I'd eat it
or at least jump up and down
on it a few times
The oldest one would strut up and down
in front of the world, scolding the world
about its ancient corruption

She'd fast
By the time the question reached
you
the world would have run out of
bones

Phoebe

Phoebe is the 9th satellite
of Saturn
Phoebe is the moon
bending the golden blades
of El Cerrito
A voice brighter than the
lights of the harness racing
fields
Snow has returned to the Sierras
snow has returned to the Rockies
Mount Shasta of opium-
headed Lemurian ceremony
Altars made of whalebone
five thousand years old
California tumbled into the
Pacific
The Indians wrote:
I am burning for snow
said Mount Diablo

Once, because I missed
the snow I made a yellow
streak to Montpelier, Vermont
to witness a white rainbow
to entwist myself in a white rainbow
my Montpelier, population one
she used to belong to a
fisherman

Untitled

I know of a man who treated his body like a dog
the dog ran away

The Middle Class Blues

MONOLOGUE

I can't believe it's 1994. Back in 84 it meant something, but nowadays being middle class and a nickel won't buy you a cup of coffee. During the rest of the 80s the frig was still full and you could always mambo in Guadalajara during the discount off seasons. But by the beginning of the 90s, the only difference between us and the poor was that everything they owned was on their backs while everything we owned was being lent to us by the banks. The banks were on our backs. I was over my head in billy dues. Me and the Mrs. argued so about money that one day she just upped and left. And these were supposed to be our golden years. Some golden years. I can't seem to save over a couple of hundred dollars and I'm spending a third more than I'm making. It's only a matter of time before I have to visit one of those bankruptcy consultants. Talking about the new poor. Never thought it would happen to me. What happened to the old poor? I dunno. They were kicked out of the bus stations, the parks and the welfare hotels a long time ago. Some say they went South. Others say that the society people had them shipped to Central America because down there they know how to handle the poor. Wherever they are, they must have been desperate. They left behind their blues. I'm lucky I guess. I can still afford a martini.

I

I got the middle class blues
I play by middle class rules
O, this middle class life
Is a life full of strife
The bourgeois state can be
A sweet and sour pill
When the first rolls around
You gotta deal with the bills

So hey, Mr. Bartender,
Bring me a dry vermouth and gin
Fix me a black olive and a big martini
Before I hit the wind

II
I constantly get headaches
And my back is often sore
Being the first one on the freeway
Is becoming such a chore
At work they got a robot
That soon will have my job
I'm too old to start all over
Too old to learn to rob

So hey, Mr. Bartender
Bring me a dry vermouth and gin
Fix me a black olive and a big martini
Before I hit the wind

III
The roof is always leaking
The plumbing needs some screws
Everybody on the block, it seems
Knows how to bar-b-cue
My next door neighbors are ticked at me
My lawn is turning brown
There's always something that must be fixed
Everytime you turn around

Hey, hey, Mr. Bartender
Bring me a dry vermouth and gin
Fix me a black olive and a big martini
Before I hit the wind

IV
My son is getting married
To a woman older than me
He just turned twenty the other
week
She's going on sixty-three

My daughter's on narcotics
Her eyes are always red
The car wouldn't start this morning
And I toss and turn in bed

So hey, Mr. Bartender
Bring me a dry vermouth and gin
Fix me a black olive and a big martini
Before I hit the wind

V

The communists say I'm an ingrate
The capitalists took my house
The old people say I neglect them
The young call me a louse
The tax man sent me a letter
He's coming here tonight
Sometimes it gets so heavy
At home, I'm never right

So hey, Mr. Bartender
Bring me a dry vermouth and gin
Fix me a black olive and a big martini
Before I hit the wind

VI

The Doctor says it's no good
To have this stress and mess
The ulcers that will get you
A classy middle class nest
A cat that won't eat store food
Must have its abalone
And don't forget the deadline
To pay the alimony

So hey, Mr. Bartender
Bring me a dry vermouth and gin
Fix me a black olive and a big martini
Before I hit the wind

VII

Well, I'm tired of paying the dentist
And going under the knife
And doing all the things you do
To stay the bourgeois life
The rich they live in heaven
The poor they live in hell
And I live somewhere in between
A sign outside says for sale

So hey, Mr. Bartender
Bring me a dry vermouth and gin
Fix me a black olive and a big martini
Let me go on get this wind

Oakland Blues

Well it's six o'clock in Oakland
and the sun is full of wine
I say, it's six o'clock in Oakland
and the sun is red with wine
We buried you this morning, baby
in the shadow of a vine

Well, they told you of the sickness
almost eighteen months ago
Yes, they told you of the sickness
almost eighteen months ago
You went down fighting, daddy. Yes
You fought Death toe to toe

O, the egrets fly over Lake Merritt
and the blackbirds roost in trees
O, the egrets fly over Lake Merritt
and the blackbirds roost in trees
Without you little papa
what O, what will become of me

O, it's hard to come home, baby
To a house that's still and stark
O, it's hard to come home, baby
To a house that's still and stark
All I hear is myself
thinking
and footsteps in the dark

Martine's Keen Eyes

"I take them with me to the fights
every night," Martine says
On the top floor of the Chelsea
In a two room, one kitchen apartment
with white walls, Martine lives with
Elvin Jones records and *Paris Match*
and wall to wall boxers, staring out
at you from the blacks and whites of
Martine's keen eyes, and the people
stop by, to tell her how much they
love her pictures, and how they moved
them so: The curly gray-haired black
woman who wanders about New York in a
rent hospital gown, her only friend
a milk-stained overcoat.
The gang members with creole faces,
smiling, in front of a Chevrolet, all
but one, dead within six months
wax-faced in Puerto Rican coffins
bussed by comrades; the sassy
bathing-suited little black girl who
charmed an adoring fire hydrant into
spouting her a lake; the pint-sized
dynamite who spars in front of Martine's
mirrors for hours at a time, and the
Inca-faced four year old who never lost
a fight, in the clubs smelling of pizza
and hotdogs where the fight people drink
beer for hours in the fight clubs
watching the fights

St. Louis Woman

He loves to see that orbed heat collapse behind the white Jefferson arc
as the downtown St. Louis sun temples burst
    Orange as the inside of a Balaban's lobster they cater in the room
of Renoirish Third Reich Speer-room nude portraits where Wash. U.
grad student waiters resemble the t.v. crew filming a restaurant scene
in "As the World Turns." On a stool outside a black man in little
boy's cap and white butcher's coat attracts customers with the gleam-
ing stars of his gold teeth. For four days a storebought apricotheaded
St. Louis woman in poor white powder and tobacco-road mascaraed
eyelashes told the other waitresses in the Forest Park Hotel to quit
putting cream and sugar in his coffee because "He looks spoiled. Big
and spoiled."
    Daughters of Davy Crockett and Dan Boone with high-Cherokee
cheekbones, St. Louis women call closeted plantations with monop-
oly-board street names, "home" behind fake second empire gates
which are locked at night to keep out the townies, Riding bicycles,
their eyes buried in the streets, the only blacks wear supermarket
names on their t-shirts
    They stand on the street's dividing line selling rush hour copies
of the St. Louis Post Dispatch like the apple-capped Irish lads in a
book about the life and times of Jacob Reiss
    They are the last people in the nation who take out their billfolds
to show you their relatives and their girlfriends' and boyfriends' rel-
atives and that time they went to Atlantic City
    St. Louis is surrounded by ninety municipalities. Only a Filipino
with a Harvard M.A. in business can untangle the town, Emile said.
Emile said that St. Louis women are dumb blondes who stand you
up. Equal rights to them means the right to tantalize but not to put
out, Emile said.
    "Are you Bruce Lee?" they asked Emile when he landed in Har-
lem.
    Feeling tomorrow and twenty-two, a St. Louis woman told him
she could run a whole radio station. She knew where you could fetch

a Gucci raincoat for one hundred dollars. In her poetry she is "a black rose." He told her that if her skin really needed a flower why not an African violet to go with her yellow eyes. He told her that her eyes were all the evidence we needed to prove that ancient Asiatics reached Madagascar. He told her that a black rose was common and that she was anything but common and that she was as rare as a white tiger rarely seen in the jungles of India or rare as the image of a white owl carrying off a white ermine in the Bird Book we saw in the museum off Big Bend where we learned that the first words said on the telephone constituted a cry for help.

In the Steinberg auditorium he asked the Dalai Lama's stand in why there were black gods with nigger minstrel white lips and great Nigerian mound noses in Nepalese paintings dated 3,000 B.C.

Before rushing to the next question he said they represented Time. He told the "black rose" that she was as rare as Time hung on a monastery wall, while outside buddhists blow conch horns and chant like a chorus of frogs.

St. Louis women are rabbit-furred hookers who hustle to star wars in the steeple chase room of the chase park hotel where Gorgeous George dressed in sequined Evel Knievel jumpsuit discos to Elvis Presley and the hogged-necked bouncers in blazers threaten to break your arm. There are portraits in that room of horses, skins shining like chestnuts, life-sized statues of jockeys in polka-dotted blouses. The lamps are shaped like racing horns.

St. Louis women write body poetry, play the harp for the symphony and take up archery.

St. Louis women wash cook and clean for St. Louis women who write body poetry, play the harp for the symphony, and take up archery.

A St. Louis woman is the automatic writing hand for a spirit named Ida Mae of the red dress cult who rises from the Mississippi each night to check out the saloons before last call.

She rises from the big river G. Redmond calls Black River, Mike Castro's River Styx, and every body knows about Muddy Waters; St. Louis women are daughters of Episcopalian ministers who couldn't sit still for Grant Wood

Sternly scarfed they stare straight ahead inside Doberman Pinscher station wagons. Their husbands work for McDonnell Douglas, Ralston-Purina, and Anheuser-Busch.

(They still talk about how old man Busch was so rich that when his son killed a man it was the trial judge who served time)

The great grandfather of a St. Louis woman appears in the 100 years of lynching horror book because he owned 300 acres and white men wanted those acres

The grandmother of a St. Louis woman told her that no man can say "I Love You" like a black man. "Velvet be dripping from his lips," a unique experience like the one recounted by a man in the bar of the St. Louis airport about the time when Nanette Fabray came into the audience and sat on his lap, New Year's Eve, The Mark Hopkins Hotel, San Francisco

On Sunday he stuffed the frig with dungeness crabs

You can find the quilts of St. Louis women patched with real chipmunks and birds in the Jefferson museum next to the Lindbergh collection "Nothing like flying across the Atlantic in a one-seater" he said, "When she rocks, you rock, when you thrust so does she, and when she dives it's as if your soul bought the circus and you owned all the ferris wheels, *The Spirit of St. Louis!*"

A black man wrote a song about a St. Louis woman that go Hello Central, give me five o'nine, hello central give me five o' nine, the St. Louis woman said she liked my line about a man entering a woman's love pond, she thought i said love mine.

like a Mississippi school boy loves his mint and rye i love to see that evening sun go down when the St. Louis women come calling around

Many St. Louis women are from Kansas City

The year was 1914
W. C. Handy wrote a ragtime march with a blues
tango introduction (The Tango, derived from
the African Tangenda, was once banned all the
way down to the Argentinian South Pole)
but there was something missing.
"What this music needs is a Vamp," the trombonist
said, and that's how "St. Louis Woman" came into
being
The big publishers wouldn't chance her
They were only interested in Whiteman's blues
and so, at the age of 40, W. C. Handy went to
bat for his Vamp, publishing 10,000
copies of "St. Louis Blues" at his own expense

Handy flew up the Fatty Grimes diamond
from Memphis and presented it to her
(Hippolite's "Mystical Marriage")
He chauffeured her across the nation in
a whale-length white cadillac like the
one i once saw Bob Hope get out of
He introduced her to a Carnegie Hall
sell-out audience which she delighted
with her shanty-town ways
Sometimes she was as icy as the Portage glacier
in Portage, Alaska,
at other times she was tropical as the
Miami airport at 5:30 when the Santeria
jets sweep in

Resting under that mellow creole
river in a silver satin slip
the color of an enshrined coronet
mooning on the silky meat of a giant
clam
guarded by chocolate dandies
Irises on their creamy waistcoats
and a Tennessee billygoat covered with
cowrie shells
St. Louis Woman

Bitter Chocolate

I
Only the red–skins know what
I know, and they ain't talkin
So I keep good friends with
turkey whiskey
Or try to do some walkin
Don't want no lovin
Ain't anxious to play
And you want to know how
I got that way
Bitter Chocolate
Bitter Chocolate
Blood like ice water
Kisses taste like snuff
Why are all of my women
so jive and full of stuff

They call me a runaway father
But they won't give me no job
They say I'm a thief
when I'm the one gettin
robbed
Most of me was missing when
They brought me back from
Nam
My mama and my sister
cried for me
But my government didn't give
a damn
Bitter Chocolate
Bitter Chocolate
Sullied and sullen black
man

II

When they come to lynch somebody
Always breaking down my door
When they lay somebody off
I'm the first one off the floor
Bitter Chocolate
Bitter Chocolate
Veins full of brine
Skin sweatin turpentine
Cold and unfriendly
Got ways like a lizard

III

Well, it's winter in Chicago on
a February day
O'Hare airport is empty and
I call you on the line
It's 9:00 a.m. where you are
and the phone rings seven times
Hello, who is this? you say
in a sleeping heaving sigh
Your woman in the background yells
Who in the hell is that guy
Bitter Chocolate
Bitter Chocolate
I'm standing in the rain
All my love is all squeezed
out
All that I can give is pain
All that I can give is pain

The Smiley School

July 2, 1982—Juneau. Today the Rotterdam is in port. "We don't make any money from tourists," Andy says. "They just come into town, buy trinkets, and return to their ship." Randall Ackley is driving me to the Lemon Creek jail, where I instruct my class of two: Cornboy and Sanchez. Cornboy writes about the town in Iowa, where people drive tractors on the highway and wear levi shorts. "The midwestern maize grows as tall as a basketball player," Cornboy says. Cornboy says he knows more about the Eagle Dance than the Indians.

Sanchez writes about Nam. His lines crackle and ignite as though they were participants in a literary firefight. They bite like the pesky snake the Ghanians called "Dead Yesterday," it was so quick. His invective is as violent as the black G.I. he told us about, who splattered the mess hall walls with officers' brains. "I dunno, he just went berserk. Docile one minute, like a park deer, next minute, a mad minute."

In the lower forty-eight, the jails are filled with blacks.

Mexican Americans, Puerto Ricans, Cubans and Indians. Up here in Lemon Creek it's Eskimos and Indians.

Randall's Swedish grandmother lives in Sweden. For her, the Italians, French, and British are black people. The Irish, descendants of a crew whose fishing boat wandered too far from the coast of North Africa. Like the Smiley family. The Smileys were part Indian and part black. They didn't want to go to the black school, and they didn't want to go to the Indian school and so down in North Carolina there's a white school, a black school, and a Smiley school.

July 1st 1982

What do you do in a town where
11:00 p.m. looks like noon
and the streets are deserted
What do you do in a town
where space is so tight that
people build houses on boggy ground
or beneath avalanche-prone mountains
covered with Holstein hides
Suicide the therapist said at
Auke Lake
There's suicide up here
knifings in bars
Alcoholism
Up here it's like the
war without the sound effects
In the Viet Nam War
58,000 Americans died by homicide
59,000 Americans died by suicide

Ice Age

Like a gargantuan tongue, coated blue from the millions of tons of pressure, a man decapitating ice monster, calving upon those who defy it the Mendenhall Glacier glowers at visitors from where it lies, pouring forth into a sapphire colored pool, at Tongass National Forest. Two tipsy soldiers, intoxicated from Ranier Ale (green death) wandered too close to it and were "eaten." Like all of Yeil's creatures, it contracts in anger from the teenaged jeers, and beer cans, lying upon its great white royal coat, extending backwards to hundreds of miles

The glacialist warned them. The young glacialist said that all of Yeil's creatures demand respect, but the City Elders laughed at the glacier's impudence and the glacialist's hippie clothes

On the last day of Juneau the sky was as blue as a Harlem Monday. Small planes squatted upon the water like mosquitoes, Alaska's state bird

A ship, the Royal Viking, reposed majestically in the port as its baby boats ferried people into the city

At Dingby Dave's the folks were enjoying the clam chowder that was hot from start to finish

Exiled New Englanders were trying out their new indoor tennis courts, and transplanted Californians were in the sauna.

People were chatting and tasting smoked salmon behind Robert's Mountain

The guys and gals were hoisting a few in the Red Dog Saloon

Cars were lined up for a half-mile as passengers awaited their turn at

mining for McNuggets at the new McDonald's

In the House of Wickersham tourists were sampling the flaming sourdough and a mother spanked her son for tinkering with the Chickering grand piano, the one that Judge Wickersham brought from Baranof castle in Sitka. Inside the Lemon Creek jail, the prisoners

were having a potlatch supper of muk tuk seal fat seal oil herring eggs
smoked salmon and halibut cheeks

The congregation of the Russian Orthodox Church was split
down the middle

Some wanted to remain loyal to Moscow, others wanted inde-
pendence (the Catholic Bishop for the area dresses like a lumberjack)
All at once, the sky grew as white as Alaska Cotton
as the Mendenhall Glacier fired its frozen chunks upon
the town
The only exit from Juneau is by air
but nobody would be flying that day
The Bears prayed to the Bear God
the mountain goats climbed higher
and from his shack in the mountains
the glacialist's eyes followed the
Mendenhall glacier as it
crept towards Canada

But Nobody Was There

I heard a crying child in the other room
I entered the room, but nobody was there
I heard a spider crawl across the silverware
I opened the drawer, but nobody was there
I heard your steps creeping up the stairs
I opened the door, but nobody was there
But nobody was there, but nobody, but nobody
But nobody was there

I saw your spirit sitting in a chair
I turned my head, but nobody was there
I heard a knock and the doorknob turned
I answered the door, but nobody was there
I saw my love in her funeral bier
I turned on the lights, but nobody was there
But nobody was there, but nobody, but nobody
But nobody was there

I heard your laughter on the summer's air
I called your name, but nobody was there
I saw you bare, riding your favorite black mare
I ran to the woods, but nobody was there
I saw you by the moon, you were combing your
hair, I rushed outside, but nobody was there
But nobody was there, but nobody, but nobody
But nobody was there

Slaveship, German Model

I

A pout is a thing with scales
Even when gliding across a marble
floor and tailored by Adolfo
I am in a room of pouts
the clothes they wear would set me
back three months rent
> Off camera, he displays a mink ring
> On camera, he talks about his
> "disenfranchisement
> his oppression"; a word that once
had its hand out has gone and gotten
a manicurist

II

He said that he bought a Mercedes
because the holes on the side
reminded him of a slaveship

At the entrance to J.F.K.
there should be a sign:
"Welcome to New York
a rhetoric delicatessen"

Lake Bud

Lake Merritt is Bud Powell's piano
The sun tingles its waters
Snuff-jawed pelicans descend
tumbling over each other like
Bud's hands playing Tea For Two
or Two For Tea

Big Mac Containers, tortilla chip, Baby Ruth
wrappers, bloated dead cats, milkshake
cups, and automobile tires
float on its surface
Seeing Lake Merritt this way is
like being unable to hear
Bud Powell at Birdland
Because people are talking
Clinking glasses of whiskey and
shouting
"Hey, waiter"

Home Sweet Earth

Home Sweet Earth
Home Sweet Earth
Our first class berth in space
Stomping ground of the human race
Designer of Dorothy Dandridge's face
Of siamese cats, and Max Roach sets
Of beaches, incredibly sandy
Home Sweet Earth
Home Sweet Earth
Your waters are chicken soup
To our souls
You give us goldenrod and
Breakfast rolls
Italian spaghetti and Dizzy
Gillespie
Zimbabwe, and Lady Day
Home Sweet Earth
Home Sweet Earth
Thank you for French Fries
and Creme de Menthe
For Rock and Roll
For the Super Bowl
For scallops and the Alps
For George Clinton's funk
For Thelonius Monk
For Trumpets and trombones
For the Cathedral of Cologne
For Ka.Bah's black stone
Home Sweet Earth
Home Sweet Earth
Mother of legba and Damballah
Of kinky haired Jesus

Of Muhammed and Gautama
Of Confucius, and Krishna
Of Siva and Vishnu
Home Sweet Earth
Home Sweet Earth
May you be shamrock green again
May you stay out of the way of
Black holes
May you spin forever without
End
May you survive the nuclear deals
May you survive the chemical spills
May you survive the bio-technology
May you survive the peckerwood theology
May the Big Crunch theory be all wet!
May you survive man
May you survive man
Home Sweet Earth
Home Sweet Earth
You give us something to stand on

I'm Running For The Office Of Love

I'm running for the office of love
My heart is in the ring
I'm bad at making speeches
So I guess I'll have to sing
A tune of moons and flowers
And things that go with Spring
And things that go with Spring

Love is so political
I don't remember it this way
They'll curse you if you play it straight
And kill you if you're gay
They say that love is dangerous
That it's best to do without
So somebody has to speak for love
That's why I'm singing out

I'm running for the office of love
My heart is in the ring
I'm bad at making speeches
So I guess I'll have to sing
A tune of moons and flowers
And things that go with Spring
And things that go with Spring

Love is like a loaded gun
A fool stands in its way
There was one man who was on the run
He was trying to get away
But love took careful aim at him
She brought him in her sights
He bought her wine and perfume

And all her favorite delights
He hadn't been paying attention
And given love her due
She took away his peace of mind
And plagued him with the blues
I'm running for the office of love
My heart is in the ring
I'm bad at making speeches
So I guess I'll have to sing
A tune of moons and flowers
And things that go with Spring
And things that go with Spring

They say that love is dangerous
It's on the radio
That holding hands is fatal
A kiss can bring you low
The papers they keep shouting
That "LOVE MEANS DOOM AND GLOOM"
So love is lying low for awhile
Until her next big bloom
Until her next big bloom

I'm running for the office of love
My heart is in the ring
I'm bad at making speeches
So I guess I'll have to sing
A tune of moons and flowers
And things that go with Spring
And things that go with Spring

Life Is A Screwball Comedy

Life is a screwball comedy
life is a screwball comedy
It's Cary Grant leaning too
far back in a chair
It's Bill Cosby with a
nose full of hair
It's Richard Pryor
with his heart on fire
Life is a screwball comedy
life is a screwball comedy
It's Moms Mabley leaving her
dentures home
It's the adventures of Hope and Bing
It's Bert Williams doin' a buck and wing
It's Stepin Fechit sauntering before
a mule
It's matches in your shoes
It's April Fool
Life is a screwball comedy
Life is a screwball comedy
It's Scatman Crothers with his
sexy grin
It's W. C. Fields with a bottle
of gin
It's Maggie gettin' in her digs
at Jiggs
It's Desi and Lucy having a doozy
of a fight
It's Pigmeat Martin and Slappy White
Life is a Screwball Comedy
Life is a Screwball Comedy
It's Will Rogers twirling a rope

It's Buster Keaton wearing his
famous mope
It's Fatty Arbuckle in a leaking
boat
It's a scared rabbit
And a tricky Coyote
Life is a screwball comedy
Life is a screwball comedy
It's Eddie Murphy's howl
It's Whoopie Goldberg's stroll
It's Fred Allen's jowls
Its Pee-Wee Herman's clothes
It's Hardy giving Laurel a hard time
It's Chaplin up on his toes
Life is a screwball comedy
life is a screwball comedy
life is a screwball comedy
And the joke's on us

Ishmael Reed grew up in working-class neighborhoods in Buffalo, New York. He attended Buffalo public schools and the University of Buffalo. As well as being a novelist, poet, and essayist, he is a songwriter, television producer, publisher, magazine editor, playwright, and founder of the Before Columbus Foundation and There City Cinema, both of which are located in Northern California. Among his honors, fellowships, and prizes is the Lewis H. Michaux Literary Prize awarded to him in 1978 by the Studio Museum in Harlem. He has taught at Harvard, Yale, and Dartmouth and for twenty years has been a lecturer at the University of California at Berkeley. He lives in Oakland, California.

The Issa Valley

The Issa Valley

CZESLAW MILOSZ

Translated from the Polish by

LOUIS IRIBARNE

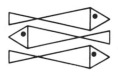

Farrar Straus Giroux

NEW YORK

Library of Congress Cataloging in Publication Data
Miłosz, Czesław. The Issa Valley.
Translation of: Dolina Issy.
I. Title. PG7158.M553D613 1981
891.8'537 81–5087 AACR2

Portions of this translation appeared, in slightly different
form, in World Literature Today, *and in* The Kenyon Review

The Issa Valley

I should begin with the Land of Lakes, the place where Thomas lived. This part of Europe was long covered with glaciers, and the landscape has much of the severity of the north. The soil is sandy and rocky and suitable only for growing potatoes, rye, oats, and flax. This explains why such care was taken not to spoil the forests, which helped to soften the climate and offered protection against the Baltic winds. The forests are predominantly of pine and spruce, though birch, oak, and hornbeam are also in abundance, but not beech, the border of its domain running farther to the south. Here you can wander for long hours without tiring the eye, for, like human cities, the tree colonies have their own distinct character—forming islands, zones, and archipelagoes—and are set off by wagon ruts in the sand, by a forester's cottage, or by an old distillery with crumbling, weed-infested furnaces. From almost any hilltop you can glimpse a blue sheet of lake with a white, barely perceptible smudge of grebe, with a string of ducks winging over the reeds. The marshlands abound in every species of waterfowl, and in spring the pale sky reverberates with the whir of snipe—a *whew-whew-whew* —made by the air in their tail feathers as they perform their monotonous acrobatics, signifying love.

In the meadows the faint whir of snipe, the gabble of blackcock, so like a bubbling on the horizon, and the croaking of frogs (the number of which has something to do with the storks that nest on the rooftops of cottages and barns) are the voices of that season when a sudden thaw gives way to the blossoming of cowslips and daphne—tiny pink and lilac blossoms on bushes as yet without leaves. The two seasons most appropriate to this land are spring

and autumn—a long and sunny autumn, thick with the smell of rain-soaked flax, the clatter of swingles, and distant echoes. This is the time when the geese show signs of restlessness, leaping clumsily to fly after their wild brethren summoning from on high; when someone would bring home a stork with a broken wing—a creature spared the sort of death by pecking such as is meted out by those guardians of the law on those not fit for the trip to the Nile; when word would get around that a wolf had made off with someone's suckling pig; and the woods would hear the music of the hounds—always a soprano, a bass, and a baritone—barking in pursuit of wild game, their pitch signaling whether they were on the track of a hare or a buck.

The fauna of this region is mixed, not entirely that of the north. Ptarmigan are not uncommon, but then neither are partridge. In winter the squirrels have a grayish coat, the shade of which may vary from red to clear gray. There are two species of hare: the first, the common variety, looks the same in summer and in winter; the second, the white hare, changes its color and is indistinguishable from the snow. The proximity of these two species has given the experts food for thought, though the matter is further complicated because, as any hunter will testify, the common hare has two subspecies—the wood hare and the field hare, the latter sometimes crossbreeding with the white.

Until recently, everything a man needed was manufactured at home. His clothes were made of coarse homespun, which women had spread on the grass and bleached in the sun. In late autumn, during that time of day given to tales and songs, fingers turned hanks of wool into yarn in rhythm to the measured beat of the spinning-wheel pedals. With this yarn the housewives wove dresses on homemade looms, jealously guarding the secret of their patterns: this one in a herringbone, that one in a twill; this color for the warp, that one for the woof. Spoons, vats, and household utensils were hand-carved, as were clogs. In summer, bast

moccasins from linden bark were worn. Not until the First World War, when dairy cooperatives and meat and grain markets were introduced, did the villagers' necessities of life begin to change.

Cottages are of wood, their roofs shingled rather than straw-thatched. Cranes, consisting of a beam braced against a forked post and stone-weighted at one end, are used for drawing well water. The small flower garden at the entrance to the house is a woman's pride and joy. Here the women tend their dahlias and mallows—a plant that flourishes along the wall, not one that graces only the earth and can't be seen through the fence.

It's time to pass from the general landscape to the Valley itself, which in many ways is an anomaly in the Land of Lakes. The Issa is a deep, black river with a lazy current, thickly bordered with reeds; a river whose surface is barely visible in places under the lily pads, which winds through meadows and between gentle slopes noted for their fecundity. The Valley is blessed with an abundance of black earth—a rarity for us—with the lushness of its orchards, and possibly with its remoteness from the world, something that has never seemed to bother its inhabitants. The villages in these parts are more prosperous than elsewhere, being situated either along the only major road skirting the river, or high above it on terraces; and at night they eye one another with their window lights across an expanse that echoes like an echo chamber every hammer blow, dog bark, and voice—which may explain why the Valley is celebrated for its ancient songs, songs that are never performed in unison but divided into parts, with one village always trying to outdo a neighboring one with a more mellifluous and gradual ending of a phrase. Collectors of folklore have noted a variety of motifs along the Issa going back to pagan times, like the story of the Moon (which in our language is of masculine gender) rising up from his nuptial bed, where he sleeps with his wife, the Sun.

2

❧♪❋♪❋♪❋♪❦

THE ISSA VALLEY has the distinction of being
inhabited by an unusually large number of devils. It
may be that the hollow willows, mills, and thickets lining
the riverbanks provide a convenient cover for those crea-
tures who reveal themselves only when it suits them. Those
who have seen them say that the devil is rather short, about
the size of a nine-year-old; that he wears a green frock
coat, a jabot, his hair in a pigtail, white stockings, and tries
to conceal his hoofs, which are an embarrassment to him,
with high-heeled slippers. Such tales should be treated with
a certain caution. It is possible that, knowing the supersti-
tious awe in which the Germans are held—they being
people of commerce, inventions, and science—the devils
seek to lend themselves an air of gravity by dressing up in
the manner of Immanuel Kant of Königsberg. It's no coin-
cidence that along the Issa another name for the Evil Spirit
is the "Little German"—implying that the devil is on the
side of progress. Still, it's hard to believe they were in the
habit of wearing such a costume for everyday. If one of
their favorite pastimes was dancing in the empty scutching
sheds near the farm buildings, how could they possibly
kick up clouds of grain dust without showing due regard
for their appearance? And why, if they are endowed with a
certain immortality, would they be apt to choose a costume
from the eighteenth century?

There is no predicting whom they might impersonate.
A girl lights two candles on St. Andrew's Eve, gazes into
the mirror, and her future is revealed: the face of the man
with whom her life will be joined, or the face of death. Is

this the devil in disguise, or could it be the work of other magical forces? And how is one to tell them apart, those creatures coinciding with the advent of Christianity from those native inhabitants of bygone days, like the forest witch who switches children in their cradles, or the little people who stray at night from their palaces under the roots of the elder bushes? Are the devils and those other creatures joined in a pact, or do they simply exist side by side like the jay, the sparrow, and the crow? And where is that realm where both species would take refuge when the earth was plowed up by the tracks of tanks; when those who were about to be executed dug their own shallow graves by the river; and when, in blood and tears, Industrialization rose up, surrounded by the halo of History?

One can easily imagine a parliamentary session being convened in caverns deep inside the earth, so deep that it is warmed by the fires of the earth's molten center. The session is attended by hundreds of thousands of tiny devils in frock coats, who listen solemnly to speakers representing the Central Committee of Infernos. The speakers announce that, in the interest of the cause, all dancing in the forests and meadows will have to cease; that from now on, highly qualified specialists will have to operate in such a way that the minds of mortals will never suspect their presence. There is applause but it is strained, for those present realize that they were necessary only during the preparatory stage, that progress has consigned them to gloomy chasms, and that they will never again witness the setting of the sun, the flight of kingfishers, the glitter of stars, and all the other wonders of the uncircumscribable earth.

The peasant farmers along the Issa used to place, by the entrance to their cottages, a bowl of milk for the water snakes, which were not afraid of humans. In time, the inhabitants became fervent Catholics and the presence of the devils made them recall the struggle being waged for dominion over the human soul. What will they become

tomorrow? In narrating such a story, one never knows whether to use the past or present tense, as if what has passed has not really passed as long as it survives in the memory of generations—or in the memory of one chronicler, at least.

Or were the devils attracted to the Issa because of its water? It is said that it possesses properties affecting the personalities of those born along its shores, who are inclined to be eccentric, are far from being at peace with themselves, and whose blue eyes, blond hair, and somewhat sturdy build only give a semblance of Nordic health.

3

ℵ♪⁕♪⁕♪⁕♪⁕K

THOMAS WAS born in the village of Gine at that time of year when a ripe apple thumps to the ground during the afternoon lull and when vats of freshly brewed ale stand in the hallway after the autumnal harvest. Gine was not much more than a hill, thickly wooded with oaks. That a wooden church was built there betrays a hostility toward the religious practices of the past, or may testify to a desire for peaceful transition, for it was here that rites were once performed in honor of the god of thunder and lightning. The church was buttressed by a stone wall at the back, and from the green in front, one could see river bends; a barge ferrying a cart, moving along a cable pulled by a ferryman's hand to a steady rhythm (there was no bridge at this point in the river); and through the trees, some cottage roofs. A little to one side stood the rectory, with its gray-shingled roof reminiscent of Noah's Ark. After mounting a few steps and pressing the door latch, the visitor crossed a parquet floor of worn tiles laid in a her-

ringbone pattern, while the light fell from above through red, green, and yellow panes, filling the children with awe.

On a slope, in a clump of oak, was the cemetery where Thomas's maternal ancestors lay in a chained-off square, the chains joined by four stone posts. Bordering the cemetery on one side were several mounds, where, in summer, lizards flitted in and out of the wild thyme. These were called the Swedish Ramparts, and were built either by the Swedes, who had journeyed here from across the sea, or by their adversaries in battle. Occasionally, the remnants of armor would be unearthed among the ruins.

Past the Ramparts were the park trees, skirted by a steep road that was often turned into a riverbed by the thaw. By the roadside, the arms of a cross protruded from an eerie clump of hawthorn. To reach the cross, you had to climb through weeds and over the ruins of stairs before coming to the round hole of a spring, where a frog might stare up goggle-eyed from below the rim, and where, by kneeling and pushing aside the duckweed, you could feast your eyes on the eddy below. Craning your neck, you beheld a wooden, moss-covered Christ—one arm clasping his knee, the other supporting his chin in an attitude of sorrow —sitting in what looked to be a shrine.

A lane branching off from the road led homeward. Thick with lindens, it was more like a tunnel, descending all the way to the pond near the granary. It was called the Black Pond because the sun never shone on it. It was a spooky place at night; the black pig had been sighted there more than once, grunting and stamping its hoofs on the paths, vanishing only after someone made the sign of the cross over it. Across the pond, the lane climbed again, opening out onto a brilliant green lawn. The house was white and built so low to the ground that the roof, its shingles here and there tufted with grass and moss, seemed to be crushing it with its weight. Wild grapevine, whose berries made your tongue curl, wound about the windows

and the two small porch columns. Another wing had been built onto the rear of the building; here they used to set up winter quarters, as the front of the house was rotting and sinking from the dampness seeping from underneath the foundation. The wing was divided into a number of rooms, housing the spinning wheels, looms, and ironing presses.

Thomas's cradle stood in the old part of the house, facing the garden, and birdsongs were most likely the first sounds to greet him. When he could walk, he spent most of his time exploring the house. In the dining room he was reluctant to approach the oilcloth sofa—less because of the portrait of a man clad in armor with purple trim, and so stern of gaze, than of the two horribly twisted ceramic faces standing on the mantel. He never ventured into the part of the house referred to as the "salon," and even as a grown boy he felt ill at ease there. Just off the hallway, the "salon" was always empty, the parquet floor and the furniture squeaked even in the silence, and somehow the room always bespoke a human presence. But the larder was the place he liked most to visit, which happened rarely. His grandmother's hand would turn the key in a door painted bright red and release a rush of odors: the smell of smoked sausage and hams hanging from the rafters, mingled with others emanating from the little drawers stacked along the walls. Sometimes his grandmother pulled out the drawers and let him sniff their contents. "This is cinnamon," she would say, "this is coffee and these are cloves." Higher up, in a place where only grownups could reach, shimmered little dark-gold pots that aroused one's desire, mortars, an almond-grinding machine, and a mouse trap—a tin box big enough for a mouse to climb onto by crossing a little bridge notched with stairs; when it reached the bacon, a trapdoor opened and sent it plummeting into the water. The pantry had a grated opening, and the room was always cool and shady. Thomas was also fond of the room off the corridor, next to the kitchen—the "cloakroom," as

it was called—where the cheeses were aged and the butter churned. He loved to take part in the churning, to move the stick up and down, the buttermilk hissing at the opening, though he soon tired of it: it took so long before one could lift the lid and see the yellow chunks clinging to the little cross at the end of the stick.

The house, the fruit garden in back, and the little lawn in front were Thomas's earliest discoveries. On the lawn, three agaves, a large one in the middle, flanked by two smaller ones, were bursting out of their tubs, whose staves bore traces of rusty hoops above and below. The agaves seemed to merge with the tops of the spruce trees at the bottom of the park, and between them loomed the world. As a little boy, he was permitted to run down to the river and the village only when accompanied by Antonina as, a wooden trough braced against her hip, a paddle—or, as it can also be called, a *kijanka*—balanced on top, she went to do the laundry.

4

Thomas's ancestors belonged to the landowning gentry. How they had become squires was now lost from memory. They had worn helmets and swords, and the local villagers had been forced to work their fields. Their wealth was measured more by the number of "souls," or serfs, in their possession than by the size of their landholdings. In the past, the villages had rendered tribute in kind; later it was discovered that the grain which was loaded onto barges and shipped down the Niemen to the sea could bring handsome profits and that it paid to cultivate the land. It was around this time that those in servitude began staging revolts and massacring their masters;

they were led by the elders, who shared a common hatred for both the squires and Christianity, the coming of which coincided with the loss of freedom.

By the time Thomas was born, the manor was already in decline. All that was left was a modest tract of land that was plowed, sown, and harvested by a few families of farm laborers. Payment was mainly in the form of potatoes and grain, and the yearly allotment was entered in the books under the heading of *ordinaria*. Aside from the laborers, a few farmhands were kept "at the manorial table."

Thomas's grandfather, Casimir Surkont, bore not the slightest resemblance to those men of yore whose passion was the judging of horseflesh and wrangling over the merits of this or that weapon. Short, somewhat sluggish, he spent most of his time in his armchair, dozing with his chin propped on his chest, the gray wisps on his rosy-pink bald patch slipping down, his pince-nez dangling at the end of a silken cord. He had a child's complexion (only his nose would take on a plumlike color when the weather turned chilly) and blue, red-veined eyes. He was quite susceptible to colds and preferred his room to open spaces. He neither smoked nor drank, and, though he was expected to wear knee boots and even spurs to demonstrate his readiness to jump into the saddle, he preferred going around in long breeches bagged at the knees and in laced-up shoes. He kept no hunting dogs on the estate, and packs of all breeds, idled without the chase, moiled about the barn, scratching and plucking for fleas. Nor were any firearms kept. Grandfather Surkont valued above all his peace and his books on gardening. He behaved toward people much as he did toward plants, and was not easily swayed by the passions of others. He was understanding, but his reputation for being "too softhearted," along with his aversion for card playing and carousing, alienated him from his peers, who, unable to reproach him with anything in particular, would pronounce his name with a shrug. Visitors to the manor

were always treated graciously, regardless of rank or calling. While it was customary for a gentleman to be treated differently from a Jew, a Jew differently from a peasant, Grandfather paid little heed to this custom—even when it came to the terrifying Chaim. Every few weeks, Chaim showed up in his britska and, whip in hand, dressed in his black caftan, his trousers hanging over the tops of his boots and his beard sticking out like a scorched plank, entered the house. He began by negotiating the price of rye or calves, but this was just a prologue, because then, wailing and gesticulating, he commenced chasing members of the household from one room to another, pulling his hair and predicting bankruptcy if he paid what they asked. It was as if he considered it a dereliction of duty on the part of a good merchant to go away without staging these little dramas of despair. And it always amazed Thomas how quickly these tantrums subsided, and how afterward, with something like a smile playing in the corners of his mouth, Chaim would settle down with Grandpa for a good, neighborly chat.

Surkont's benign way did not imply that he was apt to make concessions. The ancient feuds between the village of Gine and the manor were a thing of the past, and the lay of the land was such that it had not given rise to any quarrels. The same could not be said of Pogirai, a village to the other side, bordering on the forest, where the villagers bickered endlessly over the right to pasture. They would meet, wrangle, get riled up, and in the end appoint a delegation of elders. But the moment they sat down with Surkont to a table graced with vodka and cold meats, all their carefully rehearsed arguments faded. Stroking the back of his hand with his palm, Grandfather would state his case, slowly and sincerely; plainly, his self-assurance was aimed only at finding an equitable solution. They would yield ground, soften their position, compromise, and only on the way back would they recall all they had ne-

glected to say, rankling at how, once again, they had been charmed and embarrassed in the eyes of the whole village.

As a young man, Surkont had studied in the city and read the works of Auguste Comte and John Stuart Mill, of whom hardly anyone on the Issa had ever heard. His grandfather liked to reminisce, but the stories that stood out in Thomas's memory were the ones about the formal balls attended by men in frock coats. Grandfather and a friend had shared the same coat; while one danced, the other had waited at home, trading places a few hours later.

He had two daughters. Helen married a local landowner; the other, Tekla, a man from the city. Tekla, who later became Thomas's mother, came to Gine for several months out of the year, and then only rarely; most of the time she had to accompany her husband on his travels, at first in search of work, later because of the war. For Thomas she was almost too beautiful to be real, and he gulped with love at the sight of her. His father was practically a stranger to him, and he was constantly surrounded by women; first by Pola, during infancy, and later by Antonina. Pola was white skin, flaxen hair, and the sensation of softness, and his affection for her was later transferred to a country bearing a similar name. Antonina had a protruding belly, wore striped aprons, and always carried a bunch of keys on her belt. Her laugh was more like a horse's whinny, and her heart bore malice toward none. She spoke a mixture of both languages, Lithuanian being her mother tongue and Polish an acquired one.

Thomas was very fond of his grandfather. He had a nice smell about him and the gray bristles above his lip tickled his cheek. He lived in a little room where a print showing people tied to stakes, with half-naked men putting torches to the stakes, hung above his bed. One of Thomas's first reading exercises was to read aloud, syllable by syllable, the inscription: *The Torches of Nero*. In this way he came to know the name of that vicious tyrant, the name he

later gave to one of the pups when the grownups, after examining the pup's mouth, had said it was bound to be fierce because it had a dark palate. Nero grew up showing not ferocity as much as cunning—he was shrewd enough to eat plums that had fallen from the tree; when none lay on the ground, he leaned against the trunk and shook it with his forepaws. On Grandfather's table were many books, illustrated with roots, leaves, and flowers. Sometimes his grandfather took him into the "salon" and lifted a piano lid the color of chestnuts. His fingers, somewhat swollen, tapered, skipped along the keyboard with a motion that astounded Thomas no less than did the sprinkling drops of sound.

Grandfather was frequently seen consulting with his steward, Shatybelko, who wore a parted goatee, which he had a habit of stroking and spreading apart while he spoke. A dwarfish man, he went around with knees bent and legs sticking out of his oversized boot tops. He smoked a pipe —huge in comparison with his size—with a curved stem and a perforated metal lid. His lodgings, situated at the far end of the same building housing the stable, coach house, and servants' quarters, were always shaded green by the geraniums planted in flowerpots and tin cans. The walls of the room were decorated with religious pictures, which his wife, Paulina, festooned with paper flowers. Mopsy, his little dog, trailed Shatybelko wherever he went. If his master was detained in Grandfather's room, the dog waited outside anxiously, for it was one of those dogs that, surrounded by a world of people and larger dogs, was forever in need of protection.

Except for Chaim or farmers on business, visitors were rare, seldom coming to the manor more than once or twice a year. The master of the house was neither on the lookout for them nor was he annoyed when they came, though the arrival of almost anyone was enough to throw Grandmother into a pout.

5

─────────────

❧ʃ❋ʃ❋ʃ❋ʃ❋✠

Grandmother Michalina, or Misia as she was
called, never treated Thomas to anything and never doted
over him, but what a character she was—slamming doors,
cussing at everyone in sight, not in the least fazed by what
others thought. During one of her tantrums, she was apt to
retreat to her room for days on end. Catching her alone,
Thomas rejoiced, much as if he had surprised a squirrel
or marten in the brush, for, like them, she belonged to the
species of forest animal. Her generous straight nose, nearly
lost behind bulging cheeks, even bore a certain resemblance
to theirs. Nut-brown eyes, smoothly combed dark hair—
full of health and purity. In late May she launched the first
of her expeditions to the river, in summer she took several
baths daily, and in autumn she broke the ice with her foot.
In winter, too, she devoted much of her time to ablutions of
every sort. She was no less attentive to the house, or rather to
that part of the house she regarded as her private domain.
Otherwise, she was a woman of few needs.

Thomas seldom ate at the table with his grandparents,
as his grandmother was not one to observe regular meals,
something she regarded as a silly convention. If she had a
yen to eat, she would duck into the kitchen for a crock of
buttermilk, a snack of salted cucumbers or pickled cabbage
(she had a positive weakness for anything sour or salty).
Her distaste for the ritual of plates and dishes—how much
nicer to sneak into a corner and munch something on the
sly—sprang from a conviction that far too much time was
squandered on ceremonies, and not least from stinginess.

Guests were a constant irritation, since they had to be fed and entertained, even when one felt no inclination to do so.

She wore no jerkins, woolen underwear, or corsets. In winter her favorite pastime was to stand by the tiled stove, skirt hiked, and warm her posterior—a pose that meant she was ready to engage in conversation. Thomas was greatly impressed by such gestures carried out in defiance of accepted customs.

Grandmother's tantrums were only on the surface; inwardly, protected by her aloofness, she must have enjoyed herself richly. Thomas was of the suspicion she was made of some durable substance, that inside her ticked some self-winding machine, completely oblivious to the world outside. And what pretexts she could invent to curl up inside herself.

Her ruling passion was magic, the world of spirits and the hereafter. The only books she ever read were the lives of the saints, though it was not the religious message as much as the language, the sound of those pious and god-fearing sentences that charmed her. (She never thought to instruct Thomas in morality.) In the morning, emerging from her warren, which always smelled of wax and soap, she and Antonina would sit and interpret one another's dreams. At news that someone had been visited by a devil, that a house was feared to be uninhabitable owing to reports of clanking chains and rolling barrels, she was all smiles. Any sign from the other world—a proof that man was never alone on this earth but always in company—was enough to brighten her spirits. She divined the clues and admonitions of various Powers in the most trivial events. For only through canniness, through vigilance, could the Powers be beneficial. Grandmother had such an abiding curiosity about those beings who swarm about us, and whom, unknowingly, we continuously brush against, that

she gave special treatment to women said to be in possession of secrets and magical incantations, going so far as to loosen their tongues with a piece of cloth or kielbasa.

She showed little interest in the farm, and if she did, it was only to ensure that Grandfather, who preferred to steal rather than risk a scene, wasn't slipping things to his protégés on the sly. Not having to be of service to anyone —the needs of others rarely crossed her mind—freed of any guilt where family obligations were concerned, she was content simply to live.

Thomas, if he was lucky enough to visit her in bed— her bed stood in a corner behind a curtain, a prie-dieu with a carved rest and a red velvet cushion adjacent to it— would sit at her feet, bracing himself against her knees bent under the blanket (she couldn't stand quilted coverlets); and if wrinkles gathered around her eyes and her apple cheeks began to quiver more than was usual, that meant she was in the mood for telling funny stories. Occasionally, she might grump over some prank of his, call him a rascal or a clown, but he never took it to heart, knowing how fond she was of him.

On Sundays she dressed for church in dark blouses buttoned to the neck over a jabot. She wore a little golden chain with links the size of pinheads, and kept a locket in a little pocket on her belt, which she would open on request (it was quite empty).

6

VARIOUS POWERS would observe Thomas in the sun and greenery and pass judgment on him, each according to his province. Those able to step outside of

time would shake their diaphanous heads in dismay, for they could foresee the effects of the ecstatic state in which he lived. Such Powers were familiar with the works of composers desirous of expressing felicity; but it was enough to crouch beside the bed of a child who wakes on a summer morning to the oriole's song outside his window, to a chorus of quacks, cackling, and gaggling from the barnyard, to a steady stream of voices bathed in never-ending light, to appreciate the futility of such musical exertions. Touch was also a kind of ecstasy—the feel of naked feet racing over smooth boards onto the cool of a corridor's tiled floor, over a garden path's circular flagstones still wet with dew. And, let us also note, he was an only child in a kingdom that could be transformed at will. Devils, rapidly shrinking and taking cover under leaves at the sound of his footsteps, were forever imitating hens when, all in a flutter, they crane their necks and reveal a moronic look in their eye.

In spring, the lawn was covered with flowers known as the "keys of St. Peter," or cowslips. Thomas was wild about them, that sudden burst of bright yellow on a field of green, the way they clung to their naked stems so like a bunch of keys, and in each a little ring of red. The lower leaves were wrinkly, pleasant to the touch, chamoislike. As soon as the peonies were in bloom, Antonina would cut a bunch for church. Thomas loved to immerse his gaze in them, straining his whole body to enter their rose-colored palace, as the sun filtered through their petal walls and little bugs wallowed in the yellow pollen—once, when he sniffed too hard, a bug ran up his nose. When Antonina went to fetch meat from the storage cellar in the garden, he tagged along, hopping on one leg, crawling down the ladder, and savoring with his toes the slab of ice taken from the Issa and sprinkled with straw. A scorcher above, but so cool below—amazing! He found it hard to believe the cellar did not stretch beyond the stone foundation spotted

with dampness. And the snails. After a rain shower, they shunted across the wet pathways, from one green patch to another, trailing a silver streak. Cupped in your hand, they retreated into their shells, reappearing the moment you said: "Snail, snail, give us a look-see and I'll buy you a cookie." Whatever pleasure the grownups took in such pastimes, it was always, as the Powers could easily attest, with a slight embarrassment, and they were not likely to be found contemplating the little white band on a snail's shell.

For Thomas, the river was gigantic and always full of echoes: the *thwack-thwack-thwack* of the wash paddles, immediately echoed by others, as if rehearsed. A whole orchestra, never a missed cue, the newcomer always sure to join in at the same tempo. Hidden in the bushes, Thomas would shinny up a willow and wile away the hours, listening and staring down at the water—at the water spiders, their legs ringed by little pools, engaging in their endless pursuit; at the beetles, those drops of metal so smooth the water never clung to them as they danced their continuous round, always a round. Sunbeams revealed whole forests at the bottom, traversed by schools of fish that darted helter-skelter, only to band together again with a flick of the tail, a scattering motion, then another flick . . . Now and then, a larger fish meandered from the deep into the light, and Thomas's heart throbbed with excitement. At the sound of a splash out in the deep, at the sight of a flash and a spreading of ripples, he was up on all fours on his tree perch. Dugouts were rarely seen on the river, appearing and disappearing so quickly they almost escaped notice. The fisherman, paddling with a double-bladed oar, a line trailing behind, sat so low he seemed to skim the water.

Thomas, who made his first pole at an early age, was a patient but unlucky fisherman. Until the Akulonis children, Józiuk and Onutè, taught him how to tie a hook. At first, he made only brief visits to their cottage on the outskirts of the village; later these visits became so routine

that, if he was not at home, his whereabouts were never a secret. In the afternoon, he was handed a wooden spoon and told to sit down at the table; there he helped himself to *bonduki* and sour cream from the same bowl used by the rest of the family. Akulonis was an imposing man, with a back so flat it amazed Thomas: he had never known anyone who could hold himself so erect. The homespun pants legs around his calves were bound by strips of bast, wrapped all the way to the knees. Fishing was one of his passions; but most important of all—he owned a dugout. Behind the apple trees by the granary, the ground sloped down to a cove rank with sweet flag, through which the dugout had cleared a passage and where it lay beached. Forbidden to take it out into the water, the children pretended they were out canoeing by rocking back and forth at one end. Capsizable, the dugout, a hollowed-out trunk, was fitted with a pair of outriggers. Akulonis fished for pike in it, first letting out the line with the spinner, then looping it around one ear. At night he would set up the night poles, one of which he gave Thomas. This was a rod fastened with hazel forks; the forks were wound with line, one end threaded through a slit, a double hook going on the loose end. The ideal bait was a young perch, because once the hook was stuck in the small knife slit in its side, it could swim around the whole night; any other fish would have lacked the vitality, would have died too soon.

Credit for what followed must go to Akulonis, for it was he who picked out the spot and cast the line. Unable to sleep, Thomas sprang out of bed early the next day and bolted down to the river before the morning fog had lifted. Above the rosy, mist-covered, glasslike surface, he spotted the forks: empty. In disbelief, he began reeling in the line, yanked on it, felt it strain, then heard the splashing. Ecstatic, he darted back up the hill, eager to show everyone his fish the size of a man's arm. People huddled around. It turned out to be, not a pike, but another kind, one that

Akulonis said was a rare catch. Nothing even remotely similar had ever happened to Thomas, and years later he still spoke of it with pride.

He felt drawn to Akulonis's wife, whose fair skin reminded him of Pola, and went out of his way to be fondled by her. At home they spoke Lithuanian, slipping imperceptibly from one language into another. The children spoke a mixture, except when certain communal acts demanded certain time-honored exclamations, such as when the boys charged naked into the river, yelling: *"Ei virai!"* or "Forward, men!" *Vir*, as Thomas later discovered, meant the same in Latin, though Lithuanian was decidedly more archaic.

But all summers must come to an end. Then come the rains, noses pressed against windows, the boredom among the older children . . . And evenings in the kitchen, when the girls gathered around Antonina to spin or shuck beans, when everyone looked forward to new stories and would be disappointed if, as sometimes happened, something intruded to spoil their fun. Thomas, listening to their songs, was especially intrigued by one, all the more so when Antonina took on an air of secrecy, warning that such songs were not meant for him. In his presence she sang only the refrain:

Hey, little dress, spin all night,
Hey, little miss, have no fright!

The rest he caught only in snatches. The song was about a knight who had gone off to war, fallen in battle, and one night returned to his sweetheart as a ghost, mounting her on his horse and taking her away to his castle. There was no castle, of course, only a grave in the cemetery.

One song, sung by a girl from the Poniewież region, was about some carpenters, or at least that is what Thomas imagined it to be about:

> Boss, I'll thank you for my fee,
> 'Cause it's quittin' time for me.
> Just give me my pay,
> And I'll be on my way.

The last word was held for a long time, to show that the way was far indeed. The shorter songs were a little on the happier side.

> He grabbed his bottle and he grabbed his glass
> And made his way to High Ridge Pass
> And from High Ridge Pass to the county seat
> He rode in search of a wife so sweet
> With a thumpety-thump on his pony dear
> Till he and his horse at the church did appear—
> And I won't marry a soul, I swear,
> 'Less it's me Mike, oh dear, oh dear!

Or:

> Hop to the reel
> But don't bust your heel!
> My brother's name is Scratch,
> His shoes need a patch!
> Got me a hound named Black,
> Lose your shoes and he'll fetch 'em back!

During the fortune-telling, as the wax is poured, the most exciting moment comes when it sizzles in the cold water and starts to assume the various shapes of Fate. One by one, the figures are turned and their silhouettes studied, setting off a chorus of "ooh's" and "aah's" as the wreaths, animals, crosses, and mountains are gradually deciphered. For Thomas, one St. Andrew's Eve augured genuine horror. Only girls were permitted to look into the mirror, and at midnight, with a solemn air, to shut themselves up in their rooms. Once, as a joke, he tried to mimic them, but when the mirror reflected a pair of red horns, it ended in tears. Horns, or just the embroidery on a girl's blouse flash-

ing in the background? No telling, but for a long time after that, he gave every mirror a wide berth.

One winter—there was always that first morning when you went tracking through the snow that had fallen the night before—Thomas spotted an ermine on the Issa. Frost and sunlight made the twigs of the bushes on the steep shore of the opposite bank stand out like bouquets of gold, lightly tinged with gray and bluish purple. It was then that a ballet dancer of remarkable grace and agility made her appearance, a white sickle, arching and straightening. With a gaping mouth, Thomas stared in awe and ached with desire. To have. If he'd had a rifle with him he would have shot it, because one could not simply stand idle when one's wonder demanded that the thing arousing it be preserved forever. But what good would that have done? Then there would have been neither ermine nor any sense of wonder, just dead matter lying on the ground; no, it was better to feast one's eyes and to let it go at that.

In spring, when the lilacs were in bloom, they used to take off their shoes and let their feet squirm, every pebble stabbing like a nail. But it didn't take long for the skin to toughen, and from then until the first frost, Thomas would traipse barefoot on the trails, so that on Sundays his feet would roast and he couldn't wait to chuck his shoes after Mass.

7

NOT EVERYONE can be the hero of an adventure such as befell Pakenas. Thomas had always approached him with reverence. Perchlike, with a shiny, sharp nose, Pakenas worked as a weaver in the large workshop,

where he operated the ironing press used to press home-spun cloth between sheets of cardboard, which long use and the absorption of dyes had turned pitch-black. (People from the surrounding villages brought their homespun to the manor for beating and ironing.) Although the incident took place long ago, it has not been forgotten, and there was living proof that it was not merely rumored to have happened, since Pakenas was always on hand to testify, albeit reluctantly, to its veracity.

It all began in the Borek, a clump of pine along the Issa and a favorite nesting place of the rooks that cawed and circled above the treetops. The Borek had an evil reputation. An old shepherd believed to have choked to death on a piece of cheese was buried there.

"Choked to death?" asked Thomas. "How so?"

"Choked to death, that's how—while eating his supper in the pasture." The unusual circumstances of his death may explain why he was never buried in the cemetery. A chest left behind by Napoleon's army was buried there as well; according to legend, they had stumbled on its iron lid while digging the shepherd's grave.

"And why wasn't it taken out of the ground?"

"Couldn't get a grip on it, ran out of time and energy—" Here the explanations became rather vague.

Late one night, around midnight, Pakenas was making his way back from a village dance on the far side of the river. Finding the dugout where he'd hidden it in the bushes, he paddled across the river. But he wasn't a few steps across the field when a column of vapor started in his direction. He broke into a run, the column at his heels. His hair on end, he ran faster, but the column kept pace. Pakenas bounded uphill to the park and, howling in mortal terror, banged on Shatybelko's door for help.

The slight embarrassment with which Pakenas later recalled the incident had to do with some of the goings-on at the dance. The appearance of the shepherd's ghost he

took as a punishment, a sign—he was, as they say, inclined to superstition. If he had emigrated to America like his brother and gone to work in a dry cleaners on some bleak Brooklyn street, all recollection of that night would have faded. The same might have happened if he'd been drafted into the army. But the treetops of the Borek—he could see them every day on his way from his room in the granary to the workshop—stood as a constant reminder. But, then, it is not for a chronicler to lavish details on every character who crosses his field of vision. A life such as Pakenas's can never be plumbed, and if we have alluded to it, it was only to state that once upon a time a certain Pakenas existed, at a much later date than many a learned man with his treatises disputing the existence of ghosts and gods. Suffice it to say that both his scruples and his timidity prevented Pakenas from ever marrying, and when Antonina and the girls chided him for clinging to his bachelor's ways, he would merely snuffle.

A waistcoat, a triangle of white shirt, clasped at the neck by a red-embroidered collar; a blank expression, a certain irritability accompanying his gestures—especially at the loosening of threads on his loom. Pakenas also had custody of the key to the granary. On his way out, he hid it in a crack under the doorsill. Once inside the granary—this, after Thomas mastered the trick of opening the iron-studded door—the feet crossed a floor sprinkled with grain and black rat droppings, and in the bins you could sit and shower your feet with the cool stuff. A tiny window in the loft—the outer wall was so thick the window was more like a tunnel—commanded a view of the entire valley. Pakenas's room was furnished with flour sacks and a bed; above the bed was a cross and a tin holy-water font, and draped over one arm of the cross, an aspergillum.

Every so often, while playing with Józiuk and Onutè in the geese pasture, Thomas ventured up to the edge of

the Borek. The wind whistling overhead, the cawing, the dead silence below: it was an eerie, forbidding place. Once, plucking up their courage, they made it as far as the shepherd's grave, now overrun by a thick patch of nettles and wild raspberries. It was from this same patch that, summoned by the moonlight, a white pillar had risen up and slithered off among the trees. Had the leaves on the nettle bushes swayed, wondered Thomas.

8

THE WAY to the church cut across the Swedish Ramparts. Thomas, wearing a short jacket of prickly homespun, followed the movements of the altar boys in their surplices. The boys went right up to the altar, all shimmering in gold, swung the censers, answered the priest without the slightest unease, and handed him bottles with spouts resembling the beaklike tips of a crescent moon. Could these be the same loudmouthed boys who hunted knee-deep in the water for crayfish, grabbed each other by the hair, and got tanned at home? How he envied them that, once a week, they could be other than what they were.

Several church fairs were held annually in Gine. Peddlers set up their canvas stalls by the roadside, at the foot of the hill, hugging the path leading down from the cemetery oaks. They sold gingerbread hearts and clay-rooster whistles, but Thomas was most enthralled by the little violet, red, and black squares of the scapulars, by the clusters of rosaries, and by the color and multiplicity of tiny objects.

Of all the holidays, none could compete with Easter, not only because that was the time of year when poppy seeds were ground in earthenware bowls and Easter cakes raided for their nuts. All during Holy Week, when the pictures and statues inside the church were shrouded, and bells replaced by the hollow clatter of rattles, people made a pilgrimage to Jesus' tomb. The grotto was guarded by sentries, each armed with a lance and a halbred, each in a silver helmet festooned with comb and plume. Jesus' body lay on top of an elevated platform, the same body that normally hung on the crucifix, only now the arms were covered with myrtle leaves.

The most eagerly awaited event of the season was the performance on Holy Saturday. Fifteen- and sixteen-year-old boys, after weeks of rehearsing, came running into the church with a roar, bearing dead crows lashed to poles. Devout old women, exhausted by a strict observance of the fast and by endless prayer, their heads drooping lower and lower, were suddenly roused from their drowsy meditations by a dead crow dangled before their noses; those who had brought eggs in bundles to be blessed were similarly taunted. The skits were staged on the church lawn. Thomas's favorite was the persecution of Judas. First they ran him off his legs, corralled him, showered him with insults, hung him till his tongue bulged, then pulled down the corpse; but lest he got off too lightly, he was flipped over on his belly, pinched till he groaned, his drawers lowered, his rear end stuffed with straw, a soul blown into him, until finally Judas jumped to his feet, screaming that he was alive.

When Thomas was a little older, Antonina and his grandmother took him to Sunrise Mass at Easter. After a few doleful songs and litanies, the choir burst into an "Alleluia" and the procession got under way: a filing toward the door, a lingering darkness outside, candles flickering in

the breeze, branches overhead, a matinal chill, the women's kerchiefs shimmering in the light, the bare heads of the men—ending with a procession around the church and along the little stone wall. In time, all this became associated in Thomas's mind with the advent of spring.

Then came the sleepy holiday patter, the sweet taste of rolls—and the egg-rolling contests. The children's course was made of turf, slightly curved to the inside and lined with strips of tin to increase the momentum. No two eggs rolled alike, and you had to guess by its shape whether to position it on the right, left, or in the middle of the rut. And just when the coast was clear, just as your egg started catching up with the others, spread out like a herd of cows; when it was on the verge of hitting another egg and making its owner a winner, it would suddenly take to wobbling and, obeying its own private whim, either skirt it by a finger or stop just short of it.

On Corpus Christi, the church was decorated with oak and maple leaf garlands suspended from the rafters above the heads of the congregation. All during May, flowers were placed at the foot of the statue of the Virgin Mary, but now it was the altar's turn to be decked. The children were crowded into the sacristy and handed little baskets of rose or peony petals. Thomas's grandmother made him take part in the procession. They marched with their backs to the canopy, under which the priest carried the monstrance, and one had to step cautiously to avoid tripping over a rock. Corpus Christi almost always fell on a hot day; by the time it was over, everyone was drenched, wrought from carrying all the banners and the reliquaries. But it was still one of the most festive of feast days: bright skies, the twitter of swallows, the chiming of bells, and lots of white, red, and gold.

9

THE WORLD was at war, and barely had it begun than the Russian Tsar, with his army now in retreat, ceased to have dominion over the Land of Lakes. Thomas saw the Germans only once. There were three, all on beautiful mounts. They came riding into the courtyard where Thomas sat next to old Gregory, who, too old to work, passed the time weaving baskets. A young officer, narrow in the waist and ruddy-faced as a schoolgirl, jumped down from his horse, gave it a clap on the neck, and helped himself to a drink from the milk can. The servant girls crowded around him, but old Gregory sat still, not taking his whittling knife from the branch. The sight of a man dressed in such colorful clothes—his uniform was a grassy green—came as a shock to Thomas. Strapped to his belt was a leather holster, and in the holster an enormous gun with a protruding metal butt and a long barrel. Thomas all but fell in love with his agility, and with something else not quite definable. The officer returned the can, sprang back into the saddle, saluted, and rode off with his soldiers by way of the cow barn and the linden lane.

What remains to be told is the story of the man's fate, a fate that, though only imagined, is hardly beyond the realm of plausibility. On one visit to the church, he leaned against the little stone wall and drew furiously in his notebook. Possibly he was reminded of a similar wooden *Kirche* he had seen in Norway before the war. As he mounted his horse and dropped down into the stirrups, to a creaking of saddle straps, he inhaled the fragrance of the meadows along the Issa, possibly recalling the landscape of

devastation on the Western Front, in France, where he had recently seen combat. He never noticed Thomas, not then or—why not?—twenty years later as he sat in a general's car, surrounded by comfort rugs and thermos bottles, his corpulent chin propped against the collar of his uniform, and was chauffered through the streets of an East European city freshly conquered by the Führer's army. Clenching his fists in his pockets (we can assume he did), Thomas refused to recognize in the conqueror the object of his short-lived affection.

The war had only one effect on Gine: it meant no more shopping trips to town, since there was now nothing to buy. The result was a number of new and exciting domestic enterprises. Like the making of soap. A bonfire in the orchard, a kettle on a tripod, a brownish mash mixed with a pole. Phew! It was a stench to beat all stenches, but what excitement, what a lot of wrangling over the outcome. Once the mash had hardened, it was carved up into pieces. Or the making of candles. For that you needed cut-off bottles, tallow, and a wick. A piece of string, soaked in kerosene, severed the tops; by wrapping the string around the neck and setting fire to it, you could get the glass to crack all the way around in exactly the desired place. They also bought two carbide lamps, whose shape and odor intrigued Thomas. To make up for the lack of tea, Grandmother began to use wild strawberry leaves. Honey was substituted for sugar, but it wasn't long before she discovered saccharin, and from then on, she never went back to using sugar, saccharin being just as sweet-tasting—and cheaper.

It was time for Thomas to begin his studies, but with no one at home to take charge of his education, he was sent to the village, to Joseph, nicknamed "the Black." And black he was: brows like thick brushstrokes, a drawn face, and graying at the temples. He lived with his brother and helped out with the farming, devoting all his spare time to

various hobbies. He was always receiving books, drying plants between sheets of pressed newspaper, writing letters for people—and talking politics. He had once served a prison term for those politics, and had worked at a number of trades, though he did not behave at all in the manner of townspeople, and the embroidery on his shirts proclaimed that he was still a peasant. He belonged to that tribe on which our chroniclers of today have bestowed the name of "nationalists"; that is, he was dedicated to serving the glory of the Cause. And that was his downfall, the root of his undoing. For while his sympathies were clearly on the side of Lithuania, he was nonetheless obliged to teach Thomas how to read and write in Polish. That the Surkonts—the surname could not have been more Lithuanian—regarded themselves as Poles he took to be an act of treason. His hatred for the Polish landowners (because they were land-owners, because they had switched languages to distinguish themselves from the people), coupled with his inability to hate the man who had entrusted his grandson to him, and all that combined with his hope of opening Thomas's eyes to the splendor of the Cause—such was the tangle of emotion implicit in the fit of coughing that overtook him every time the boy opened his reader in front of him.

Grandmother was not at all happy with these lessons, with this fraternizing with "country bumpkins" (she had never accepted the Lithuanians, although her photograph might have served to illustrate a book on the country's original inhabitants). But since hiring a tutor would have been too uppity, she finally consented to Joseph, grumbling they were bound to make a yokel of him. Thomas was ignorant of all these complexities and antagonisms, and when at last he did understand, he thought of it as something exceptional. Had he crossed paths with a young Englishman brought up in Ireland or with a young Swede raised in Finland, he might have found many analogies.

But those lands beyond the Issa Valley were enveloped by fog, and what little he knew came from his grandmother's stories—how the English ate compote for breakfast (which may have explained his attraction to them), how the Russians had exiled Grandfather Arthur to Siberia, how one should love the Polish kings whose tombs were located in Cracow. To Grandmother, Cracow—"When you're a big boy, you'll go there"—was the most beautiful city in the world. His grandmother's patriotism for something so distant; the tolerance practiced by his grandfather, so unconcerned with nationality; and Joseph's constant invoking of the words "we" and "our country" nurtured in Thomas his later distrust whenever heated reference was made in his presence to any flags or emblems.

The lessons with Joseph dragged on, due to the chaos of the intervening years, out of which chaos the tiny republic of Lithuania was born. Thanks to Joseph, construction on the first school in Gine was begun, and he eventually became one of its teachers.

The war was abating, its progress measured by what one saw down on the road—from one of the rotting benches, say, situated at the park's edge. From far away, from beyond the lakes, from the cities they came, all fleeing from hunger, their backs strapped with sacks and bundles, many of them pulling their children in little wooden carts. One such family, a mother and two boys, was taken into the manor on the insistence of Antonina, whom the practically grown-up Stasiek had charmed with his beautiful harmonica playing, his city songs, and above all with his pure Mazovian Polish. "What a fancy talker!" she squealed, squinting with delight. Stasiek, with his big ears and skinny neck, failed to gain Thomas's affections, even though the boy had made him a crossbow with a butt similar to one on a real carbine. Those evenings were full of girlish giggling coming from under the linden tree, and even when Stasiek sat alone with Antonina, Thomas would

squirm and fidget in his seat, and eventually leave them—
bored, and somehow irked, as when the afternoon sun
suddenly ducks behind a cloud.

10

❦❦❦❦❦❦

IF ANYONE was hounded by devils, it was
Balthazar, even though he had the look of a man born for
joy. A gypsy's complexion, white teeth, over six feet tall,
pie-faced, with a light down for a beard. Whenever he
presented himself at the manor—dressed in a tightly
cinched tunic, his navy-blue cap cocked back, revealing a
bushy thatch—Thomas would come on the run to meet
him, yelling all the way. With him he carried either a bas-
ket of mushrooms—boletuses and honey mushrooms, their
tops the shade of a cut alder, their sides a dappled white—
or some game: a snipe or a black grouse with a little red
stripe over the eye. Balthazar was a forester, though not in
the strict sense. He was neither paid nor was he obligated
to pay, but made his home in the forest (built with a free
allotment of timber), cultivated a few potato and rye
fields, and plowed a little piece of farmland every year. His
arrival at the manor was enough to give Grandmother a
migraine. Sometimes Thomas caught her scolding his
grandfather: "It's your favorite again! Don't you dare try
to slip him anything!"

People were envious of Balthazar, and with good
reason. Before he became a forester, he had nothing; now
he had a farm, some livestock, and not just a cottage but a
house with a plank floor, a porch, and four outbuildings.
He later married the daughter of a prosperous farmer from
Gine and had two children by her. Surkont was a push-

over for any of Balthazar's requests, to the point of ex-
posing himself to ridicule. The forester made few enemies,
for he knew how to act with discretion: while he made sure
no trees in the old oak forest were cut down, he would not
object if someone from Pogirai felled a spruce or a horn-
beam, as long as the stump was covered with moss.

For Balthazar, happiness was lounging on the front
porch, a jug of homemade beer beside him on the floor—
swigging from his mug, smacking his lips, yawning and
scratching. A contented cat; but it was on just such occa-
sions that he was given to fits. From time to time, Grand-
father sat Thomas down beside him in the britska and rode
out past the manorial fields to the forester's cottage. The
britska was a buggy put to frequent use, as was the *linijka*
—a kind of board on wheels, mounted horseback-style.
Still other vehicles were kept stored in the coach house: a
carriage, dust-covered and cobwebbed; another on run-
ners, an open sledge; and one called the "spider," a long
carriage painted a garish yellow, with enormous front
wheels and smaller ones in back, an elevated seat for a
driver or footman; and stretching the full length of the
"spider" (which rather reminded one of a wasp), a bed of
planks that, when jumped on, flipped high into the air.

Grandfather grabbed him by the waist every time the
britska lurched. Past the fields came the grasslands and
moors. Black pools in the grass-choked ruts concealed
potholes deep enough for a wagon to sink up to its axle.
Smoke, curling upward against a clump of hornbeam, sig-
naled the barking of dogs, a rooftop and a well hoist. In
the wilderness, alone, among animals that craned their
necks from the brush and spied on the barnyard bustle—
that was the life for Thomas. Balthazar's place smelled of
resin, and the virgin wood made it gleam as though forged
from copper.

Balthazar sat there, grinning, while his wife enter-
tained them with food and drink, passing round the cold

meats with a persistent "Please—help yourselves." Slight of build, with a jutting jaw, she uttered not another word the rest of the evening.

Thomas sometimes left the grownups and ran off to spy on the jays or wild pigeons—so many species of bird were to be found there. Once, among a pile of rocks in the brush, he discovered a nest of hoopoes; reaching inside, he caught one in his hand, a fledgling, which tried to frighten him by fanning its head feathers. When he brought it indoors, the hoopoe wouldn't eat, preferring to flit along the walls instead. In the end, he had to let it go.

Whatever was tormenting Balthazar, he would never have told Thomas. Not even he knew the nature of his affliction, only that it was getting worse. As long as he was putting up the house, everything was fine. But later, pausing behind his plow to roll a cigarette, he would lose all sense of where he was; when he came to, his fingers would be clenched, the tobacco spilled all over the ground. As a last resort, he doubled his work load, but his innate laziness made him finish any job in half the time it took normally; and the moment he stretched out on a bench with his jug of beer, his insides would go soft, do a slow somersault, and in a trance, as though half asleep, he would try to scream through clenched jaws. No luck. Sometimes he had an urge to jump up, bang his fist on the table, and take off for parts unknown. At times the whispering merged with the limpness, and Balthazar would fling his beer mug at his tormentor, who either crawled inside him or mocked him from a distance. When this happened, his wife took off his boots and helped him into bed. Balthazar submitted to her, as he did to everything else, with apathy and the feeling that something was wrong, that he had somehow been cheated. He was repulsed by her homeliness, which was hardly noticeable in the dark but inescapable during the day. Sleep brought relief, but not for long, and at night he would awaken with the sensation of lying at the bottom of

a pit barricaded by high walls, from which there was no escape.

There were times when he did bang the table and break away. But then it was only to embark on a real binge, lasting no fewer than three or four days, during which time he would drink till the vodka burned his insides and the innkeeper's wife, a Jew, had to squat over him and piss in his face—a notorious, though incriminating, method of revival. Word would then get around that Balthazar was at it again, some claiming that it came from a life of fat and plenty, others that he was conniving with the devil— which was not idle gossip, because Balthazar was heard to blab many things during his drunken ravings.

Years later, after he had left Gine, Thomas had occasion to think of Balthazar, to sum up all that he had heard about him, with its blending of fact and legend, and to recall the stone-hard biceps (Balthazar was a man of herculean strength) and roelike eyes. No amount of success or providence, he decided, could protect a man from such an affliction of the soul, and whenever the example of Balthazar came to mind, it always made him fearful of his own fate and of all that lay ahead of him.

I I

A GOATEE, a flickering glance, the meekly folded hands of a city dweller, elbows propped on the table: thus did Herr Doktor, the "Little German," manifest himself. "Scat," Balthazar muttered under his breath, trying to make the sign of the cross and scratching his chest instead, while the other went on, cajolingly, his words falling with the rustle of dry leaves.

"But, my dear Balthazar," he said, "I only want to

help you. You're forever worrying, and for no reason. You're worried about the farm, aren't you? You're worried sick because the land doesn't belong to you. Yours and not yours. Here today, gone tomorrow, right? You think someone else will take over the manor and turn you out."

Balthazar moaned.

"But does the land really mean that much to you? Well, admit it. No, deep down you're hiding something. Right now, this very minute, you'd like to make a clean break with everything. Oh, the world is such a big place, Balthazar. Big cities, nights of laughter, music . . . You fall asleep on some riverbank, alone, free, all your bridges burned behind you, one life finished and another just beginning. No more guilty conscience, a new world before you, one that's never to be . . . Because you're scared, Balthazar. You're trembling over your property, over your hogs. 'What,' you say to yourself, 'am I to be a nothing again?' All right, but of all the Balthazars, why choose the dumbest one? Wouldn't you like to know what the other Balthazar is like?"

"Oh, God."

"There's no relief in sight. Autumn comes, winter, spring, summer . . . then autumn again, and so it goes till the grave—that's it, Balthazar, drown your troubles in drink. And you know what the nights are like. But it wasn't I who advised you to get married against your better judgment, to pick out the ugliest girl because she had a rich father. Fear, Balthazar, that's what did it. You wanted security. And are you any happier now than you were at twenty? Remember the parties? The days when your hand took easily to the ax, your feet to dancing, your throat to singing? How you and your friends used to live it up in grand style? Now you're alone. A farmer. Though it's true, they might take away that house of yours."

Balthazar was paralyzed, a sack of sawdust inside. The other was on to him.

"You're out at the crack of dawn, dew on the grass, birds singing—but is that the life for you? No, you're counting. For you it's just another day, a day like any other. On and on, like a plow horse. And in the old days? You used to sing. But now? You look at the oaks, but they might as well be hemp. Or not even there. It's all there in the books, Balthazar. But you, you'll never know what's in the books. Better to hang yourself than to keep such a mess buried inside. Otherwise, how can you be sure life isn't just a dream? That's what it says in the books. Would you hang yourself? I doubt it."

"Why is everyone else so lucky and not me?"

"Because, my friend, to each is given a certain thread, and that thread is a man's fate. Either a person catches hold of it and is content with it, or he doesn't. You were unlucky. You weren't looking for your own thread, you were too busy trying to copy others. What makes others happy makes you unhappy."

"What am I to do? Tell me."

"Nothing. It's too late. Too late for Balthazar. You're losing more and more of your nerve. The nerve to hang yourself or run away. You'll rot."

The beer came out of the jug in a muddy stream. He was drinking and at the same time burning on the inside. The other grinned.

"And no sense worrying over that secret of yours. No one will ever be the wiser. It's strictly between us. Everybody has to die, right? A little sooner or a little later—what's the difference? True, he was young. But he'd been fighting so long he was almost forgotten in the village. His wife will cry for a while, but she'll get over it. So what if he had a plump baby boy to hug him; he was much too small to remember his father. Only you shouldn't go around crying in your beer about having some sort of crime on your conscience."

"But the priest . . ."

"Yes, I know, you went to confession. But you're not so dumb as to believe you can make a clean breast of it in the confessional. You lied. It's bad to be refused absolution. You were lying when you said you killed him because he jumped you with an ax. All right, he jumped you. But then what? Well, Balthazar? You shot him while he sat there eating in the bushes. You threw in the bloodstained biscuits after him, and that's how you buried him. Isn't that so?"

Balthazar howled and let fly with the mug. The intercession of the "Little German" also accounted for his later hell-raising in the taverns as he went about overturning tables and smashing lamps.

12

THE GROUND in the fir hollow being the quickest to heal, Balthazar had carved out a piece of turf, then packed it down again with the shovel. He would come just before nightfall, sit, and listen to the shrieking of the jays and scurrying of the thrushes. It was easier to endure the pain here than to brood over it from a distance. He was almost envious of the person lying there. Such a peaceful spot, clouds drifting above the trees . . . And how many years did he still have ahead of him?

After stashing the rifle in the trunk of an oak, he never touched it again. A converted army rifle with a sawed-off barrel, it had fit easily under his overcoat, leading the other man to believe he was unarmed. He had jumped him from the bushes lining the trail, his ax held high, and yelled: "Hands up!" A red beard, a Russian greatcoat much the worse for wear: a POW from a Ger-

man prison camp, trying to escape through the woods. Why the ambush? To rob him of his civilian clothes, club him to death, or just some madman on the loose? The moment Balthazar swung the rifle to his hip, the intruder spun around and fled so fast the bushes swished. But he didn't know his way around the forest, wasn't familiar with its many tunnels and crossings. And once an animal starts circling, it'll always wind up where it should. Taking his time, Balthazar started stalking him. If the prisoner went that way, he figured, then he had to come out in the pine clearing and stop to catch his breath. What was pushing him? Revenge? Fear that the man wasn't alone, that he might attack at night? Or was it just his hunter's instinct, the urge to track down the animal, to get even with him? Sneaking up, crouching low, he glimpsed the gray coat more or less where he had expected to find it. Leaving him for a moment, he circled round by way of some saplings to get in closer range, then trained the barrel on the man's stooped shoulder—he was sitting sideways to Balthazar— his neck, and finally on his head with the visorless cap. Later, with all his might, he tried to remember why he had pulled the trigger, but just when he was sure of the reason, another took its place.

The Russian fell face down. Balthazar waited; it was quiet except for the hawks crying overhead. Not a sign of any movement. Satisfied the man was dead, he zigzagged up to the body and turned it over. Bright blue eyes stared up at the spring sky, a louse crawled out of the hem of the dead man's coat. Next to him, on the ground—a bag of biscuits, untied and spotted with blood. The heels of his boots were worn smooth, evidence of his long trek from Prussia. He went through the man's pockets but found only a pocketknife and two German postage stamps. He covered the body, along with the ax and other things, with some fir branches until he could come back with the shovel later that evening.

He made up his mind while brooding at the scene of the crime one day. He was almost willing to believe the idea was communicated to him by the Russian. Maybe the killing was meant to be. That night he slept well, and was out of the house at daybreak.

The wizard Masiulis owned a large flock of sheep, and gate after gate had to be opened before entering the yard. Balthazar displayed his gifts: a tub of butter and several wreaths of sausage. The old man adjusted his wire-rimmed spectacles. His skin looked almost smoked, gray bristles showed in his ears and nostrils. They began by swapping the latest neighborhood gossip, but when it came time to reveal the purpose of his visit, Balthazar was tongue-tied. At last, he pointed to his heart, made a gesture as if to rip it out, then muttered, bearlike: "They're torturing me." The sorcerer said nothing, nodded, and led him into the orchard, out past the beehive, where an old forge, rank with weeds, stood among the apple trees. Taking down some sacks that hung on poles, he gathered a handful of dried twigs lying in a corner, made four little piles, and sat Balthazar down on a log in the center. Then he lighted the twigs, and, to a low patter, began sprinkling herbs from the little sacks onto the fire. The smoke grew fiercer and headier, as the bespectacled face, all the while intoning some prayer, loomed up on one side and then the other. When he stood him up and brought him back to the house, Balthazar lowered his eyes under the other man's gaze.

"No, Balthazar," the old man said at last. "I can't help you. What's fit for a king is a king, an emperor for an emperor. Every power has its equal, but this is one power I don't have. Maybe you'll find someone who has what it takes. Wait and see."

Thus did his hopes vanish. And to those who tried not to guess his secret, Balthazar smiled blithely, baring his teeth.

13

THE PRIEST seldom visited the manor, and
Thomas first came to know the rectory the day he and
Antonina, nervously fingering the fold of her kerchief,
stood on the front steps, staring up at the magical window.
The parish priest, a stooped, rumpled man, was nicknamed
—after one of his pet phrases—Father "Well, well." The
priest had him recite the Our Father, the Hail Mary, and
the Creed, and rewarded him with a holy picture. The
Virgin Mary in the picture reminded him of the swallows
that nested above the hay ladders and in the barn rafters.
A blue dress, a bronzed face, surrounded by a disk of real
gold. He kept the picture in an almanac, approaching its
colors with delight every time he leafed through its pages.

He had little trouble learning the catechism, though
his sympathies were not evenly divided. First came God
the Father, bearded and frowning and towering above the
clouds. Then Jesus, with his gentle gaze, one finger point-
ing to a heart spoked with rays—but Jesus had gone back
up to heaven and so He, too, was far away. But not so the
Holy Ghost, that eternally living dove shooting shafts of
light down on people's heads. As he prepared himself for
confession, he prayed to the Holy Ghost to hover over
him—it was so hard keeping track of one's sins. He added
them up on his fingers, lost count, and had to start all over
again. Brushing his lips against the much worn and pol-
ished grating of the confessional, listening to the priest's
heavy breathing, he recited the list as fast as he could.
But by the time he reached the Swedish Ramparts, he was
suddenly doubt-stricken, slackened his pace, broke out cry-

ing in the lane, and, full of despair, ran to his grandmother: what to do about all the sins he had forgotten? She told him to go back, and he cried the harder, now from shame. At her wit's end, she took him by the hand and brought him to the priest. Her presence had a calming effect, and embarrassing as it was, it was better than having to face it alone.

From the start, therefore, Thomas had the makings of what theologians call a "scrupulous conscience," the cause, in their view, of many of the devil's triumphs. Try as he would not to omit anything, he was always careful not to include a certain secret among his offenses. Unable to see it from the outside, he never imagined that it was both his—his and Onutè Akulonis's—and that it existed, so to speak, apart from them, in the sense that it had been invented before them. It went far beyond the usual—using foul language, say, or spying on girls swimming naked in the river, at the black crows beneath their navels, or spooking them on Saturday nights when they squatted in the orchard between dances and hiked their skirts.

Slipping away from their playmates, Onutè and he would retreat to their secret hideout on the Issa, crawling on all fours through a tunnel of blackthorn and then branching off—one had to know exactly where. There, on a sandy mound, safely huddled in seclusion, drawn together by the danger, they conversed in muffled voices and listened to the fish splashing, to the whacking of the wash paddles, and to the rumble of cart wheels on the road. Naked, their heads turned toward each other and the shade falling on their arms, they would find in this inaccessible palace an even smaller sanctuary in which to dwell in mystery. Like her mother (and like Pola), Onutè had blond hair, worn in a braid. And this is how It was performed: Onutè would lie flat on her back, pull him toward her, and squeeze him with her knees. And they stayed that way, as the sun rolled across the sky, and he knew that all the time

she was waiting, waiting for him to touch her, and it made him feel *sweet* all over. Yet this was not just any girl, but Onutè, and nothing could have prevailed on him to confess their secret.

Taking Holy Communion early in the morning, on an empty stomach, made him woozy and gave him stomach cramps. He came back up the aisle from Communion with his hands crossed on his chest and his eyes glued to his shoe tips. It was hard to visualize the wafer stuck to his palate—and which his tongue would shyly peel off—as the body of Jesus. But he was noticeably changed by it: for one whole day he was actually quiet and well-behaved. What appealed most to his imagination were the priest's words comparing the soul to a room that had to be cleaned and made worthy of receiving its Guest. He imagined that, after the wafer had melted, it was later healed in the soul, returning to its place in the chalice that stood among the greenery on the altar. That he, Thomas, was privileged to carry around such a room filled him with pride, and he was careful not to sully or damage it.

The day was approaching when, as had been promised, he was to be made an altar boy. He had even begun memorizing those inscrutable Latin responses, when the old pastor was suddenly transferred to another parish. The new priest—young, imposing, with a prominent chin, and brows joined at the bridge of his nose—alarmed people by his impulsiveness. He kept those who were already altar boys and refused to take on any new ones, as he had more important duties to attend to.

His sermons were a far cry from that endless prating, larded with hemming, with that monotonous "Well, well . . ." to which the people of Gine were accustomed. Although not always able to follow them, Thomas like everyone else froze in expectation when the new priest stepped into the pulpit. He began informally, in a voice barely above a patter, but soon, at regular intervals, he rose to a loud and

booming exclamation, and the effect was musical. Then came a raising of the arms and a vociferating to set the church walls to trembling. He fulminated against their sins, his finger pointed into the crowd, and everyone quaked, believing himself or herself to be the object of his wrath. And then—abrupt silence, as he stood, flushed and excited, and stared; leaning on the edge of the pulpit, he bent down and in a low, soothing, heart-to-heart voice presented them with visions of the happiness awaiting those who were saved. At that point, his listeners began to sniffle. Soon the fame of Father Peiksva began to spread beyond Gine and the neighboring villages, and people from out of the parish began coming to him for confession, and he was forever surrounded by kerchiefs, seen bowing low every time his female admirers went to kiss his stole or hands.

He was adored by Akulonis's wife, by the servant girls, and above all by Antonina ("When he cleanses your sins," she sighed, "it's like he was scrubbin' your insides with a steel brush"). Even Grandmother, though opposed in principle to Lithuanian sermons, became a convert of his after hearing one of his orations delivered in Polish. But the fervor didn't last long. Now the women's boast to outsiders that a great honor had been bestowed on Gine was accompanied by a scowl, and they would immediately change the subject. Nor did it take Thomas and the children from the village long to realize that it was better to steer clear of the rectory.

14

❧ ♪ ❋ ♪ ❋ ♪ ❧

MAGDALENA'S COFFIN was delivered to the cemetery a few days before the Feast of the Assumption. The coffin, shrouded with an ornamented blanket, lay in

a big wagon on a bed of straw. Pausing in the shade of the lindens, the horses buried their heads in their feed bags, lapped up the oats, and drowsily swished away the flies: they had come a long way. The news spread so fast that the driver had no sooner tied the reins to the fence than people began milling around in anticipation. Father Peiksva made his appearance on the smooth flagstone path farther up the hill—motionless, as if unable to decide whether to come down, as if bracing himself. At last, he began to make his way down, slowly, only to stop again, pull out his handkerchief, and stand there, twisting and crumpling it in his fingers.

The scandal involving Magdalena had lasted some six months, and she had no one but herself to blame. Peiksva had inherited her as the rectory housekeeper, and their relationship was strictly private—a priest was only human, after all—until she began acting improperly, strutting about with her chin up and swiveling her hips like a dancer. She took such obvious pleasure in flaunting herself before him, in dropping hints so as to put the other women on notice: you may kiss his hands and robes, but I have *all* of him. Words led to visions—of how the man who stood before the altar used to lie in bed naked with her, of conversations, of moments of intimacy . . . Granted, much can be forgiven in such matters, as long as one is not nagged by all sorts of images.

Looking back over Magdalena's behavior prior to that (for two years she had served as the old pastor's housekeeper), the inhabitants of Gine, after long discussion, soon discovered other improprieties. Had her marriage plans fallen through and her fiancé immediately married someone else because of her age—she was going on twenty-five at the time—or even because she was poor, the daughter of landless peasants? Her fiancé, against everyone's advice, against even his parents' wishes, was ready to marry her, owing obviously to Magdalena's spe-

cial powers. But at the last moment, frightened by her passionate nature, he had a change of heart. Similarly, other things, one corroborating the other, began to appear in a new light. And for those who still had any doubts, there was now the coffin.

Because Antonina used to spit every time she uttered Magdalena's name, Thomas, even though she had done nothing to deserve it, was already prejudiced against her. Whenever he came to the rectory to visit Father "Well, well," he was lured into the kitchen and treated to a piece of cake. He was even enthralled by her, would get a lump in his throat at the sight of her. When she leaned over the stove to sample one of her dishes with a spoon, her skirts (they pinched her waist they were cinched so tightly) rustled, a lock of hair slipped down over one ear, and a breast shifted inside her blouse. Though she was unaware of it, they were joined together because he knew what she looked like. True, he had confessed the sin, but he had seen her—from his leafy perch in a low-hanging tree on the river, his heart racing, wondering whether she would ever come, the Issa slowly turning pink in the setting sun, the fish jumping . . . He was craning up at a flight of ducks when she appeared, testing the water with her foot. She entered the water not like a *baba* who plops down once or twice with a splash, but slowly, step by step, her breasts splayed, not too black under the belly, more like a smudge. Kicking up an occasional fountain as she went, she had dog-paddled over to the water-lily pads, then swam back and washed herself with soap.

Thomas was both shocked and confused by all the gossip. It was inconceivable to him that the same person who thundered against the fires of hell could himself be a sinner. If the person who granted absolution was no different from anyone else, then what was the good of absolution? (Such questions were never posed openly.) Thus did Magdalena acquire for him the magic of forbidden things.

But the grownups were resentful of her; they were able to make distinctions where Thomas was not: a woman was one thing, a priest in a surplice another. She had broken the covenant, disturbed their peace, and spoiled for them the pleasure of listening to the sermons.

Father Peiksva, accompanied by stares, came down the hill. What would he have them do with the coffin? As he approached the wagon, they looked the other way. Tears were streaming down his cheeks, his lips pressed together to stop them from twitching. Only once did he open his mouth, and that was to ask that the body be carried up to the church for the Christian burial he meant to give it. The blanket was removed, revealing a coffin of white pine. Four of the villagers hoisted it to their shoulders and began climbing uphill, so that Magdalena stood up perfectly straight.

15

IT TAKES a fairly desperate person to swallow rat poison, a surrendering to one's own thoughts so complete as to make one oblivious to everything but one's fate. Magdalena might have lived to know many cities, countries, people, inventions, books, and all the incarnations of a lifetime. She might have, but try explaining that to her, try proving by a wave of the wand that there have been millions of women in the same predicament as she. Nothing would have stopped her, not even the despair of all those who, at the very moment she was taking her own life, were fighting for another hour, another minute. Once the mind has surrendered, once the body finds itself face to face with the supreme horror, it's already too late.

Nor should one overlook her wrought state shortly before the old pastor's departure. Her fiancé had broken off the engagement, which had numbed her, convincing her that nothing would ever change, that things would remain irrevocably the same. She rebelled at such a future—day in and day out, month after month, year after year, until she woke to find herself an old spinster. At daybreak she lay in bed, horrified at the thought of getting up and going about her daily chores. Sitting on the edge of the bed, she cupped her breasts; spurned like herself, they would share her life of celibacy and wither idly away. And then what? Latch on to boys at village dances, go for a tumble in the hay, become a prey to their dirty jokes . . . ? By the time Father Peiksva took over the rectory, she had worked herself into a state of utter despair.

When you're on a swing, there comes a moment of suspended motion, followed by a breathtaking downward rush. For Magdalena, earth and sky suddenly changed places; the tree outside, even the clouds, lost their old familiarity, and every animate thing seemed suffused with pure gold. Never had she dreamed that life could be so transfigured. She was to be rewarded for her suffering; and even if it meant eternal pain, it was worth it. Not the least of her exultation sprang from satiated pride; poor and illiterate as she was, she had been singled out by such an educated man, a man head and shoulders above the rest.

And then—it should be borne in mind—she was driven out into the cold, this time for good. Peiksva, aware of the scandal and forced to choose, had found her a housekeeper's position with a pastor in a parish so distant everyone could see the break was final. In that house overlooking the lake, with only a carping old man for company, Magdalena did not wait long before surrendering to dark despair—a despair she had known before her brief interlude of happiness. She swallowed the rat poison while the wind was whistling in the reeds, traces of white foam

were being washed up on the shingle, and waves lapped against the boats moored to the landing.

The pastor of the other parish refused to bury her, washing his hands of the affair by donating his wagon, a few horses, and a driver.

Magdalena's last journey—before she entered that realm where highbred ladies belonging to a bygone era were on hand to greet her—began early in the morning. Under fleecy clouds the horses trotted briskly along, the men stood sharpening their scythes for the second mowing, and whetstone chimed against metal. They traveled down a sandy road, through groves of juniper and pine, then climbed uphill before coming to a crossroad overlooking three stretches of water, joined by green clasps like a necklace of translucent stones. Again downhill and into the woods—into a village street, where Magdalena spent the afternoon hours staring up at the leaves of an old maple, till evening shadows began to fall and the heat let up and it was time to resume the journey. The wagon wheels bounced across the log-covered dam; before long, the thrushes began their evening concert, and a starry sky unfolded with a refulgence of moving spheres and universes. An immense calm, a deep blue space—and whoever was looking down from there, did he behold a tiny solitary creature who had discovered how to stop the beating of her heart, the circulation of her blood, and of her own volition turn herself into an inanimate object? A horse smell, a driver's idle patter—and so it went until late into the night. Came morning and it was over hills again, through oak forests, the wagon all the time drawing closer to its destination. Gradually they descended into the Issa Valley, while across the way, with a view on the river gleaming through the osiers, Father Peiksva recited his breviary and waited.

Decomposition sets in quickly in summer, and people wondered why he was delaying the ceremony, almost as if unwilling to surrender her to the earth. Yet no unpleasant

odor was detected when it came time to lift her from the wagon—a fact duly noted later on. The priest had her buried on the outskirts of the cemetery, on the slope, where the loose ground was held in place by clusters of roots.

Father Peiksva's sermon on the Feast of the Assumption was brief, and was delivered in a calm and steady voice. He described how she who was without blemish had risen into heaven, not in spirit alone but with her whole body, just as she had been while on earth; how at first her feet had barely touched the grass, then how she had slowly ascended without moving them, higher and higher, the breeze playing with her long robe, such as was worn in Judea at the time, till she became a minute speck among the clouds; and how she was granted that with which we sinners—if we are worthy—shall be rewarded in the valley of Josephat; and how, with all her earthly senses and in possession of eternal youth, she now beholds the face of God the Almighty.

Shortly afterward Father Peiksva left Gine, never to be heard from again.

16

AMONG THE WOMEN it was a subject of back-yard gossip. The men, on the other hand, observed silence; their eyes fixed on a pinch of tobacco, they licked the paper and pretended to be focusing all their attention on the thing at hand. With the gossip came a mounting anxiety, though for a time the people were content to pon-

der it, were careful to avoid using certain dangerous expressions.

The person who contributed most to the spreading of rumors was the new priest, Father Monkiewicz, a rotund, baldheaded, high-strung man, who could hardly contain his unease when he could find no natural explanation for a continual knocking on the wall (always three knocks in a row). After all he had heard, he was never comfortable at home; his nerves couldn't take whatever was manifesting itself in all the knocking. At the sound of someone's hand on the door latch, he would jump up, open the door, only to find no one there. He had hoped that these weird intrusions would cease of themselves, but things only got worse. The sexton was invited to sleep in the rectory, and from that moment on, there could be no more room for speculation. Father Monkiewicz, beside himself, appealed to the local villagers, and at night, in two's and three's, they stood guard in the kitchen.

It seems that Magdalena's ghost was loath to leave the place where it had known happiness. Using an invisible cleaver, it split invisible logs and started a fire that crackled and blazed like the real thing. It moved pans, broke eggs, and scrambled them on an otherwise cold and empty stove. What did it use for tools and utensils? Or were these only echoes, a whole register of sounds imitating nature? Or does a ghost have access to another kind of kitchen, one equipped with a universal bucket, a universal frying pan, a universal woodpile, that are but the essence of all the buckets, frying pans, and logs that ever were? A mystery— nothing to do but be vigilant and try not to believe the evidence of one's senses. Not even holy water had any effect. The priest sprinkled the water, there was a letup, but not for long, because then it resumed, every night a little louder and more obtrusive, sometimes to the sound of splashing water and a clanging of pots and pans. Worse,

the mysterious interventions soon shifted to the bedroom. To the continual knocking and tampering with door latches were added footfalls, the sound of papers and books being hurled to the floor, and something else—something bordering on muffled laughter. Father Monkiewicz made the sign of the cross, sprinkling first one corner, then another—not a sound; but as soon as he came to the fourth, he would hear giggling, followed by the sort of whistling made by blowing into a hollow nutshell.

News of the incidents traveled quickly to the neighboring villages, and if the people of Gine hadn't made it their own business, there would have been not three of them sitting around at night in the kitchen but three hundred. Barred from it, outsiders fell to gossiping so that the parish fairly teemed with the wildest rumors.

It was Balthazar who helped persuade people that Magdalena's ghost had outgrown the priest's house. His story might have been sloughed off as absurd, or treated with that sham gullibility with which one assents to the tales of drunkards so as not to risk offending them—were it not for one detail. Balthazar claimed, no less, to having seen Magdalena ride down from the cemetery to the river on a white horse. She was stark naked, he said, and both she and the horse had glowed in the dark. When a crowd later assembled at his father-in-law's place, he repeated the story, taking offense at the merest insinuation that he might have been seeing things. Someone suggested going to the pastor's stable to see whether the priest's bay was there. Sure enough, they found it—all lathered up as if just returned from a long gallop.

Naturally, the manor house was all astir at the news, a fresh installment of which was delivered daily by Antonina. "How awful," Grandmother Misia would say, and secretly delighted by these otherworldly pranks, she would invite the priest over to hear the litany of his woes. When,

noisily gulping down his strawberry-leaf tea, he conceded with a worried look that his health was failing, that unless these manifestations stopped he would ask to be transferred to another parish, Grandmother's triumph would be complete; and implicit in her "Oh, do be serious, Father!" was a cheerful vindication, since, after all, she was on the side of the spirits, not men.

Then another incident, this one quite close to home, arose. One day, allowed into Shatybelko's bedroom when the steward had nearly recovered from a sudden illness, Thomas got the creeps. The sick man, his beard spread out fanlike on the quilt, his dog curled up on the bedside rug, could muster only a few words in a feeble voice. Although Mopsy had disgraced himself—he had run off, his stump of a tail tucked between his legs—the old man bore him no grudge. What had happened was this: during the threshing season, the boiler engine was parked in the shed by the barn, and after the day's work the precious transmission belt was stored in the shed, under lock and key. That evening Shatybelko had already settled down with his slippers and pipe when he was suddenly seized with doubt: had he or had he not turned the key in the lock? That he couldn't recall was enough to give him the jitters. At last, afraid someone might steal the belt, cursing under his breath, he pulled on his boots, slipped into his sheepskin coat, grabbed the lantern, and gave up a warm room for the cold and rain outside. It was so dark all he could see was the patch illuminated by the lantern. As he had suspected, the shed was unlocked. He went inside, squeezed through the narrow passage between wall and boiler, and checked: the belt was still there. But just as he was about to head back, he was visited by a monster. Shatybelko described it as a sort of bumpy log that moved sideways, level with the ground, and which was mounted with three heads—all with Tartar features, he said—baring their teeth in hideous

grimaces. As the ogre slowly advanced, he made the sign of the cross and started backing into the shed, aware that by doing so, he was cutting off his only escape. So, waving the lantern, he tried to maneuver around it and in the process trod on the monster's body—a body "soft as a bag of chaff," he said later. Once outside, he wanted to run, but did not dare turn his back on the creature. Step by step, he backed across the yard separating the farm buildings from his door, the three infernal heads constantly twisting and writhing on that legless trunk—and gasping, keeled over onto his front doorstep. The entire episode could not have lasted more than a quarter of an hour, but despite his previous good health, he suddenly came down with a fever.

Grandmother claimed it was the ghost of a Mohammedan, descended from the hill known as the Tartar Cemetery. (If not for that name, all recollection of those Tartar prisoners of war who had worked in Gine centuries ago would have vanished.) But why now—unless someone had put him up to it, ordered him to sow more turmoil? And who else could that someone have been if not Magdalena, in command of subterranean forces.

In time, all these episodes led to a straining of relations between Father Monkiewicz and the village. Now that all were agreed as to the cause, they argued logically that what remained was to remove the cause. At first they merely insinuated as much in his presence, discreetly, relying on parables and circumlocutions. When that didn't work, they came right out and declared it was time to put an end to all these spooky goings-on, and that there was only one way to do it. The priest waved his arms and screamed he would never condone it, never, and he denounced them as pagans. Once his mind was made up, he was adamant. There were those who were in favor of going ahead anyway, with or without his consent, though no one

believed they would ever have the nerve. A stalemate. Meanwhile, another priest came to the rectory. During his brief stay, the rites of exorcism were performed.

17

THOMAS WAS AFRAID to stay out after dark —up until the time of his dream. It was a sweet and powerful dream, but also horrifying, and it was impossible to say which of these emotions prevailed. Words could not describe it, not the morning after, nor later on. Words cannot capture that mixture of smells, those indefinable qualities that attract us to certain people, much less the sensation of falling down a well, of sailing clear through to the other side of existence.

He saw Magdalena in the earth, in the solitude of the immense earth, where she had been dwelling for years and would go on dwelling forever. Her dress had rotted away, shreds of cloth had merged with dry bones, while the strand of hair that used to slip down over her cheek as she bent over the kitchen stove was now stuck fast to her skull. But at the same time she was close to him, looking exactly as she had that day he had seen her wade into the water, and this merging was like the recognition of another time. He had the same lump in his throat, the shape of her breasts and neck was unspoiled, while her touch became transmuted into a kind of dirge: "Oh, why must I fade, why must my arms and legs fade away? Why am I alive, yet not alive—I, who once lived, just once, from the beginning till the end of the world? Oh, the sky and the sun will still be there when I am long gone. Only these bones will be

left . . . Oh, nothing, nothing is mine." And together they sank into the silent depths beneath the earth's many crusts, to which worms make their way and pebbles slide; only now it was he who was turning into a handful of rotten bones, lamenting through Magdalena's lips, and discovering such questions as "Why am I me? Why am I destined to die, to stop being myself, when I possess a body, warmth, a hand, fingers?" Or perhaps it was not a dream, for even as he lay at the bottom, under the surface of reality, he could still feel his bodily self—his doomed, disintegrating, and posthumous self; and even as he was taking part in the annihilation, he perceived that the person below was the same as the one above. He woke up screaming. But the objects outlined in the dark now became a part of the nightmare, defying definition. He was immediately plunged back into the same delirium, the same visions as before, but in ever new variations. Relief came at daybreak. Anxiously, he opened his eyes; he was returning from faraway places. Gradually, the light illuminated the crossbar joining the legs of the table—the bench, the chair. What a relief to rediscover the real world of objects, things made of wood, iron, and brick, so solid and full-bodied and rough to the touch. Things that only yesterday he had spurned were now a welcome sight, his private treasure. He feasted his eyes on all the knots, cracks, and crevices. Of that other world there remained only a delicious headiness, the remembrance of lands whose existence he had never dreamed possible.

From then on, he swore never to scream if Magdalena ever approached him in the dark, confident that she would do him no harm. He even wished at times she *would* appear, though the mere thought of it happening was enough to give him goose pimples—the good kind, the kind he used to get when he ran his hand over a velvet ribbon. But not a word about the dream did he breathe to anyone.

18

WHAT WAS DONE was done in secret, and it was some time before Thomas learned of the affair, which provoked in him feelings of great horror and sorrow.

Only the village elders, a dozen or so farm owners, were made a part of the conspiracy. They convened toward evening and drank their fill of vodka to quell their unease and to bolster their courage. Permission had been granted; that is to say, Father Monkiewicz had said, "Do as you please"—a tacit admission that all the means at his disposal had failed. Shortly after the other priest had left— that night, except for the sexton and the old housekeeper, the rectory was empty, the expectation being that the exorcisms had rid them of Magdalena—a loud cry was heard in the bedroom, and Monkiewicz appeared in the doorway, his long nightshirt in shreds. Magdalena had pulled off his blanket and started ripping the shirt off his back. When he later came down with erysipelas, everybody, including himself, attributed it to a bad case of fright, for which there was only one effective cure: magical incantations. A medicine woman was summoned to work her spells on him. These were people known to possess powers capable of exorcising any illness from the body; laced with threats, snatches of Christian prayers, and with chants of even greater antiquity, their incantations contained words that, once revealed, immediately lost their power, and whoever knew them was allowed to transmit them before death to only one person. The priest submitted to these remedies grudgingly, but who will say no, who will doubt them, if there's a chance of his being cured? A similar moment of

weakness, coupled with the faint hope that the haunting would soon cease, made him acquiesce in that other matter as well.

Tradition dictated that it be undertaken at night. Although not necessarily a rule, it was something that had to be performed with a certain reverence—meaning, above all, in silence, without any spectators, attended by only a few solemn and trustworthy individuals. After testing the blades of their shovels, they lit their lanterns and slipped out by way of the orchards, singly and in two's.

There was a strong wind, a rattling of dry oak leaves. The lights in the village were already out, so that it was pitch-dark and quiet except for the leaves. As soon as all were gathered on the little square in front of the church, they set out for the appointed place and formed a circle as best they could on the steep slope. The flames inside their stovepipe lanterns pitched and tossed in the wind.

First came the cross, which had been stuck in the ground so that it would last as long as the wood held out, leaving only the buried part to rot and crumble, and eventually the whole to topple. They pulled it out of the ground and carefully laid it on its side. Then they leveled the mound of dirt on top of the untended grave—not a single flower was to be seen on it—and went to work in a hurry, so as not to prolong the eeriness. A body is laid to rest for an eternity; to open a grave after several months to see what has happened to it is a violation of nature, tantamount to planting an acorn or chestnut and then scraping the ground to see whether it has taken root. But perhaps they only meant to prove by their actions that a show of strength and willpower was necessary to counteract those doings so contrary to the natural order.

The sound of loose gravel signaled that the moment was at hand. A shovel clanged, but closer inspection with the lantern showed that it was only a rock. At last they struck wood, dug out the coffin, and cleared away the dirt

so they could raise the lid. The vodka had done what it was supposed to do, supplying the sort of inner warmth that allowed them to feel superior to creatures less alive than themselves, not to speak of the trees, the rocks, the howling wind, and the phantoms of the night.

What they found bore out their suspicions. For one thing, the body showed absolutely no signs of decomposition. Later they reported that it was so well preserved it looked as if it had been buried only yesterday. This was proof enough, as only the bodies of saints and ghosts were endowed with such powers. Secondly, Magdalena was found lying not on her back but face down, which was also a sign. But even without such evidence, they were ready to do the prescribed thing. The presence of such signs only facilitated their task, relieving them of any doubts.

After the body was rolled over, one of them took the sharpest shovel and, bearing down with all his might, lopped off Magdalena's head. A spike carved from an alder was placed upright on her chest and hammered with the dull end of an ax till the point went clean through the bottom of the coffin and deep into the ground. Next they grabbed the head by the hair, stuck it between her feet, replaced the lid, and lowered the coffin again—now so relieved that they were laughing, as sometimes happens after moments of great tension.

Possibly Magdalena had been so terrified of decaying, so desperately unwilling to enter eternity that, ready to pay any price, she had consented to haunt the living, and in return was granted the privilege of preserving her inviolable body. The men swore up and down that her lips had been bright crimson. By cutting off her head and crushing her ribs, they had put an end to her bodily pride, to that pagan attachment to her own lips, arms, and belly. Skewered like a butterfly on a pin, her skull brushing the soles of the little shoes given to her by Father Peiksva as a present, she surely must have realized that she, like every-

one else, was meant to dissolve into the saps of the earth.

After that, no more disturbances were reported by the rectory, and nothing was ever heard of Magdalena staging any more of her exhibitions. And why should she have, for it appears she had discovered that, even more effectively than by cooking on invisible stoves, by knocking on walls or by whistling, she could prolong her life simply by invading Thomas's dreams, as he never forgot her.

19

THAT AUTUMN—the autumn Magdalena was haunting the land—there was an exceptionally good fruit harvest, but for want of any market it ended up as pig feed, only the best of the crop going for canning and domestic use. Piles of apples and pears lay rotting in the grass, attracting wasps and swarms of hornets. Thomas paid for one such pear with a stung lip and a swollen face, because once a wasp tunneled its way into the pulp, its presence was hard to detect, and only by giving the pear a good shake could you get it to show its striped and pulsating belly. Thomas helped with the fruit-picking by climbing up the trees, secretly flattered that none of the grownups could match his skill in shinnying up, cat-fashion, even onto the skinniest branches. And every year there was a crop of new ones, each bearing a different name: sugar pears, butter pears, honey pears, bergamots . . .

During the summer–autumnal lull, Thomas got into the library. Until now, this corner room, with its painted walls and where even in hot weather it was shivering cold, had failed to arouse his curiosity. But by badgering he got hold of the keys to the bookcases, from whose shelves he

was always pulling down new wonders. In one of them, a glass-paneled one, he found several red-bound illustrated books embossed with gold. Although unable to make out the captions under the drawings—they were written in French—he figured out that the girl in the long, lace-trimmed knickers was called Sophie. From another case, this one set back in the wall, under a cobweb and several scrolls of yellowed paper, he dug out a volume bearing the title *Shakespeare's Tragedies*, in whose company he spent long hours on the edge of the lawn, next to a green hedge-row redolent of moss and wild mint. This was also the favorite nesting place of ants—the large, red, biting kind—and it was not unusual to see him furiously rubbing one calf against the other. Between the spruce tops the air shimmered on the far side of the valley, and from where he lay he could see tiny horse-drawn coaches trailing long columns of dust.

The book was illustrated with men in armor holding crossed swords, or scantily dressed men (were their legs naked, or did they wear tight-fitting pants?) being stabbed to death, and the mildewed pages gave off a musty smell. He ran his finger along the rows of letters, but although the text was in Polish, in time he gave up, conceding that such things were only for big people.

He had more fun with the travel books. Negroes, armed with bows and arrows, were shown standing naked in reed boats, or towing a hippopotamus familiar to him from his natural-history book. He often wondered whether their bodies were really striped, or just painted, and dreamed of accompanying them on a long voyage to distant waters, and, among papyrus plants standing taller than a man, of building a village inaccessible to outsiders. Two of these books were written in Polish, and he read them both from cover to cover (it was from them that he learned how to read, that's how intrigued he was). Thus began a new era in his life.

He used hazel branches for making bows, but not those that were crooked from exposure to the sun. Instead, he crawled into the shady underbrush, among matted layers of dead leaves, where kinglets flitted with a tremulous *cheep-cheep-cheep*. The naked saplings that grew straight up to the light, not bending an inch, were the best. These dark grottoes also made excellent hideouts and arsenals for his weapons.

Armed with homemade arrows—for greater stability, he tacked on turkey feathers—he set out on hunting expeditions, freely inventing his game, a gooseberry patch often sufficing. His favorite stand was a footbridge—not on the Black Pond, but on another, situated between the wing facing the garden and the farm buildings—used for loading the water cans. Pretending he was in a dugout, he stood on the footbridge and took potshots at the ducks. This once led to an investigation when one of the ducks was found dead in the middle of the pond and he refused to take the blame. Since the Indians were known for hunting fish with a bow and arrow, he was constantly on the lookout for fish along the river shoals (so as not to lose any arrows), but they always got away in time.

On rainy days he sat at a little table bolted to the floor of the porch and practiced drawing swords, spears, and fishing poles. Here a certain quirk of his should be noted, for no sooner would he commence sketching a bow than he stopped and tore up the drawing. Bows were his great passion, and somehow he had formed the idea that one should avoid showing the things one loved, that they should be guarded in absolute privacy.

One day his grandmother took him along to the attic and showed him a box brimming with all sorts of odds and ends, mostly junk, except for one thing—books! Adventure books! One was about a stowaway on a sailing vessel who hid under the deck, kept himself alive on hardtack,

and was constantly menaced by rats. The water which he later found in some barrels was called "sweet water." Did that mean it had been sweetened with sugar? So Thomas imagined, for how else could he explain the boy's ecstasy when he managed to bore a hole in the barrel?

The best place for daydreaming about these and other adventures was the outhouse, which stood at the end of a pathway sheltered by a canopy of currants. The outhouse door was latched from the inside, and the heart-shaped opening could be used as a peephole to spot anyone heading for the privy. A few cracks let in the sunlight, and there was always the music of flies, bees, and bumblebees. Now and then a hairy bumblebee, droning heavily, meandered from behind into the pit (whose stench Thomas inhaled with gusto). The corners were always full of spiders spinning their nets, the crossbeam dotted with patches of stearin left by the candles. There were also cracks in the side walls, through which, except for the leaves of a black elder, there was nothing to be seen.

Seeing Antonina flit past the heart in the door, he would snap out of his daydreaming and button his pants in a hurry. At the other end of the path was a garbage pit, the place where Antonina butchered the chickens. Her lips puckered and cheeks bulging, she cocked the arm holding the cleaver and maneuvered the chicken into position on the stump with the other; only mildly flustered, the chicken seemed pensive, whether from idle curiosity or indifference was hard to say. The cleaver flashed, Antonina's face wrinkled with pain, even a faint smirk, and a feathery clump was next seen flopping aimlessly on the ground. Thomas shuddered to see it, and just because he shuddered, he remained a spectator to it. One such beheading turned out to be extraordinary. A rooster, an enormous bird bristling with shimmering gold feathers, tried to take off without his head, with only his red stump of a neck

sticking out. His speechless flight caused Antonina to drop her jaw in amazement—and in tribute, for the rooster fell only after colliding with the trunk of a linden.

Thomas seldom made any more fishing trips to the river, and seldom ran off to see the Akulonis children— partly because of Magdalena, partly because of his books. The more secluded places along the Issa now seemed forbidding. As for bow-and-arrow hunting, that was not to be shared with one of his companions and run the risk of ridicule: that wasn't dignified enough, not like fishing or carving reed pipes from willows. There were some games he preferred no one else to watch—games that might have been thought of as too childish for a boy his age. One was a game of war between two stick armies planted in the sand, with Thomas taking turns bombarding one and then the other side with rocks.

20

❦❦❦❦❦❦

EARLY THAT WINTER, Grandmother Dilbin arrived from Dorpat, Estonia, and the room where she slept exerted a strong attraction on Thomas. Not much taller than he, ruddy-skinned, she was, unlike Grandmother Misia, a real busybody. She darned his socks and mended his pants, tutored him, and made him recite his catechism. She was, above all, different. She smoked cigarettes, the long-tipped Russian kind, a habit she had acquired from constant fretting—as she put it—which cigarettes had a way of relieving. From her trunk she removed a flat clothes box, revealing a wealth of tiny tins and wooden cases, minuscule packages bound with ribbons, and sundry trinkets meticulously wrapped in newspaper.

The rite of unpacking, just because it was such a rare occurrence, preserved its ceremonial character. For Thomas there was always some little present, some novelty, like a bar of genuine Chinese ink, the purpose of which was explained to him by his grandmother, though he was captivated more by its shape, its deep black color, and the clean angularity of its corners.

From her he learned, as never before, something of the ways of the world. Having spent her youth in Riga, his grandmother could tell him stories of the trips to Majorenhof, of swimming in the Baltic, and of the time she was nearly swept out to sea; about her father, Thomas's great-grandfather, Dr. Ritter, who treated children and waived his fee if their parents were poor; of his great popularity and his reputation as a practical joker, famous for his impersonations and disguises so convincing that even his mother, taking him for a beggar, had once tossed a coin into his hat. Thomas also heard talk of the theater and the opera, of swans that bobbed up and down as if truly waterborne. The name of a vocalist—Adelina Patti—was invariably pronounced with a sigh. She sighed, too, when reminiscing about the parties in Riga, about the crowds of young people, the games, the singing, the *tableaux vivants*. Not to mention the trips out into the countryside, to the Imbrody estate, near Düneburg, which had belonged to her mother's family, the Mohls. About the coach rides through brigand-infested woods, the secluded inns with conniving innkeepers. About "the guillotine"—a bed whose canopy fell at night, killing the unsuspecting traveler and then disappearing along with the corpse through a trapdoor in the floor. Of how, when a coach was ferried across the river, the horses would panic and drown its occupants. Then there was the servant girl at Imbrody whom the boys once spooked, installing long tobacco pipes behind the mirror—where she was fond of posing—and blowing big puffs of smoke her way. Once, as she slept, they made off with

her bed and put it down in the lake; she later woke with a scream. And the boat trips on the lake, in the white sailboat . . . Of all the names and incidents mentioned, these were the ones that stuck in Thomas's mind.

He also had his grandmother to thank for tales of Bitowt and his comic exploits—Bitowt, a glutton and eccentric madcap celebrated all over Lithuania. In summer, Bitowt would get his cart into shape, load up the back with horse feed, put on his cape, take his place behind the driver, and shove off on a journey that usually lasted several months. He drifted from manor to manor, where he was always treated royally because of the fear aroused by his malicious tongue. He smoked cigars as he rode, tossing the butts behind him—once he barely made his escape after setting the rear of the wagon ablaze. Another time, at an open market in a little town, he went up to an orange peddler, a Jew. "How many oranges can a man tuck away at one go?" The Jew: "Five." Bitowt to that: "Sixty!" The Jew: "Free oranges to the man who can!" As Bitowt was starting on his fifth dozen, the Jew yelled: "Help! Many dozen oranges ze man has eaten! He vill die for sure!" At home he had a first-class cook, and they were always squabbling. In the evening, Bitowt would summon him to his bedroom and growl: "You rascal! You're through, finished! You've done it again! Your cooking is too good; I'm so stuffed I can't sleep!" But then he would call him back and ask him for the next day's menu.

Thomas, by chatting with his grandmother, managed to pick up a little history. A copper relief of the Virgin Mary, delivered up from her trunk, hung over her bed; above the nightstand was a portrait of a girl—beautiful, bare-necked, with an open collar. The girl's name was Emilia Plater, a distant relative of Thomas, on the Mohl side, which was supposed to be a source of great pride, as she was remembered as a heroine of the Polish Insurrection. In 1831 she had mounted a horse and taken com-

mand of a detachment of insurgents in the forest. She later died of wounds suffered in a battle against the Russians. As for the copper relief, it was once the property of his grandfather Arthur Dilbin, who in his youth had also chosen the forest. That was in the year 1863 ("Remember, Thomas—eighteen hundred and sixty-three . . ."). The battle cry of the insurgents, "For our freedom and yours!" had meant that they were fighting for the liberty of the Russians as well; but the Tsar was very powerful and their only weapons had been shotguns and swords. Grandfather's commanding officer, Sierakowski, was hung by the Tsar, but Grandfather was exiled to Siberia, from where he made his way back many years later and married. Presently Thomas's father and uncle were serving in the Polish army; they, too, were fighting against the Russians.

Around the house, Grandmother Dilbin dressed city-style, even with an amber brooch. Underneath—Thomas used to spy on her—she wore several woolen petticoats and cinched her waist with a sort of whalebone corset. Her pale blue eyes bulged, her mouth assumed a look of utter dismay whenever Misia hiked her skirt in front of the tiled stove. What exasperated her was the way she had of mocking the emotions of others. Gossiping about someone in love with one of the local girls, she would ask, in her usual Lithuanian drawl, as she rubbed her rump against the tiles, "Now what, pray tell, can he possibly see in her?" Over and over again: "What, pray tell?"—as if it was not enough that human beings longed, yearned, suffered. Grandmother would respond with an angry shrug, mumble something about how "pagan customs are slow to die"— which was true enough; yet privately Thomas seldom sided with her, sensing in her, kindhearted as she was, a certain weakness. At the mere sight of him she wrung her hands in despair, complaining that he was neglected, shabbily clothed, and wild as a savage. And did she ever spoil him. Until then, he had not thought twice about sewing on his

own buttons with the help of Antonina's needle and thread; but now that he had someone to pamper him, he had to be waited on constantly.

There was something fragile in the curvature of Grandmother Dilbin's round shoulders, in the veins around her temples. Peeking into her room at five or six o'clock in the morning, he found her sitting up in bed, saying her prayers in a loud, keening voice, a vacant stare in her eyes, her cheeks bearing traces of two little wet streams. (Misia, on the other hand, slept till ten in winter, woke, and stretched with feline contentment.) Footfalls sounded in Dilbin's room till late in the evening, as, pacing the floor, she smoked cigarette after cigarette. The monotonous sound of her padding feet traveled through the house, lulling Thomas to sleep. Subject to chronic dizzy spells, in the daytime she never went for a walk in the garden unless accompanied by her grandson; often she would stop in the middle of a path, stretch out her hands, and beg him for his arm. Once they rode out in the carriage to visit neighbors; at the place where the road skirted a cliff, she shut her eyes, keeping them closed until she was sure the danger had passed.

Thomas was constantly tempted to tease and test her. Sometimes, when she pleaded for his arm on one of their garden strolls, he ducked behind a tree, deliberately provoking that round and pink little creature to tearful supplications.

21

THE DAUGHTER of Graf von Mohl was given in marriage to Dr. Ritter, and from that marriage six daughters were born, the youngest of which, Bronislawa,

was destined to become Grandmother Dilbin. From that period of warmth, love, and happiness, lasting until her eighteenth birthday, a number of copybooks, inscribed with minuscule writing, had been preserved in her trunk— verses composed as a young girl. Several dried-out flowers had outlived those closest to her.

Constantine had played the piano beautifully, sung in a baritone, and was famous for his recitations of patriotic poetry at all the Riga soirées. But her parents were resolutely opposed: he was too young, too impractical, and, most damaging of all, penniless. Soon after they parted, there was another suitor, and Broncia, as she was called for short, experienced her first nights of solitary weeping, the terror that accompanied the sealing of one's fate. Arthur Dilbin, no longer in his prime, with a reputation for being rather staid in his ways, was surrounded by an aura of martyrdom: for his having taken part in the Uprising, his estate had been confiscated, though his management of the family property assured him of a steady income. He was found acceptable, and Broncia gave up the city of her youth for a remote country village, for a life of domestic chores and bookkeeping on quiet evenings, under the same lampshade where Arthur sat smoking his pipe.

A portrait of the man: broad forehead, narrow face, an expression of feral pride; hollow cheeks accentuated by a bushy blond mustache, big-shouldered, sober-minded, hand stuck in a buckled leather belt. At the manor he kept a pack of hounds, devoting all his leisure to hunting. He also had a passion for harness racing, that test of strength between a driver and his horses, when the pull of the reins can tear the skin from a man's hands. He was a gentle, discreet man, slipping payments to the mothers of his illegitimate children so that his wife was never the wiser. These children dated, for the most part, from his bachelor days. As a young blade he was credited with having saved a certain aristocratic family from extinction, thanks to vis-

its to a local countess married to a senile husband. Such gossip did him no disservice; and whenever he passed the young count, he would size him up on the sly, stroking his mustache with approval.

Then the settling down, the burden of responsibility. And children. Bronislawa lavished all her affection on her children. When the older boy, Theodore, was seven, she brought him for the summer to Majorenhof, to the seaside, though she failed to recover the beauty she had once known there. Their younger son was born the same year that Arthur died of a cold caught while hunting. He was named Constantine.

However far back one searched in the history of the Dilbins, Ritters, and Mohls, Constantine bore no physical resemblance to any of his ancestors. Black eyes, pitch-black hair encroaching on a low forehead, an aquiline nose; the swarthy complexion of a southerner. Skinny and high-strung, he was a winning child with a heart of gold: ask him for something—anything—and he was ready to hand over what was his, down to his coat and jacket. He also showed signs of being exceptionally gifted. But when Bronislawa later moved to Vilno so that her sons could receive a proper education—which, left to her own resources, was no easy task Constantine showed a reluctance to learn. The slightest effort enervated him. His mother pleaded with him, went down on her knees, promised him presents, cajoled him. But he knew her better than to believe in her bullying threats, and as for presents, he knew there was nothing his mother would deny him. He soon fell into bad company, cavorting with gamblers and people of loose morals, drinking, running up debts, and began taking up with girls from the clubs. His education came to an abrupt halt when he was expelled from the Gymnasium in his fourth year.

His older brother, Theodore, had studied veterinary medicine in Dorpat, and after graduating, he began sup-

porting both his mother and his brother. Heir to his father's build and facial features, he was quieter and more given to romantic dreams. Burdened by his sense of responsibility and honesty, he felt the urge to travel, to seek adventure— all the Dilbins had been something of adventurers, one of them having served in Napoleon's army, taking part in both the Italian and the Spanish campaigns. Theodore married Tekla Surkont, whom he met while vacationing at the house of his cousin, in the vicinity of Gine. He later became Thomas's father. The outbreak of war he welcomed as a portent of change, as that "war of nations" prophesied nearly a century ago and promising to destroy the might of the Northern Tyrant.

Bronislawa's tears, although swallowed privately at first, streamed more and more openly down her cheeks, and she prayed to God to have mercy on Constantine and for the forgiveness of her sins if they were the cause of his suffering. Her pleas had risen in the early-morning hours —once, after she discovered that he had forged his brother's signature on some checks, and later, when after being drafted into the Russian army he was assigned to an NCO's school and from there transferred to the front. She trembled for his safety when he saw combat at the front, but not for Theodore's, who, as a professional man, was mostly stationed at the rear. Finally she received word that he had been wounded and taken prisoner. From then on, it was packages made of plywood, bound with canvas, and addressed to the Red Cross, reaching him at some unknown destination in Germany. She counted the days from one package to the next, sewing little sacks for sugar and cocoa, devising ways to squeeze the most into a package. She did this until the year 1918, until the day she received a letter from him telling her that his shrapnel wound had healed, leaving only a chest scar, and that he had been caught trying to tunnel his way out of a POW camp, but that he was free now and had enlisted in the Polish cavalry.

There was still a war on, this time between Poland and Russia, and the Tsar had been assassinated. Theodore, accompanied by his wife, had visited Bronislawa in Dorpat, stopping off on his way south, from up around Pskov, to fulfill his patriotic duty. Fingering her rosary beads, she tried to imagine the night marches, her son Constantine bent over his saddle in the sleet and rain, the charges with raised swords; his chest, already wounded once, ready to stop a bullet. She was haunted by visions of corpses—the Germans, in occupying Dorpat, had executed a number of Bolshevik commissars, dumping their bodies in the square and leaving them to lie there, glazed with frost, until orders were finally given for their burial.

She prayed that Constantine's life would be spared. But during the pre-dawn hours she would be seized by another fear, the terror of time, of both the past and the future. All the lies he had told, the sneaking into Theodore's bureau drawer, the banknotes lifted on the sly; her trembling as she confronted him with it. And the way he had blushed, pitied her, and then that dreaded moment when he had tossed back his head and assumed an expression of defiance, believing even in his own lies—that, for her, had been the most painful part. Resident in him was an inability to experience the world as it really was, the need to embellish it with fantastic schemes, always confident of discovering some new ticket to success serving to justify these occasional perfidies. She knew that it was too late for him to mend his ways. Her supplications for his return were not altogether pure. Her mind constantly swarmed with images of the consequences of his weakness, of his lack of perseverance and vocation. The sleazy, big-city haunts, the cardsharps with their fawning whores— and there, among them, her little Constantine. No, her incantations were not pure, and that made her feel guilty, that made her raise her voice and rock back and forth as she recited the words of the litany, by which gesture she

hoped to exorcise her grief. Such was the intent of phrases like "O Tower of Ivory," "O Ark of the Covenant" that Thomas heard through the door.

Her sins? What sins she had committed, no one would ever know. Perhaps deep down, in the pulsations of her blood, in the very depths of her corporeal being, whose essence no tongue could ever convey, she had discovered the flaw, the guilty residue of her existence, of her having begotten children. Possibly. It was from her, in all probability, that Thomas had inherited his scrupulous conscience, a tendency to reproach himself for each and every thing, and his teasing of her was a revenge for the guilt aroused in him by her lamentations of "Oyey, oyey."

22

SPRING WAS in the air. The ice on the pond was melting, and the traces left by Thomas's blades were slowly being effaced where only a short time ago he had skated or amused himself by stamping his feet on the green slabs embedded with insects and algae. Showing signs of weariness, the snow dripped from the rooftops in the afternoons, the drops drilling little dotted lines along the sides of the house. In the evening, the bright pastel pink on the white hills would thicken into yellow and carmine, the tracks of animals and people darken with moisture.

Thomas, encouraged by Grandmother Dilbin's supply of illustrated German magazines, acquired a passion for sketching. He was especially inspired by pictures of artillery, tanks, and his very favorite plane—the Taube. Twice a Taube had flown over Gine, but at high altitude, causing people to congregate and point up at the sky, the source of

the buzzing racket. Now, in magazines, Thomas could see what it looked like in action. His drawings showed soldiers charging (legs in motion were easily rendered by dashes bent at the knee) and hitting the dirt; rifles sent forth sheaves of straight lines, broken to mark the bullets. And sailing by overhead—the Taube.

Before moving on to the incident that is somehow related to these scenes, we must first describe the floor plan of the house. In winter, only the wing facing the orchard was occupied; that is, the part looking out across the angle formed by the old manor and the annex. First came the weaving room (where Pakenas worked), then nothing, then a storage room for wool and seed, then Grandmother Dilbin's room, then Thomas's, followed by Misia's little cubbyhole and, at the far end, by Grandfather's room. Awakened by a chill early one morning, Thomas curled into a ball, but there was no escaping the draft. He turned so his back faced the window, pulled the blanket up to his neck, and pondered the sunlight on the wall. Some flour, set out to dry on a canvas sheet, lay on the floor. Letting his eyes roam lazily over the surface, he became intrigued by the sight of something sparkling like ice or salt crystals. He jumped out of bed, crouched down, and lightly fingered it: glass. Mystified, he turned and glanced out the window. The pane was punctured by a hole the size of two fists, its jagged outline shaped like a star. He ran immediately to Misia's room, yelling that someone had thrown a rock from the garden.

It turned out he was mistaken. They searched high and low, until finally, under Thomas's bed, in the very corner, Grandfather flushed out a black object, which he warned everyone not to touch. They sent for one of the villagers, an army veteran. The black object, which Thomas later had a chance to examine at his leisure, had the shape of a large egg, only heavier, with a notched flange wrapped around the middle. In the orchard, below

the window, they found boot tracks and a grenade pin. They recalled, too, how the dog-barking that night had been more fierce than usual.

The grenade had not exploded, but it might have, in which case Thomas would have been laid to rest under the oak trees, a stone's throw from Magdalena's grave. The world would have gone on as before; swallows, storks, and starlings would have winged their way back from their annual migrations beyond the seas; wasps and hornets would have gone on sucking pears for their sweet juice. Why it had failed to explode is not for us to judge. It had hit a wall, bounced to the floor, and rolled over to Thomas's bed, where the decision to explode or not to explode had ripened inside it.

Grandfather was sorely grieved. At news of another manor being attacked, inspired by what was happening farther to the east, he would quietly clear his throat and try to turn the latest scare into a joke. Not even when the woods had been infested with marauding bands of Russian POW's had he taken any special precautions. And which of his neighbors had cause to attack him? They had known him since childhood. Had he ever done anyone any harm? Even accidentally? And as for the traditional animosity between Pole and Lithuanian, wasn't it he who argued that the Lithuanians were entitled to their own state, and that those who spoke Polish were as much *gente Lithuani* as he? Still, there it was—the grenade. Someone had thrown it. Who? And for whom was it intended? They counted the windows: one in Grandfather's room, two in Misia's, and two in Thomas's room. Anyone well acquainted with the house would not have aimed for the boy's room, so it was either an outsider or someone who knew his way around but had simply miscalculated.

Grandmother Misia was not at all fazed that *she* could have been the object of such hostility. As usual, she let Grandfather have it, blaming it on his Lithuanian and

peasant sympathies. Nor was she the least bit concerned for her own safety, though, in her case, protection would have been difficult: the wooden shutters to her room closed from the outside. Not so with Grandmother Dilbin, who was panic-stricken, so much so that her windows had to be padlocked. After Thomas's miraculous escape, she indulged him more than ever, taking from her trunk—which seemed to contain an inexhaustible store of treasure—a slender box full of watercolors and a paintbrush. His first painting was of a bullfinch, the reason being that bullfinches—they were forever husking seeds in the bushes by the house—were a big splotch of red, tinged with streaks of blue, gray, and black. Bullfinches and the speckled, red-hooded woodpecker, whose pecking brought down white patches of snow from high up in the trees, were among winter's greatest surprises.

The grenade affair failed to enter the realm of Thomas's military and travel fantasies. Even though tracks in the snow inspired visions of long boots, tightly cinched jackets, and hushed deliberations, his soldiers and pirates were not a surreptitious force, had nothing of the darkness of the night. He became suspicious, flinching whenever he met up with any of the local farmhands, whom the war had lent a somewhat menacing air. It had started the summer before, with Thomas sneaking down Indian-style to the Issa because of the way they sat in the bushes, whistling, making catcalls, and firing their army carbines so that the bullets skipped across the water like pebbles. They were not very popular in the village, and they kept to themselves. Akulonis used to threaten them with his fist and call them "jailbirds" because they scared the fish. Once, when they went so far as to fish with grenades, they provoked widespread indignation: that was too easy, a violation of the code.

To be on the safe side, a bed was put up in the weaving room, where Pakenas, now shifted from the granary,

took up quarters. Not that he afforded any real protection; indeed, he had a reputation for being a terrific coward, probably dating back to his tumultuous escape from the shepherd's ghost. Imputations of this sort are generally promoted by a person's physiognomy, in Pakenas's case by a pair of bulging, lobsterlike eyes. Besides his knotted walking stick, Pakenas also had custody of an old revolver, the bullets to which, alas, were missing.

23

JOSEPH THE BLACK climbed the road leading up from the village and occasionally got mired in the snowy slush mixed with horse manure. Water trickled in the wagon ruts burnished by sleigh runners. He unbuttoned his gray homespun jacket, and as he passed by the roadside crucifix, he doffed his cap and squinted from the glare cast by the white slope, and higher up, at the park's edge, by the granary's white wall. Down below, in one of the Issa's inland coves, crows circled the Borek forest, their cawing a portent of spring.

Instead of turning into the lane, he passed the exit and, skirting the orchard, steered for the cottages. Once upon a time, these huts lining the road had been occupied by farmhands working the manorial estate. Only a few were inhabited now, the rest having been invaded by itinerant laborers. Joseph responded politely when greeted, but was in too great a hurry to stop. Past the cottages, near the cross under the tin-roofed lean-to, he swung to the right in the direction of Pogirai and the forest's dark border.

Pogirai was a long village, stretching well over a

kilometer, with one main street and one cross street. Fairly prosperous, it was distinguished by the absence of any thatched roofs or chimneyless hovels. Its orchards were as plentiful as those in Gine, and it was known for its apiaries, for the dark honey collected in fields of buckwheat, clover, and open forest meadows. When he came to the third cottage past the green farm belonging to Baloudis, the American, Joseph stopped and peered over a picket fence. An old man in a brown woolen caftan—brown and black sheep were a Pogirai specialty—was trimming a log. Joseph shoved open the gate, and as they stood shaking hands, he complimented the man on his choice of fir. The old man nodded and said it was for bracing the crib. The tree, no doubt, had made its way there thanks to Balthazar, but Joseph had other things on his mind than poaching.

Just then, the younger Wackonis, heavy with sleep, came crawling out of nowhere. He ran his fingers through his hair to comb out the straw and feathers, and somewhat shyly, eyeing him nervously, paid Joseph his respects. He had on a pair of navy-blue pants and a military tunic. His broad face turned sullen when Joseph said he had a little matter to discuss with him.

Putting down his tin cup and wiping his mustache with the back of his hand, Joseph stared at him in silence. At last he propped both elbows on the table and said: "Yeah, yeah—I know."

Sitting on the end of the bench, Wackonis fluttered his eyelids, then lowered them drowsily. A shrug of the shoulders. "Ain't nothin' to know."

"Maybe there is and maybe there isn't. I picked you because you're a simpleton. Remember who taught you how to read? Or have you forgotten?"

"You did."

"Well, now, is that any reason to start pitching grenades at folks?"

Wackonis lifted his eyelids. His face was now that of a grown man—serious, grim. "And what if it was me? Those ain't folks—they's gentlefolk."

Joseph laid a birchwood snuffbox on the table, rolled himself a cigarette, fitted it into a holder, lit up, and took a puff. "Ever see me siding with gentlefolk?"

"Nope, never did. But I do now."

"Your father, he won't tell you, but I will. You'd better listen to people with more brains than you."

Wackonis folded his arms on his chest; his cheek muscles twitched. "The gentlefolk sucked us dry, we don't need their kind round here. Kill one, two—they'll git on back to their Poland. Then the land'll be ours."

Joseph shook his head mockingly. "We don't need no gentlefolk in Lithuania, the land will be ours. Where did you pick that up? From me, that's who. And now you're going to teach *me*, huh? You want to go around butchering and burning like a Russian?"

"They don't have no more Tsar."

"Not now, but one day they will. You're a Lithuanian. We'll get it back one day."

"And who's gonna get it back?"

"Lithuania. The Slavs—Poles or Russians, what's the difference—they're all sons-of-bitches. I worked in Sweden —now that's the life for us!"

"The Poles are our enemies."

"The Surkonts have been Lithuanians for centuries."

Wackonis chuckled. "How can Surkont be a Lithuanian when he's a gentleman?"

Joseph reached for the beer pitcher, filled his mug, and asked, "Is that who you were aiming for?"

The young man's face emptied. "Naah—I didn't much care who it hit."

Joseph again wagged his head. "Oh boy, that's just fine. You can thank the Lord it didn't go off. And you know who it almost killed? Did they tell you?"

"Nope."

"The boy—Thomas. They found it under his bed."

"The Dilbin kid?"

"Yep."

Silence. The mug still at his mouth, Wackonis said, "Everybody knows where his old man is. Like father, like son."

"You jackass! How would you like to have been at the kid's funeral?"

"What for?"

Joseph curled his lip, baring his teeth, and blushed. "Listen here, Wackonis. I know who put you up to it, and I know who kept you company out there that night. Those pals of yours, those 'Iron Wolves,' they don't scare me, see? Oh, you know how to fight, all right—against women and kids."

Wackonis sprang to his feet. "None of your darned business whose idea it was!"

Joseph leaned back, fixed him with a stare, and sneered: "Spoken with all the arrogance of a born Pole."

24

THE ICE on the Issa broke with a cannon's roar. Then came the floes, freighting loose straw, boards, branches, dead chickens—and crows, promenading on the ice with a delicate step. This was also the pupping season, and the bitch Dusty couldn't keep her litter a secret for very long; sooner or later the whimpering pups gave her away. Thomas loved to feel their fleshy warmth against his face, to immerse his gaze in their eyes enveloped by a blue

film. Russet-colored, a cross between a wolf and a fox, her muzzle flecked with black, Dusty would quietly acquiesce, panting with a drooping tongue.

Pakenas packed the pups into a basket and Dusty was locked in the woodshed along with one of her pups, the brightest and the quickest. Thomas ran after Pakenas and caught up with him by the cliff overlooking the river. The steep bank, bright with yellow clay, was riddled with swallows' nests. The floes had moved downstream, leaving swirling little eddies in the swollen waters.

Pakenas cocked his arm and let go with one of the pups. It hit the water, a splash, then nothing, only a little pool, which was rapidly broken up and borne away by the current. A little while later, a head surfaced downstream; paddling its tiny paws, the pup again vanished from view, only to reappear as it rounded the bend. From then on, Pakenas took two at a time from the basket; throwing one, he would clutch the other against his chest. The last of them went under, but a second later came up, fighting bravely until, followed by Thomas's gaze, it too was swept out into midstream.

Going from the warmth, from a world of things they had not yet learned to distinguish, into the icy water, they were not even aware of the water's existence. Thomas walked back in a daze. Mingled with his curiosity was a shadow of his dream about Magdalena. He opened the shed door and began petting Dusty. The dog whined, sniffed him suspiciously, then bolted from his reach.

Then came the first warm spell: chickens grubbing by the woodpile, old Gregory sitting on his bench, whittling away . . . Gregory's knife, so worn down that the blade was more like a shoemaker's awl, could sever a branch at one swipe—in old Gregory's hand, that is, but not in Thomas's, who, even if he used the same knife, first had to notch one side and then the other before getting it to snap.

Mrs. Malinowski came to see Grandfather about leasing the orchard for the summer—called an *arenda*, an arrangement whereby a certain percentage of the harvest went to the landlord. An unusual request, but she said she wanted to give it a try; her son, Dominic, was now fourteen, and she was sure they could manage it together. He promised her the orchard, but the woman had come none too soon. A few days later Chaim came lumbering up to the manor in his buggy to propose some of his relatives as leaseholders. Chaim could cite professional guarantees, as well as custom, since traditionally the leaseholders were Jewish. But a promise was a promise. The scene ended with the usual pulling of hair, wailing lamentations, and clenched fists raised to heaven.

A widow, Mrs. Malinowski was the poorest in all of Gine; with no land of her own to sow or till, her only possession was a cottage down by the ferry landing. She was a squat, broadly built woman, and the crest of her kerchief towered above her freckled forehead like a peaked house roof. Her visit marked the beginning of a new friendship for Thomas.

Several months later, while he was busy exploring that part of the orchard out past the beehives (the path ran alongside the hives, within attacking range of the bees), he spotted a shed. A real cabin—not one of those trail shacks built by horse herders in the clearings—tall enough in the center for a man to stand upright, its straw roof held down by wooden poles. The peak, formed by the acute angle of an inverted V, was reinforced with nails. A small campfire was burning by the entrance, and next to it sat a boy roasting green apples on a stick. The boy showed Thomas in and around the shed.

Dominic Malinowski, freckle-faced like his mother but taller, with a shock of bushy red hair, was quick to get Thomas, for whom the privilege of addressing a nearly

grown-up person as an equal was a source of discomfort, even embarrassment, under his control. Dominic let him smoke his homemade pipe—a rifle cartridge fitted with a stem. Thomas, who had never smoked tobacco before, tried, even though it irritated his throat, to keep the rolled tobacco leaf lit, determined, then as later, to win the approval of those cold gray eyes.

Whereas it used to be that when asked for Thomas's whereabouts, Antonina could answer, "At Akulonis's, where else?" now it was: "Up at the shed." The irresistible magic of smoke winding through the trees, the smell of straw and rotting apples, and hours spent by the campfire. Dominic could spit more than a dozen meters, blow smoke through his nose, fix traps for birds and marten (which used to chase squirrels around the linden trunks in the park, though the trapping had to wait for winter) and teach Thomas the art of cussing. Since he was illiterate and had an abiding fascination with everything, he made Thomas tell him what was written in books. At first Thomas was embarrassed—in the same way he was embarrassed by his kinship with Grandmother Dilbin—because knowledge acquired from letters of the alphabet seemed to him inferior; but Dominic was persistent, asking "Why is that?" "How so?" "If, then why?" But there were some things, things that had never occurred to him until now, that lay beyond his power to explain.

Attraction. Submission. Was it an attraction for the roughshod, the forbidden? Dominic emerged as a high priest of truth, because his sense of irony, his implied mockery, was a refutation of his, Thomas's, superficial knowledge, underneath which, he knew, there teemed something real. That something went beyond the long slugs they collected and roasted over coals to make them contract; beyond the horseflies whose bellies they packed with blades of straw to make them fly like airplanes; beyond

even the rat Dominic once let loose in a tunnel of blazing coals. Far beyond that—farther and deeper. Every trip to the shed in the orchard held out the promise of some new discovery.

His instincts proved correct, for Dominic was always guarded in his presence, never revealing more than a fraction of his nature. He did not need any outward confirmation of his power over Thomas; he graciously, condescendingly accepted the homage rendered him. He spared him, in fact. Why? Perhaps he was disarmed by Thomas's naïve trust, or perhaps he found it more prudent not to jeopardize his relations with the manor house. His hemming, the way he had of wrapping his arms around his knees whenever Thomas insisted on entering forbidden territory— such gestures seemed full of implication about the very thing for which Thomas had such an urge. If, though, his reticence suddenly broke down, it was surely the fault of the devils along the Issa, or of Thomas's own stupidity— for having violated the rule that one should not always cling to those one venerates. If he was tactless, then it was because he lived with his fantasies and had never been snubbed.

Mrs. Malinowski seldom visited the shed. She would bring supper for her son in the afternoon, but not always, at which times Dominic would boil himself a batch of cabbage soup and use his jackknife to carve huge chunks from a loaf of black rye, wolfing it down with bacon bits. Not to mention apples and pears—charcoaled pears were like nothing in this world—or potatoes, roasted to a crisp, a jab with a sharp stick signaling whether they were done. Occasionally, Antonina would drop by unannounced and drag Thomas away by the scruff of the neck. Now and then, she came with baskets for the "inspection"—the term given that quota of the harvest owed the manor for the household—and their job was to help with the carrying.

Sometimes, in a lighthearted but mean sort of way, she would address Dominic with a pejorative word that meant "you relative of every conceivable kind of toad."

25

DOMINIC, if the truth be known, was a king in disguise, ruling by means of an unspoken terror, the quietness of which he carefully guarded. He had been elevated to royal office by virtue of his toughness and by his talent for giving orders. Those who had tasted his hard fist obeyed him and whispered not a word of complaint to their parents. His court, which waited on him in the village pasture, consisted, as might have been expected, of his most trusted confidants, or ministers, and of ordinary acolytes, who were used for performing such menial tasks as keeping the cows in line. Only the closest confidants were admitted to experiments of a more serious sort.

A critical mind, which took nothing on faith and demanded for everything a scientific explanation, he scrupulously attended to anything that flew, jumped, or crawled. Severing their legs and wings, he was intent on plumbing the mystery of living machines. Nor were humans overlooked, such as the time he commanded his ministers to hold up one specimen by the legs—namely, the thirteen-year-old Vera. He was equally intrigued by technological inventions, capable of devoting hours to contemplating the construction of a mill, to the point of rigging an exact replica, together with his own modifications, and installing it on one of the brooks that emptied into the Issa.

By imposing his will on others his own age, Dominic

avenged himself for the humiliation he had endured since childhood. For as long as he could remember, he and his mother had worked the property of others, mostly wealthy farmers, these being by far the worst breed, whose holdings ranged from a hundred to two hundred acres. To have to look them in the eye and, cheerfully, fawningly, anticipate their every whim, their every command; to live in constant fear of being cheated out of a promised bushel of rye or a couple of pairs of old shoes—this was the stuff on which hatred thrived, the suspicion that the entire world was predicated on a lie.

Earlier that same summer, before he was moved into the shed in the orchard, something important happened in Dominic's life. For a long time he had been content to fawn, to do the bidding of others, until one day a war veteran began letting him handle his service rifle—this in reward for keeping silent about certain matters.

Now, the arrangement about the rifle coincided with an outbreak of rabies in the village, and people suspected one dog of having been bitten by a rabid animal. All agreed that it would have to be destroyed, yet no one was eager to do the job—until Dominic volunteered. The dog was surrendered, but with reluctance—who knew, maybe the dog *hadn't* been infected. The dog—big and black, tail erect, bristles sprouting from its muzzle—started fawning on him, happy to be unleashed, to exchange a life of yawning and flea-hunting for the freedom of open spaces. Dominic, after giving the dog something to eat, took it out to a place overlooking a small pond. Situated in the middle of a peninsula formed by a bend in the Issa, the pond was fed by a muddy ditch; in spring its warm shallow waters became a spawning ground for pike, before drying up again in summer, its bed of silt suitable as a permanent dwelling place only for stickleback. A thick wall of reeds ran all the way around, reaching as high as a man on horseback; on one bank, nestled among the reeds, stood a pear tree.

Dominic tied the dog to it on a thick cord and sat down with the rifle, a little distance away. Next, removing the bullet heads from the cartridges, he inserted wooden ones, specially carved for the occasion. The dog playfully wagged its tail and yelped with joy. To shoot or not to shoot. He braced the rifle butt against his shoulder and hesitated, more to savor the freedom of choice, the fact that the hound suspected nothing, that the decision rested entirely in his, Dominic's, hands. That and the knowledge that one jerk of his finger would change it into something other than what it had been. But how? Would it fall flat, spring into the air? Not only the dog but the entire landscape would be altered. Nothing like being killed by a bullet—a calm, a hush, as if devoid of human presence, and all done so effortlessly, so coolly, just a simple: "Fire!" The reeds sighed, a moist red tongue hung from the dog's yap. The mouth snapped shut: it had caught a fly. Dominic took aim at the gleaming hide.

Fire! For a split second, the dog was convulsed by something like shocked bewilderment. Suddenly it bolted forward, stretching its cord, snarling. Angered by this gesture of defiance, Dominic fired a second shot. The dog keeled over backward, rose again to its feet—and suddenly comprehended. With hide bristling, it backed away from some appalling vision. It went on taking bullets, which came at intervals—to prolong the moment—each one having a different effect, culminating in a dragging of the hind quarters, a whining, and a convulsive waving of the paws with flank to the ground.

Sitting with Thomas by the campfire in the orchard, Dominic began entertaining thoughts of a theological nature, inspired by memories of the act just committed. If he was superior to the dog, the arbiter of its fate, wasn't God in like measure the arbiter of human fate? He felt bitter toward God. He held against Him his insensitivity to the most sincere pleas. Once, just before Christmas, when

there had not been enough bread in the house, when his mother had knelt before the holy picture, weeping and praying, he had wished for a miracle. Crawling into the attic, he had got down on his knees, made the sign of the cross, and, in his own words, said: "It can't be you don't see how worried my mother is. Perform a miracle, and I'll sacrifice myself to you. Kill me, so long as you make a miracle happen." Confident of success, he hopped down from the ladder, sat down on the bench, and calmly waited. But God responded with absolute indifference, and that night they went to bed hungry.

God, thunder-wielding God—thunder, after all, was a better weapon than a rifle—clearly favored hypocrites. Every Sunday, there they were, dressed in the latest fashions, the women in green velvet bodices, with gaudy kerchiefs tied under their chins. They sang in the choir, rolled their eyes to heaven, and piously folded their hands. But watch out when they got home! You could faint on their front doorstep before they condescended to share their cheese fritters smothered in cream and lard. And they knew just where to use a strap—out behind the granary, out of earshot. They hated each other and loved to backbite; stupid and vicious, once a week they assumed an air of virtue and piety. Divine retribution? How, when God had bestowed the greatest wealth on a man who slept with his own daughter—he had spied on them through a crack: the girl's naked knees, the panting old man, the girl's amorous groans . . .

The priest instructed them in the lessons of charity. But for men, no less than for animals, the only lesson was: kill or be killed. When he was younger, he was everybody's scapegoat. Not until he was bigger and tough enough to draw blood did they begin to respect him. God saw to it that the strong prospered and the weak suffered.

If only he could have flown to heaven and grabbed Him by the beard! They had invented flying machines, so

why not a superplane? Dominic was floundering in a maze of complexities. Who went to hell, anyway? Maybe God was only faking that nothing fazed Him, maybe He was the sly type, like a cat that looks the other way and then pounces. If it weren't for the fear of hell—boy, what a picnic! And if anyone got in the way—whamo!—let him have it with the rifle. Clasping his knees and listening condescendingly to Thomas's rambling explanations, he looked for a way out of the labyrinth. Once he was struck by an ingenious idea. What if the priests were making it all up, what if God really didn't care about the world? Of course there had to be a hell, but that was something between people and devils—spirits who, like the invisible witch, Laume, changed their appearance at will and went after those stupid enough to court them. Maybe there *was* no God, maybe no one lived in heaven. But how to be sure?

Dominic, who, as has already been noted, had the sort of mind that appreciated the value of experiments, gradually formulated the following logical proposition: If man was to a dog what God was to a man, then whenever a dog bit a man and the latter reached for a stick, that was the same as when God was wounded by a man and punished him. The trick was to find something so offensive as to force God to use one of His thunderbolts. If nothing happened, that would be a proof.

26

A SHARP AWL, the kind shoemakers use. Dominic was continually testing the blade with his finger, carrying the instrument in his pocket wherever he went.

That Sunday, a hazy sunrise gave way to clear skies laced with luminous strands of Indian summer. By one of the Issa's steep banks there stood a moss-covered boulder, with a flat, altarlike surface. Dominic's ministers, now wearing shoes and clean shirts—they had just returned from Mass —sat on the grass facing the rock, puffing on little cigars, each trying to keep a poker face. Invisible creatures may also have been in attendance, their necks craned in anticipation of the performance.

Dominic, meanwhile, stood pensively on the riverbank, skipping pebbles across the water. He could still back down. And if what the priests had said was true? Then he would be struck by lightning. He gazed skyward. Not a cloud; a noontime sun high overhead. A bolt of lightning out of a clear blue sky—he'd give anything to see it. But by then it would be too late. The ripples pursued each other in ever-widening circles, rocking the flattened leaves on the surface, until one of them buckled and its green hide was overrun. Was he scared, or what? He tossed a pebble across the river, aiming for the strip of shade on the opposite shore, squeezed his fists inside his pockets, and felt the awl.

He headed straight for the boulder. Seeing him approach, his ministers began to withdraw, and he watched them with contempt as they kept moving farther and farther away. Then he took from his pocket a crumpled blue handkerchief, carefully unfolded it, and smoothed out its corners on the rock's rough surface.

The Mass over, Thomas had tried to catch up with him but lost sight of him in the crowd. Someone had said he'd seen him heading for the pasture, and Thomas, picking up the trail, took off in the same direction. His tagging after him would have been enough to infuriate Dominic. But to show up at the climactic moment, at the instant the vertical fold between his brows expressed a firmness of will—that was unforgivable. Why did Dominic have to be

distracted from his purpose? He yelled something at Thomas, who stood there, not comprehending, though somehow he grasped the impropriety, the painful ridiculousness of his presence, as reflected in the faces of the others. At a command from their leader, they pounced on him and flipped him to the ground, belly first. He fought back, but their hands, reeking of tobacco, kept him pinned down, immobile except for his upturned chin. They ordered him not to make a sound.

The stone table reached just above Dominic's waist. Something round and white shone in the middle of the handkerchief—the Holy Eucharist. He had brought it back from Communion, his hands folded on his chest, balancing it on his tongue and deftly spitting it into his handkerchief. Now he would find out. He grabbed the awl and aimed straight down at the body of Christ. He lowered it, then raised it.

He dug it in.

Keeping the blade in the wound, he searched the sky for some sign of retribution. Nothing happened. A flock of birds shimmered overhead, winging their way from the direction of the stubble fields. Not a cloud or a wisp in sight. He bent down to see whether the wafer, still transfixed by the knife blade, was bleeding. Nothing. Then he began to stab and stab, mutilating the little white disk to bits.

The moment he was free, Thomas took off on the run, his throat convulsed. He ran with the feeling that he was fleeing from the world's manifold evil, that he had been implicated in the sacrilege; it was not only the fear of possible mortal sin. Suddenly he realized how dispensable he was, the self-deception of all those times he had imagined himself to be Dominic's friend. He was, in truth, nobody's friend. He ran for an eternity. At home he clung fitfully to Grandmother Dilbin's arm, desperate for her help, and she kept asking him what was the matter, but all

she could get out of him was spasmodic sobbing. That night, screaming he was afraid, he pleaded for the light to be left on in his room. He mumbled in his sleep, and several times his grandmother had to climb out of bed and anxiously lay her hand on his forehead.

Father Monkiewicz, to whom he immediately went to confession, not wanting to postpone it till the weekend— he could barely muster the words to describe it—was outraged by this sacrilegious act committed in his own parish. Coaxing and cajoling, the quicker to extirpate the evil, he twisted and squirmed inside the confessional. But Thomas refused to betray his former friend, despite the priest's insistence that it was his Christian duty to do so. Somehow the name refused to come to his lips. Only when absolution was granted did he feel somewhat relieved.

From now on, even though it meant missing the harvest, then at its peak, he avoided the shed in the orchard, resorting to various subterfuges when Antonina stuck a basket in his hands. This was around the time that he began disappearing, going into hiding at the mere glimpse of homespun pants through the trees. Crossing paths with Dominic, he lowered his gaze, pretending not to notice him.

In effect, that whole ritual conducted on the banks of the Issa had resolved nothing. As soon as it was over, the other boys, unable to seize the scientific relevance of the experiment, feeling somehow cheated—how different if there'd been a clap of thunder, or at least a little blood to show for it!—sat down and dealt a game of blackjack. Afterward, it should be noted, Dominic had gathered up the crumbs of wafer and eaten them: stabbing it was one thing, tossing it into the wind or trampling it underfoot was another.

Dangling his legs over the side of the cliff, he banged his heels against the clay and smoked his pipe fashioned from a cartridge shell. He was overcome by a feeling of

emptiness. Better a bullying, fist-wielding, stick-wielding father than having no one to put on trial. He was oppressed by the sorrow of orphanhood, of his double orphanhood. Alone, completely alone.

The surface of the Issa quivered. A water snake was crossing to the other bank, bearing high its perpendicular head, with tentacle-like ripples forming diagonally in its wake. Dominic measured the distance with his eye and felt in his arm the certainty of a bull's-eye. But the water snake was a sacred being: whoever killed one did so at the risk of tempting fate.

27

EVERY AUTUMN, Thomas was on hand to help with the threshing. The boiler engine: the best part was the way it started up or blew off steam. On top of the boiler, a little off-center, close to a wood-fired furnace, the two large balls rotating on metal rods resembled a pair of outstretched arms, lowered at an angle. Did the arms ever stretch upright, he wondered. He never did find out, his attention being devoted exclusively to the action of the balls. At low speed—*prrr-whack, prrr-whack*—they were easily distinguishable; but at high speed they became a whirling, spinning, almost invisible blur: *pfft-pfft-pfft* . . . A couple of benches took up one corner of the yellow-painted shed, through whose roof the boiler's smokestack shot up chimneylike. Thomas, parking on one of the benches, was often joined by the men from the barn as they took time off from the threshing for a smoke. The other bench, the one opposite, was usually taken by young Sypniewski, stretched out on his sheepskin. The nephew of

Shatybelko, Sypniewski had charge of the boiler. Drawing up his knees, he lay there, head cradled in hand, meditating about only he knew what. From time to time, he would climb down from the bench, check the pressure gauge, flip open the little door, and toss a few oak logs into the belching pit, or lubricate the engine with an oilcan, even though the blacksmith was responsible for its maintenance.

With a flushed face and a nose full of grease smell, Thomas would come out for a breath of the fresh air that ruffled the leaves of the poplar. Outside, he was fascinated by something else: the transmission belt. Close to a meter in width, made of thickly padded hide, the belt connected the boiler's big wheel to a smaller wheel mounted on the thresher. What stopped the belt from slipping off the bigger wheel, wondered Thomas. There were times, in fact, when it did come loose, caused by a slack in the revolutions, producing cries of "Keep back!"—because when it came down, it was with a bone-crushing crash. All work was immediately halted while Sypniewski and the blacksmith tried to soften the impact by applying pressure on the belt with poles. By the time they jumped back, it slipped off without a sound. A surefire sign the machine was slowing down was if the patches on the belt could be seen on its rotations.

Inside the barn: dust clouds, reverberations, a frenzy of activity. The sacks, suspended on iron hooks, swelled in no time. Thomas liked to dip his hand into the streams of cool grain. One by one, the filled sacks were hauled away by the blacksmith, over to the poplar tree and onto the weighing machine. The threshing floor, aswarm with blinding, stinging dust, was a blur of white kerchiefs and sweaty faces. A sheaf described an arc on the end of a pitchfork; the thresher swallowed it with a *grrr*, the paws at the back, their bright-red finish now a faded pink, jerked fitfully back and forth, and sifted the straw between them.

Several teams of horses were needed to move the

boiler engine or the thresher. Sometimes, though seldom, it would be transported to one of the neighboring farms, accompanied by a lot of yelling and cracking of whips and laying of branches under the wheels. The only other boiler in the region belonged to Baloudis, the American, in Pogirai; elsewhere, the threshing was done by hand, with flails. The thresher might be lent to anyone, except to those living down below by the river: downhill was easy going, but uphill was too rough on the horses.

Previously at home among the threshers, Thomas first sensed, following the incident with Dominic, that his presence was somehow unwelcome—by the palaver of the men, by the way they ignored him or somnolently spat out their tobacco spittle. The brooding Sypniewski; the women, shooing him away from the threshing floor; the other children his own age, who were assigned special chores, such as fishing out from underneath the thresher the canvas tarpaulin used to catch the chaff—all made him feel like an outsider.

Other little unpleasantries took on a new meaning. The looks of amused condescension when he tried his hand at a scythe or plow, for example, or the *baraban*—a piece of metal strung on wires, which Shatybelko banged in the morning when it was time to go to work, and later in the evening at quitting time (during the threshing season, the signals came from the boiler's whistle, a blast so shrill it made people plug their ears). Shatybelko's clanging had a definite lilt to it, and people laughed because it sounded like "booby-boss, booby-boss." They laughed good-naturedly, but it hurt nonetheless.

In the servants' quarters, Antonina and the women gossiped about their masters, about them and about their forebears, those slave drivers of old. One ancient pastime held particular fascination for Thomas: a girl was forced to climb a tree and cuckoo while the men took potshots at her. Thomas loved it when the girls shinnied up the trees at

apple- and cherry-picking time—it allowed him to peek up at the darkness under their dresses (panties were unheard-of in Gine). They giggled and called him names, but pleasure was written all over their faces. So what did they, those grandees of the past, do? Blast away from below? In Antonina's sighs he caught not only a brooding rancor but also a feeling of superiority—over him, who was, after all, one of them.

For these and other reasons he began to take refuge in Grandfather's company. Nodding, arms akimbo, he would listen to lectures on plants—how nitrogen was inhaled and oxygen exhaled, how every year forests were burned and grain sown, until the soil became barren, and how the three-field system was later introduced. In time, Grandfather became his chief companion; now, when Thomas turned the pages of his grandfather's books, he did so demanding explanations. He entered the verdant kingdom of plants at that time of year when leaves turn yellow and fall to the ground, a kingdom far removed from reality. Here was a sanctuary for him; plants were not mean or vicious, did not wound or exclude.

Nor was there anything menacing about Grandfather. Always patient, never so distracted by the affairs of grown-ups that he neglected Thomas's needs, he talked to him in earnest, always in his hemming manner—a sign denoting both amusement and affection. Even while he was washing, pomading his hair, or combing his bald patch, he was always ready to answer questions. Thomas once rubbed his hands with the pomade—a soaplike paste that came in a little paper tube—and sniffed it. Grandfather washed with warm water, with a towel wrapped around his waist, revealing a chest and stomach coated with a fine layer of grayish silver.

Grandmother Dilbin openly deplored Thomas's lack of proper schooling. Having no faith in Joseph, she began tutoring him herself, though much had changed since she

was a schoolgirl. She promised that when his mother re-
turned she would take them both away with her, but that
day was continually being deferred. And what learning he
did acquire was not very evenly distributed. If he read
well, it was only because of his curiosity. He wrote in a
chicken's scrawl and spoke the local dialect, throwing in
Lithuanian expressions at random (which later was to
cause him considerable embarrassment in school). With
his sudden turning to Grandfather, he was initiated into
botany, becoming rather knowledgeable for his age, and
his grandfather was cheered that instead of growing up to
be a soldier or pirate he might one day become a farmer.

No photographs of Thomas remain from this period,
for the simple reason that none was ever taken. Of late he
had discovered the mirror, though he still did not know
how to view himself in comparison with others. He never
thought to use a comb or brush. A thick shock of untamed,
dark-blond hair swooped down over his forehead. Chubby-
cheeked, gray-eyed; the stubby, upturned nose of a little
boar—a nose identical to the one in the lilac-tinged photo
of Great-grandfather Mohl. Tall for his age.

"Tommy has a face like a Tartar's ass," he once over-
heard one Koreva boy whisper to the other. The remark
had added insult to injury. The two boys, sons of Koreva, a
neighbor from across the Issa, had stopped over in Gine
with their parents. They had bossed him, bored him silly
with their games, and hurt his feelings with their constant
elbowing in the ribs and teasing.

The suspicion arose that he had inherited an inability
to make friends. Was it from Grandmother Surkont and
her streak of self-willed independence? Grandmother Dil-
bin's timidity? Or was it simply due to inexperience? His
grandparents once took him along on a social visit. Not
only did he eye the host's daughter suspiciously, but he
shuddered when she took him by the hand and showed him
around the garden, stiffening his whole body and holding

his breath for fear of being brushed by her skinny bare elbows. Standing on a bridge over a stream, their backs against a birch railing, he had sensed an aura of expectation, but he was mute. He was reminded of Onutè, of their mutual excursions, and was mortified.

His social manners: he blushed and shuffled his feet in company. He had been to town several times, but that hardly meant a familiarity with the world at large. On market day he stayed put in the wagon, giving Antonina a hand with displaying the apples for sale. Some of the houses in the town sat so close to the river's edge they almost touched the waterline—the Issa broadened here, almost beyond recognition—the streets were paved with cobbles big enough to sprain an ankle, and Jewish shop-keepers stood on the wooden steps of their shops, beckoning to customers. The tallest and biggest building in town was a white mansion—overlooking ponds covered with duckweed—that had once belonged to a princely family but was now in the process of being converted into a school or a hospital. The railway station lay on the outskirts, which was why he preferred the longer but smoother route home that cut across the tracks, because then he got a chance to see a real train. He looked forward to the trip. Antonina handed him the reins and he would crack the whip. If they were traveling alone, she had them hitch the most sluggish horses—automobiles were a constant hazard. To keep them from bucking, Thomas would remove the blanket covering the hay seat, jump down, race around the front, and drape the horses' heads.

With his grandfather, freed from the proprieties and the coercing that came of being among people, he wandered through the wonderland of seeds that germinated underground—of shoots, crowns, petals, pistils, and stamens. He made up his mind to learn the different species of plants, enough to start a herbarium the following summer.

28

As a baby, he was often placed on a bear-skin, at which time a sacred peace descended on him; half frightened and half enthralled, he would sit motionless, lifting his hands so as not to touch the shaggy beast. Worn and moth-eaten, the hide had come from the last bear in the region, tracked down ages ago during his grandfather's childhood. Though he knew them only from the rug and from pictures, bears nonetheless aroused in Thomas feelings of great affection. And he was not the only one, judging by the reminiscing of the older people. In former times, bears were kept on the manorial estates and were trained to perform certain chores, such as turning hand mills or hauling wood. Numerous anecdotes were told of them. One proud and self-respecting bear was still remembered in the village of Gine—a bear so partial to sweet pears that if the master of the house invited him to sit at table, he had to be careful to share everything fairly and equitably, for, if his pears were too soft or too green, the bear roared with indignation. Thomas sat up straight in his chair and was all ears when stories were told of one bear. The bear, who had a habit of strangling hens and had to be chained up, showed great cunning: sitting up on his haunches, he scattered sand around with his forepaws, and when the gullible chickens came within radius of the chain, he clubbed them unconscious, hiding his quarry beneath him and assuming a look of pious innocence. His favorite story, though, the hero of the most marvelous adventure of them all—this one was told by Grandmother Dilbin—was the bear who, seeing an empty carriage parked in front of some farm

veranda, climbed aboard. The horses bolted, but the bear, which also panicked, froze in his seat. The runaway coach and its strange passenger reached the highroad. At a junction stood a cross; the wagon careened to one side, the bear grabbed hold of the cross and, still holding on to the driver's seat with the other paw, managed to uproot it from the ground, and so arrayed rode into the village street, terrifying the villagers, for it looked like the devil's work.

One aristocratic squire, the story went, used bears to show his disrespect for the Russians. The Governor General, a Russian, once paid him a visit, and this is what he saw as he pulled up at the manor: two bears standing in front of the porch, each holding a halberd, and down below on the steps, wearing a Russian peasant blouse, the squire in the act of bowing to the ground. The Governor General, taking this to mean: "We, the Emperor's wild subjects, half beasts and half men, welcome you under our roof," clenched his jaws and ordered an about-face.

In all these tales, the bears emerged as creatures endowed with a nearly human intelligence, making their treatment at the Smorgon Training Academy, as described by his grandfather, all the more cruel. The bears, wearing wooden clogs, were paraded on a sheet-metal floor heated by a fire from below; as the floor grew hotter, music was played, and soon the poor bears were sitting up on their hind paws—the forepaws were left intentionally bare. Later the music always made them recall the scorching metal and they commenced to dance.

That such huge and powerful animals were possessed of a benign, even timid nature only deepened one's sympathy. Their cowardice was borne out by a certain peasant, at a time when bears were still in abundance in the forests. The peasant had lost a cow—a maverick, given to straying from the herd; in a fit of anger, the peasant grabbed a pole and, finding the stray lying in a raspberry

patch, began swinging. A roar told him he was mistaken. The man took off in one direction, the bear in another, so scared he dirtied the entire patch. Diarrhea in these parts is even referred to as "bear's disease."

Grandfather could recall how the bear—the one that had bequeathed his skin—was smoked after the kill and how the hounds had recognized the meat by its smell and how their hides had bristled at the mere scent of it.

In winter, Misia used to spread an elkskin by her bed, the elk being prized for its cured hide, so thick and soft to the touch. When the soles of Thomas's moccasins wore down, his grandmother took a piece of leather from the cupboard, measured off a section, then cut out the part outlined in pencil with shears. This was also a vestige of the past, as elk were now scarce, with only a few being left at the mercy of poachers in a forest located some twenty kilometers from Gine.

The bearskin was associated with one of Thomas's earliest loves. One autumnal day Balthazar showed up at the manor and announced that he had a present for Thomas in the wagon. There, lying on a bed of straw, was a cage with wooden bars, and inside the cage—an eagle owl.

Grandmother Surkont acquiesced, though not without grumbling that the bird was bound to make a mess of the house. The owl stayed. Balthazar had caught it and raised it before it had learned to fly; quite tame, it allowed itself to be taken by the stomach, screeching in a shrill, chickenlike voice, for which reason Thomas named him Squeaky. It was as unlikely a sound as one would have thought possible. Though it was no bigger than a hen, its wings, when extended, were longer than Thomas's fully outstretched arms; it had a curved beak, a powerful grip, and the claws of a killer. Then a new era began: the plucking of rats from every conceivable kind of trap. Squeaky ate like this: he clasped the meat between his claws and

tore at it with his beak. Quite capable of snapping at a hand if it came near the bars, he never went for a finger. At dusk Thomas let him out of his cage. A soundless flight, a rush of air—when suddenly, in midflight, he would drop a pile, splattering the floor (which indiscretion Thomas immediately cleaned up, to avoid angering the grownups), and then, from the top of the tiled stove, let out a real owl hoot. The flying exercise over, he was returned to his cage.

The softness of his feathers, the russet-gold eyes, the way he nodded, like a farsighted person struggling to decipher something in fine print . . . Thomas's attachment grew, to the point that he could predict certain of his habits. When the owl was placed on the elkskin, he behaved uproariously: his whole body jerked, his claws contracted, and then he started pawing the hide, shifting his weight from one leg to the other. One brush of the elk's short hide was enough to evoke memories of his ancestors that had once preyed on deer and hare. The bearskin, on the other hand, did not seem to bother him.

For Thomas, though he would have been too embarrassed to admit it, hair had many vague connotations and was close to being an obsession. Why the upraised hands when he was placed on the fluffy fur hide? And why were bears thought to be so nice and gentle? Was it because they were so hairy? And Magdalena that time in the river. And the owl. Weren't its spasms born of the same thing as what Thomas, in his dream, had felt as a shiver? By identifying with the owl, by embodying himself in him as he clawed the elk hide, he was on the verge of asking whether he had not felt an urge to claw Magdalena, or whether the sweet intoxication had come of the knowledge that she was already dead. But he didn't ask, and it was better so.

Hens screech, but then that is their nature. The owl, on the other hand, was by nature a dual personality: trust-

ful, defenseless, his heart pulsating beneath your fingers, the dangling legs, the gracelessness, veiling his eyes with his lower eyelids when he was scratched behind the ear, and a terror of the forest by night. But was he really the outlaw he was made out to be? If he was, it did not seem to affect his internal nature. Or did every Evil harbor some hidden vulnerability, a suspicion, the barest glimmer of doubt?

No sooner did Aunt Helen arrive and lay eyes on the owl than she and Grandmother Surkont began to conspire. The decision was made: they would sell him. Eagle owls commanded a good price among hunters, who, setting them out on posts as decoys, hid in blinds and shot down the owl's attackers. Thomas dutifully accepted their verdict, as if intuiting that no love should ever be extended beyond its limits. As for the money he was promised, he never saw a penny of it.

29

WHENEVER Thomas went into the library, he had to put on his little sheepskin against the cold; the room was never heated and his hands turned blue as he leafed through the sheets of parchment in the hope of finding something on plants or animals. Often, he grabbed a couple of volumes and took refuge in a warmer part of the house. One of the tomes abducted in this manner bore a title whose contorted, snakelike letters he had difficulty deciphering: "On the Office of Swordbearing . . ." Unable to cope with the rest, he went to his grandfather for an explanation of the contents. His grandfather—but not be-

fore putting on his pince-nez—read the title aloud: *The doctrines of the Church of Our Lord Jesus Christ/ being in Lithuania/ briefly summarized/ according to Holy Scripture. The defense of said office against all its adversaries having been written by Simon Budny. On the question of what is clearly prescribed by Holy Scripture/ that a Christian may own subjects, both freemen and slaves/ so long as they be treated in a God-fearing manner. This being the 1583d year A.D.*

Tapping the leather pince-nez case against the volume's musty cover, his grandfather began turning the pages. After a while he cleared his throat. "This is not a Catholic book. You see, Thomas, long, long ago there lived a man named Hieronymous Surkont. This book was his; he was a Calvinist."

Thomas knew that the word Calvinist connoted something bad, that it was even a derogatory term. But they, those infidels, who didn't go to a church but to a *Kirche*, belonged to the far-off world of cities, railroads, and machines. Protestants? Here in Gine? He regarded it as an honor to have been initiated into such a shameful secret.

"A heretic?"

Grandfather's fingers slipped the pince-nez back into its case. He looked out the window and stared at the snow. "Hm? Yes, yes, a heretic . . ."

"And this Hieronymous Surkont used to live here?"

Grandfather suddenly perked up. "Did he live here? Probably, but we know very little about him. He spent most of his time in Kedainiai, at the court of Prince Radziwiłł. That's where the Calvinists had their parish and school."

Thomas sensed some reticence on his grandfather's part, some resistance, the sort of deliberate ambiguity the grownups used when they spoke of certain family members in hushed voices, falling silent the moment anyone entered

the room. The faces of these outcasts, impossible to visualize, disappeared into the dark background as in some faded photograph, with not a trace of a brow or facial blemish left behind as a reminder. Whatever sins they had committed—grave enough to bring shame to their descendants—the age in which they lived, the degree of kinship dissolved into whispers or mild reproaches directed at the intruder. But this time it was different.

"There is a German side to the Surkont family. They are all descendants of Hieronymous. Nearly three hundred years ago, in 1655, the Swedes invaded our land. Hieronymous went over to the side of the Swedish king, Karl Gustav."

"Then he was a traitor?"

Grandfather liked to pinch the end of his purple-veined nose, puff his nostrils, then suddenly let go, producing a *pff-pff* sound.

"That he was"—*pff-pff*—"but if he'd fought against the Swedes, he would have betrayed the Prince he served. Either way, he would have been a traitor."

Thomas frowned as he contemplated the complexities of the dilemma. "So it was Prince Radziwiłł's fault," he declared at last.

"Now *there* was an ambitious man," said his grandfather. "He thought that once Karl Gustav made him a Grand Duke he would no longer be a vassal of the Polish king. As ruler of Lithuania, he could then force everyone to convert."

"And if he had," said Thomas, "we would all be Calvinists, right?"

"Probably." He scrutinized his grandson's face, grinning in a way that suggested he saw through the boy's questions, to the awareness gradually taking hold: Why are we what we are? Who or what decides? What would he have become if he were someone else? "But Hieronymous

Surkont wasn't exactly a Calvinist. He was a Socinian, another—uh—species of those who refused to recognize the Pope."

And he began telling him of the Socinians, or Arians, as they were also called, and of the new set of doctrines they had propagated—doctrines prohibiting, among other things, the holding of public office, whether that of voivode, judge, or soldier, a practice expressly condemned by Christ; and the ownership of serfs. This last point had been a cause of much dissension, many arguing that the Bible sanctioned it—this being the position of the book he had taken from the library. As for Hieronymous, following the expulsion of the Swedes he left the country, never to return, eventually settling in Prussia, somewhere around Königsberg.

Thus was the seed sown, and his grandfather had no way of knowing how long it would be nurtured in the vegetable sleep of seeds that patiently bide their time. The seed was sown: in it were contained the squeaking of wooden boards, the sound of footsteps slipping along bookshelves and numbered folios that glow among dark rows of leather bindings; elbows propped on the table in a ring of light cast by a green shade; a pencil bobbing up and down in mimicry of thought, which in the beginning is nothing but a haze, a blur without shape or outline . . . No one lives alone; he is speaking with those who are no more, their lives are incarnated in him; he is retracing their footsteps, climbing the stairs to the edifice of history. Their hopes and defeats, the signs left behind, be it a single letter carved in stone—here is the way to peace, to mitigating the judgments he imposed on himself. Happiness is given to those who have the gift. Never and nowhere will they feel alone, as they are comforted by the memory of all who have struggled, like themselves, for something unattainable. Whether or not Thomas was rewarded, such mo-

ments as those spent in the company of his grandfather abided with him, anticipating an age when voices muted by time would become precious.

30

IT TOOK the Spaniard Michael Servetus more than two hours to die. It took so long because not enough wood had been piled, and through the flames he chastised the city of Geneva for its frugality. "Poor me, I can't even die a proper death! Surely the two hundred ducats and the gold chain they confiscated should have bought enough wood to burn me alive!"*

Meanwhile, Calvin had sat unbendingly in his chair, reading the Bible in the penumbra of his room, while his vicar, Guillaume Farel, his eyes smarting from the smoke, had shouted up at the burning heretic: "Believe in Jesus Christ, the everlasting Son of God!"

Such was the fate of Michael Servetus, after his having hidden among the papists in France for twenty years— a fate willed by the very man with whom he had secretly exchanged letters and in whom he had sought refuge. But Servetus had an indomitable spirit, the tongue in his charred mouth still stirred, and his weak voice could yet testify to the sacrilegious truth: "I believe that Christ was the true Son of God, but not that he was everlasting."

---

* A record of Servetus's last days, based on no longer extant sources, is given by Wiszowaty. See Stanislaw Kot's "L'influence de Michel Servet sur le mouvement antitrinitarien en Pologne et en Transylvanie," in the collection *Autour de Michel Servet et de Sébastien Castellion*, (Alphen aan den Rijn, The Netherlands: H. D. Tjeenk Willink, 1953).

He was survived by a rumor that spread from country to country, that caused goose quills to scratch in Basel, Tübingen, Wittenberg, Strasbourg, and Cracow as they went about copying theses secretly obtained from friends attacking the Trinity. When copies of Servetus's banned writings were discovered on some Polish students in Tübingen, the Prince sneered: *"Schwärmerei!"*; the university trembled and tried to hush up the whole affair. Servetus's name was never mentioned, and even Petrus Gonesius, now returned from Padua to propagate the new doctrine among the Protestant sects in Poland and Lithuania, was careful not to utter his master's name in public. But Melanchthon wasn't fooled. "I have been reading the work of a Lithuanian who means to summon Servetus from hell," he wrote. In Transylvania and Moravia, meanwhile, Jacob Paleologus was composing his great work *Contra Calvinum pro Serveto*—quite clearly written in defense of the Spaniard. But the chest containing his manuscripts was sealed by the hand of the Holy Inquisition, following his arrest and journey to Rome, where he died a martyr's death.

In the writing of any chronicle, people and events are re-created from certain minor details. Now, it would be dishonest to say that Hieronymous Surkont was a short or tall man, dark-haired or fair, when not the slightest physical description of him, not even the dates of his birth and death, has survived. This much was certain: that Rome was for him the seat of the Antichrist; that as he rode horseback in his elkskin jacket along the road skirting the Issa, he had contemplated with sadness this people incapable of embracing the true faith. For theirs was a fake Christianity aptly fitting popish superstitions: after singing hymns in church, the women ran and offered sacrifice to snakes, convinced that if they didn't their men would not be up to fulfilling their conjugal duties. Fables took the place of Holy Scripture, fables about a god of water and a

god of wind who shook the world. And pagan rites, such as those observed when hunters assembled before the hunt. And furtive meetings under the oaks.

An inquisitive man, driven by what must have been a powerful thirst for knowledge, he had probably sought out those like himself, finding them in Kedainiai. He must have studied diligently to have felt an equal in those disputes held by candlelight, supporting his arguments with quotations from the Bible: "Your reasoning, my good sir, is fallacious, more properly deserving of the name of sophistry, because that passage in Hebrew can be interpreted otherwise." Or: "Fellow brother, is not the intent clearly evident in the Greek and Latin commentaries?" This was at a time when the Trinitarians, still loyal to Calvin, and the ditheists, and even those who, following the example of Simon Budny, refused to worship Christ, still tolerated one another, thanks to the mitigating influence of Radziwiłł, who, even though he took as his model the Church of Geneva, refrained from banning theological disputes and was even inclined toward novelties. Not a few Arians from Poland had found a haven on his estate, though, to be sure, at the price of exercising a certain caution.

Was Hieronymous Surkont submerged; that is, was he baptized as an adult, in the manner prescribed by the Brethren, who were strictly opposed to the baptism of infants? No telling, though it is known that he ceased to be a Trinitarian, remaining loyal to the memory of Servetus, nearly a hundred years after that martyr's death. That the three-headed Cerberus substituted for the One God was a heinous insult to reason he took as self-evident. He embraced the revolutionary thesis that God was one, as was Holy Scripture, which was clear and unequivocal and did not require any official exegesis; one had only to read the Gospels, to return to the age of the Apostles, to traverse centuries during which Scholasticism had sought to obscure the simple words of the prophets and of Christ. Calvin had

gone only halfway, killing Servetus in fear of the truth. Whoever failed to destroy Cerberus would never be entirely free of all the hocus-pocus, indulgences, Masses for the dead, pleas for the intercession of the saints, and all other things of a magical nature.

One can infer, from the scarcity of facts available, that in that religious controversy which for many decades divided the Brethren, Hieronymous Surkont leaned in favor of the legacy bequeathed by Petrus Gonesius. Placing all hope in Jesus Christ for the salvation of his soul ("I am a vile worm in the eyes of my Lord," Thomas deciphered in one of his books), he would have argued that Christ did not share in God's divinity; that the Logos, the invisible and immortal Word, became flesh in the Virgin's womb; in other words, that Christ was conceived of the Logos. He had embraced Christ's humanity with awe, gratitude, and joy, but not like the nonworshippers, who did not distinguish between Jeremiah, Isaiah, and Jesus, and who were more apt to invoke the Old Testament than the New.

But what of his thoughts on Gonesius's *De primatu Ecclesiae Christianae*, which he surely must have studied, and on the works of his disciples? Hieronymous Surkont could hardly have dismissed their arguments in the practical realm, arguments that had long reverberated in the synods of Lithuania. Their demands, after all, were given credence by the Gospels. For was it not written: "And unto him that smiteth thee on one cheek offer also the other; and him that taketh away thy cloak forbid not to take thy coat also." Was it not written: "Jesus said unto him, Follow me; and let the dead bury their dead." Was it not written: "And every one that heareth these sayings of mine, and doeth them not, shall be likened unto a foolish man, which built his house upon the sand: And the rain descended, and the floods came, and the winds blew, and beat upon that house; and it fell: and great was the fall of

it." Jews, Greeks, slaves, and masters are equal; all are brothers. A Christian does not shed blood, but divests himself of the sword. He frees his serfs from bondage, sells his earthly goods, and distributes his wealth among the poor. Only thus does he become worthy of salvation; only thus does he distinguish himself from the hypocrites, whose actions give the lie to their words.

The period in question came after the synods of Lithuania had rejected these uncompromising demands, giving rise to bitter dissension among the Brethren. Surkont had set out to refute their arguments with the aid of the Old Testament, as well as with examples taken from his own experience. Granted, the serfs had endured great poverty and oppression—but free them from bondage? That would have been to invite paganism, barbarism, and banditry. Look what happened during the emancipation under Rekut, starosty of Samogitia: the serfs took cover in the forests, emerging only to murder and maraud. Then, too, there was the example of their own peasant rebellion with its revival of the old gods, serving notice on the landowners inhabiting the Issa Valley. Unbelt one's sword? The disciples of Gonesius had chosen a bad time to propose so drastic a measure: to the east, beyond the Dnieper, the wars with Ivan the Terrible were still going on unabated. Outvoted in the synods, they never recovered from their defeat.

Then came Karl Gustav of Sweden, brandishing the sword on behalf of an Imperium for Protestants. And Hieronymous Surkont? Did he suffer moments of vacillation? Of indecision? His Prince had painted a powerful vision of Lithuanians living under the protection of a Swedish king; stripping the papists of both land and serfs, they were to become bearers of light to the east and to the south, all the way to the Ukraine, wherever the black robes, their mouths full of holy Byzantium but not knowing a word of Greek themselves, had succeeded in keeping

the people in ignorance. They had no choice: they were being threatened by a Jesuit invasion—the Jesuits, with their cunning methods of seduction, their theaters, schools, every year luring more and more of the faithful away; the desecration of temples, funeral processions being attacked by student mobs . . . Before long, nothing would be left of the Reformed Church in Lithuania. The Prince had played his last card, obedient to his vocation as protector of the faith. And to another ambition, off in the distance: the crown. And, who knows, even visions of Swedish, Lithuanian, and Polish armies standing at the gates of Moscow.

One suspects that he was driven not only by his loyalty to the Prince but also by his contempt for the blusterous nobility, roused by the priests to a holy war against the heretics. Never applying cold reason, never opening the Bible, guided only by blind, elemental instinct.

Faithful to the end. And the horror of it all: the initial reverses, the vacillation of even the most fervent believers, a fratricidal war, a country laid waste, the sinister indifference of allies . . . Death came to the Prince as the papists stormed the fortress, the last outpost. Then, for Hieronymous, the final hour of reckoning, the time when each man repeats after Christ: "Lord, why hast thou forsaken me," the final dissolution of pride and will.

We can assume that he found consolation in the Bible, or in the memory of their own Anti-Trinitarian martyr—his head crowned with straw drenched in sulphur; his body chained to the stake; his book, waiting for the first lick of the flames, bound to his foot. A detailed account of Servetus's death has survived, thanks to Hieronymous Surkont's co-religionists from the Protestant sects of Poland and Lithuania. It was they who copied the manuscript, otherwise not extant, bearing the title *Historia de Serveto et eius morte*, whose author was Petrus Hyperphragmus Gandavus. No, exile could not compare with bodily torture.

Surkont, nonetheless, had endured spiritual torture, the stigma of a traitor, the burden of self-doubt that came from not knowing whether he had made the right choice. Between his fealty to the King, the Res Publica, and to his Prince, who never begrudged him their theological differences. Between his contempt for the papists and his aversion for the invaders, whose successes—not defeats—he was obliged to wish for. A heretic in the eyes of the Catholics. A barely tolerated outcast among the Protestants. All he could do, in fact, was to repeat: "I am a vile worm in the sight of my Lord."

Quite by accident, it was discovered that Hieronymous's last descendant, a Lieutenant Johann von Surkont, student of theology, was killed in the year 1915, in the Vogesen. If his body lies on a slope facing the east, where thick rows of crosses descend into the valley of the Rhine, crosses that from a distance might be mistaken for vineyards, then the grass on his grave is brushed by the dry winds coming from his native Lithuania.

31

In Gine, the *bitnik*, or beekeeper (from *bitè*, Lithuanian for "bee"), was Thomas's aunt, Helen Juchniewicz. As payment for tending the beehives, she was allotted a percentage of the honey and wax—though she was a member of the family, custom dictated it. Her arrival invariably signaled the removal of utensils from a special cupboard and the donning of special vestments. Pinning up her sleeves at the elbow, she slipped a mask over her head, a sort of basket of green muslin. Though she often dispensed with gloves, she was seldom stung. Thomas was

assigned the task of loading the smoker (tin, with a wooden handle) with live coals from the kitchen, dry rot being needed to get the coals to smolder. In her mask, with a knife and pail in one hand, the billowing smoker in the other, she looked like—well, no metaphor could have possibly done her justice. With mouth agape, Thomas passionately devoured that figure trailing down the lane in the direction of the hives. Later, back at the house, she ladled out some curdled milk from a bowl, applying it to the stings. When it came time to extract the honey, Thomas got to operate the "centrifuge"—a metal pot that rotated manually on a stick, forcing the honey out of the combs.

Aunt Helen had the same large, pyramid-shaped nose and protruding apple-cheeks as Grandmother Misia, to whom, except for being somewhat larger-proportioned and blue-eyed, she bore a definite physical resemblance. She had a sugary smile and a look of piety, which obviously worked to her advantage, clothing her passions in innocence. Her ruling passion was miserliness, dictated not so much by frugality as by something so deeply engrained, so fundamental to her being, that it often sought justification in the most improbable of motives. If she had to go into town on some errand, she never took the wagon. "The weather's so lovely—I feel like a walk today," and so saying, she would hike the ten kilometers to town on foot, taking off her shoes the moment she reached the road, since, as she put it, "walking barefoot was healthier." The real reason, of course, was to avoid having to tip the driver and to save wear and tear on her shoes. When it came to dividing the honey and flour, she always made sure the choicest part went to others, except that the "choicest" part always contained some hidden flaw. Nor, if the rumors were to be believed, was she above feeding her domestic staff bad meat, worm-infested pork, for example, though no doubt she prided herself on not keeping them exclusively on a vegetarian diet.

From Misia she had inherited an iron constitution and endurance. She never took ill—but God forbid anyone calling a doctor if she had! Twenty kilometers were, for her, something of a country stroll, though at her brisk peasant pace she could easily have managed a hundred. Naturally, she didn't give up bathing in the river until well into November. Never had Thomas seen her with a book in her hands, not even a prayer book, as if she had vowed never to touch one, though the little French she knew said that she must have studied at one time or another.

The arrival of her husband, Lucas Juchniewicz, was always theatrical, contagiously so. Whooping and hollering from his carriage, he threw up his arms, jumped down, and with the flaps of his cape or cloak fluttering behind him, ready for a bear hug, came on the run, squealing in a high soprano, "Mama! Oh, oh, oh! How glad I am to see ya, what a sight for sore eyes . . . !" Smooch, smooch, mm-mm . . . But the chief attraction was the man's face: round, with a dark forelock drooping down over the forehead, a face all wrinkled with sincerity and emotion. "Good ol' Luke," Misia, by now smothered and wet, would reply, and behind his back mercifully sigh, "Good ol' loon." For Grandmother Dilbin, on the other hand, Luke was living proof that there was at least a grain of truth in the old saying: "Only fools and madmen are born along the Issa."

That summer, the summer Thomas built his herbarium (after managing to scrounge some cardboard from Pakenas), his naturalist's honor could no longer keep him from the beehives, heretofore off-limits; after considerable pestering, his aunt finally surrendered and agreed to take him with her to the apiary. He took no chances, wearing his grandfather's long pants tied at the ankles, an old mask with rusted netting, and a pair of rubber gloves. Although prized for their intelligence, although surrounded by a poetry of honey, bees assumed an altogether different aspect the moment their hives were opened—one not ex-

actly compatible with the image of them buzzing in the branches of a linden tree. An acrid smell, a fury of motion, a mad ferment, the cruel severity of law: Gine most certainly was a poor preparation for life in society if Thomas was intimidated by something as cruel and mysterious as a beehive. Charging at him with their stinging intent, they descended on his glove, their curved bellies vibrating spasmodically, their diminutive feet clinging to the rubber —all in order to perform that fatal act and expire, helplessly and convulsively, in the grass. His aunt worked at a leisurely pace, nonchalantly flicking off her attackers, now and then cautioning him: "Easy does it, Thomas." But Thomas was less affected by the pain than by the hellish pandemonium of the beehive, with its own special, persistent rhythm. He couldn't take it; he began to run, the bees in hot pursuit, a hint of murder in their buzzing drone. He squealed, waved his arms—in short, the whole enterprise, his dream of accomplishing something worthwhile in the practical realm, ended in disgrace.

Plants were better, quieter. Some, after a thick *Economic and Technical Guide to a Herbarium* had been consulted, enticed one to prepare crucibles and mortars— a whole pharmacy—so alluring were the descriptions of their medicinal properties. Visions of different colored decoctions that had to be blended and strained; extracts submerged in alcohol; jams and preserves made from roots popularly thought of as worthless. As in the family larder in Gine, the imagination was plunged into an aromatic penumbra. For now, though, Thomas was content to devote himself to less practical work: the collection of various species.

He had a weakness for orchids, which contained all the magic of creatures inhabiting warmer and more humid climates, being for northern regions emissaries of the tropical south. First there was the stem, the meatiness of their green bodies, contiguous with flowers concealing a multi-

branched candelabrum and smelling vaguely of something rotten, wild, so faintly that their fragrance had to be inhaled long enough to be named—alas, it was unnamable. In June they dotted the grasslands along the Issa, at that time of year when vapor rose from the floodwaters of the river deltas, still awash with silt and the decay of bulrushes, to mingle with the bright green efflorescence. The speckled orchid, a pale lilac-hued cone flecked with dark violet, was hard to catch in full bloom because it was immediately touched by the rust of decay. Thomas would kneel down and carve out the black earth with his pocketknife. (Pocketknives, though occasionally lost, belonged to the realm of objects marking various stages in his life; his last had been one with a wooden handle, his present one being flat and made of solid metal.) Carefully, he would lift the soil and slip out the bulb with its rough, fingerlike protrusions. Bursting from the bulb, the orchid rushed forth to meet the sun, then remained in darkness till the following year. Pressed between sheets of cardboard, the orchid gradually took on a rusty hue; the bulb began to flatten and assume the most bizarre configurations.

The white orchid had a purity of color that in a summer twilight was as luminescent as the white of the narcissus. A meadow full of orchids became, in the evening mist, a meadow inhabited by diminutive phantoms. But, when dried, the white orchid lost all its charm, retaining only its slender, roan design. The same was true of the arum. He soon discovered that plants growing in dry regions kept perfectly, undergoing hardly any discoloration, though he felt a greater attraction for the luxurious plants that thrived in wet, humid places. Even insects, armor-plated and quick of movement, bustling in hot sand and a riot of roots, lacked interest. The jungle—now that was the place for him! Why was it that a superabundance of light always resulted in a diminishment of being?

From among the many inhabitants of the sand dunes,

Thomas collected only mulleins, though they were too long for the herbarium and had to be bent zigzag fashion. Needless to say, he hunted most passionately for those flowers described by his guidebook as rare. And just because it was so rare, he especially treasured a globeflower (*Trollius*)—of the crowfoot family, similar to a yellow rose—plucked among some oaks by the cemetery.

He helped his grandfather tend the flower beds along the wall, to the right and left of the porch, weeding, transplanting the seedlings, and carrying water from the pond. Terraced steps, reinforced with stakes, led to the footbridge through a small wicket gate—why the gate was there was anyone's guess—in a fence invisible under heaps of hops and morning glory. As he dipped the watering can into the duckweed, large green frogs, startled by his intrusion, leapt in panic and took refuge among the debris afloat in the middle of the pond. Returning with the can, winded from the long walk, he would watch his grandfather water, trying to guess in advance when it was time for another trip to the pond. The evenings were redolent with the tiny bluish-gray night-scented stocks planted along the edges of the beds. Stocks, gillyflowers (with lustrous, velvetlike petals), and asters, which lasted until late autumn and the first frost, were the garden flowers Grandfather liked most to grow. Thomas's favorite was reseda because, although it was plain-looking, like orchids, it aroused an urge to inhale its insides, but also regret because it was so tiny. A reseda the size of a cabbage head—now that would have been something to smell!

Because Misia was of the belief that sickness was one of those things to which normal people were immune, the medicinal virtues of the vegetable world were never exploited. True, the larder was still called the "pharmacy," a relic of the past, but the medicines contained in its drawers had not been preserved, with the exception of arnica flowers, used for treating bruises, and dried raspberries, an

extract of which was used by Grandfather as a sudorific against colds. Thomas knew that plantain leaves were the best remedy for wounds; first you applied the leaf, then wrapped it with a cloth bandage. If it still refused to heal, Antonina would moisten a piece of bread with spit and knead it with a spiderweb—a surefire home remedy. It was Grandmother Dilbin who introduced the use of iodine.

Thomas's botanical passions were fated to last no longer than a season. His herbarium, monumentally conceived, became more rarely enriched with a new specimen, the need for cardboard less urgent, as his interest in birds and animals began to revive, soon to the exclusion of everything else. This revival was less Aunt Helen's than Romuald's doing.

32

THAT AFTERNOON, Romuald Bukowski, dressed in his work shirt and work pants, finished mowing the clover, planted his scythe beside the ditch, and went for a dip in the river. He stripped leisurely and, standing knee-deep in the water, washed himself, the black string with the holy medal dangling every time he bent down. Contentedly, he lathered his flat stomach and his thighs; he was still a man in his prime. Wet, he slipped into his clothes and, the scythe safely back on his shoulder, was homeward bound by way of the path through the orchard. Barbarka dished him up a bowl of buttermilk from the underground cooler, elbowing him good and hard in the ribs in the process (something she never did in company). To his loud clap on her rump, she squealed, "Mind you don' spill the milk, Rom!"

The hounds whimpered and whined in their pen. In high spirits, he reached for the hunting horn on the wall, which hung under a shotgun and riding whips with deer-hoof handles. Horn in hand, he went back out onto the porch and began blowing, setting the dogs to wailing and baying for their freedom and the hunt. Later, in his bachelor's quarters, he opened a medicine chest and shaved in front of a tiny mirror—a hard growth, bluish in color—and brushed his sidewhiskers. A sunburned, brick-red face, leathery skin, a black mustache streaked with white—nothing to worry about.

He pulled on his shiny knee boots and buttoned the collar of his navy-blue jacket. "Where to?" pried Barbarka. "Bear-trappin'. Fix a man somethin' to eat and hold yer tongue." From a pile of stirrups in the corner, he disentangled two saddles. "Go git Pietruk to saddle Blackie and Chestnut!" The freckle-faced Pietruk showed up a short while later, scratching his crotch through a hole in his pants. Romuald trailed after him to make sure the saddles were cinched properly. He mounted Blackie gently, his spurs jangling, and led the riderless horse by the bridle down into a little canyon, then uphill along a rocky road that cut through the woods. Whenever a hazel grouse fluttered, he bent over the horse's neck and followed it with his eyes.

On Romuald's finger was a signet ring—of some kind of metal, not gold. He wore a homespun jacket, dyed a dark blue. Starting in the sixteenth century, the Issa Valley had been colonized by settlers lured there by the Princes Radziwiłł, and the Bukowskis had come from the Kingdom of Poland in their covered wagons, through forests, across fords and uncharted wilderness, before reaching their destination in the virgin forests of Lithuania. Many fell on distant fields of battle—in the wars against the Swedes, the Turks, and the Russians. Some became impoverished, predestining their heirs for the life of a peasant or tradesman.

But Romuald had upheld the family tradition. His father had run the family farm just outside Vendigala; later, after the estate was parceled out, they migrated here. Not a fortune, but never mind: a man's worth was measured not by money.

Past a clump of woods, the road dipped down and leveled off into grazing pasture, threading a maze of fences —stakes lashed with dry branches. A well crane, steeply pitched roofs. As he rode past one of the houses, both men—the man on horseback and the one observing him— touched the visors of their caps. Masiulis, the wizard, sat with his back against the farmhouse wall, smoking his pipe. They were not on the best of terms. The magician laid claim to as much land as Romuald, but he was a peasant— a Lithuanian peasant. Masiulis followed the rider with squinting eyes, took a puff on his pipe, cleared his throat, and spat.

A mauve afterglow lingered behind the fir-notched horizon; a round wafer of a moon; the distant echo of a shepherd's song played on a wooden horn wrapped in birch bark. He let his horse break into a trot, admired the undulating earth, thought about nothing, rejoicing in the motion, his leg against the warmth, the animal's supple grace. Coming into view now were flat grasslands, fringing the park shrubbery; off in the distance, wrapped in a bluish mist, loomed the hilltops beyond the river valley.

At the park's edge, on a wooden bench overgrown with beards of gray moss, Helen Juchniewicz sat staring up at a moon gaining steadily in brightness. She had come out for a breath of summer air, and not, let it be emphasized, for a horseback ride with Romuald Bukowski; otherwise, she would have worn riding breeches. That she had jokingly, even flippantly, agreed to a rendezvous had completely slipped her mind: no sinful desires had guided *her* steps. When Romuald secured his horse to a tree down below by the roadside, climbed the hill, and made for the

bench, she let out a startled "Oh!" He greeted her gallantly, bowing and kissing her fingertips. They talked about the weather, about farming; he told a few jokes and she laughed. When he invited her for a horseback ride, she demurred, saying that she was out of practice and not properly dressed for it. In the end, she consented, placing her foot in the stirrup with all the grace of a born trooper. "Which way?" she asked. "Let's try that way," he said, pointing straight ahead.

From Gine the dusty road ran along the Issa, climbing steadily to where the terraced land sloped down more steeply, twining inlets and meadowlands, taking refuge from the highland mass in the willows by the riverside, until finally, bypassing one and then another of the little villages where long bundles of cut reeds lay before the house to dry, the road made a fork: one way led across a ford to the far bank, the other straight up the side of Mount Vilainiai. The swift river current cut through willow-thick sandbanks. The ford was a comfortable one, with the waterline well below the axles, though dangerous in autumn, during the rainy season, when the horses snorted and balked in panic, leaving the rider to trust to the horse's instincts. Mount Vilainiai, dense with boulders and juniper bushes evoking sinister silhouettes, fell steeply down into the river gorge. The summit afforded a marvelous view of the winding blue ribbon below, of the holms around the ford, which had not prevented the mountain, by far the most rugged and desolate in the region, from acquiring an evil name. The smell of warm milk drifted from the cowsheds along their way, the evening hush being occasionally disturbed by the sound of milk squirting into a bucket, by a farm woman's whining complaint provoked by a swishing tail in the face. Through the twilight, through shafts of light issuing from open cottage doors, through a baying of hounds kept behind fences, they rode. Below them, a gleaming ford, a scaly surface. The clatter

of hoofbeats on shale at the foot of the Vilainiai's steep talus caused Helen to pull up on the reins of her chestnut.

"What a spooky place," she said.

He smiled. "What's so spooky about it?"

"God help you, Romuald, if you so much as mention his name."

"Oh, *him!* I've got a way of dealing with him."

"What sort of way?"

"Well, you talk to him, see, real polite-like, then you invite him along."

"Honestly, how can you! I'm heading back!"

"Hold on, I was only teasin'."

They continued to climb, the darkness steadily thickening, a light breeze ruffling the mountainside grass. They reined in at a spot overlooking the gorge. The river shimmered faintly at their feet. Far below, the rueful cries of a bird in flight.

They sat motionless in their saddles, their bridles softly jangling. Helen sighed. Was it a sigh dictated by convention, one of those gestures well suited to the occasion? Or was it the sigh of someone wishing it could somehow have been otherwise?

The Milky Way, which in this part of the country goes by the name of the Bird's Way, was inscribing its luminous signs in the firmament.

33

WHEN ROMUALD, wearing his navy-blue visored cap, his hunting whip dangling from his saddle, rode up the lane to the veranda, Thomas had visions of a

dark statue, a mobile perpendicularity on horseback. They soon became the best of friends. At the dining table, while Aunt Helen lavished their guest with sweetmeats, Romuald and Grandfather talked crops. Still, certain imperceptible signs visible in the behavior of the older women connoted a distance. Romuald, though a welcome guest, was of a different world. Such distinctions took nothing away from the powerful charm exerted by his presence, and for Thomas those visits, those conversations full of the lore of animals, held forth the promise of new marvels.

Although Borkuny lay no more than three and a half kilometers away, this was his first trip there—now, as he accompanied Aunt Helen, who, just by chance needing to call on the medicine man for some sheep medicine, had decided to pay Mr. Bukowski a social visit. A sharp right at the crucifix, down the road from the commune, took one to Pogirai; veering slightly to the right before gradually straightening was the way to Balthazar's; the left led to Borkuny. Before them loomed the timberline, and behind the first row of trees, another world: a knoll sloping down into a glen, a clump of woods, a patch of swamp, a maze of trails, and a set of wagon ruts through bouquets of green. Behind a clump of fir, at the very bottom of the hollow, the Bukowski farmstead suddenly sprang into view. The small manor house was fronted by wooden porch columns overgrown with purple lilacs, partially obscuring an orchard, scattered alder, and rows of pine in ascending height—from saplings to full-grown. The inside of the house was rank with leather, the corners cluttered with stirrups, saddles, and harnesses. Scattered among the piles and decorating the walls were objects of an unfamiliar nature: horns, whistles, bags, cartridge belts . . . Thomas went from object to object, wanting to know the purpose of each, in one instance grabbing hold of a gun—Romuald had cracked it to make doubly sure the chambers were empty—and pulling on the trigger with a clicking sound that brought Romuald

over on the run. "You shouldn't do that, Thomas. Might damage the firing pin." It was a 16-gauge shotgun, medium caliber (a 12-gauge, broad-barreled, was for big game; a 20-gauge, for small fowl). Though antiquated—Romuald had inherited the gun from his father—it could still fire with accuracy. The entire barrel was embossed with silver ornamentation called damascene.

The table was laid with a tablecloth and they were served by a young woman with head modestly lowered. Thomas could not, as they say, tear his eyes from her, enthralled no doubt by the range of colors: a whiteness of skin that shaded, subtly, by degrees, into a ruddiness of cheeks; a braid of dark gold; a furtive glance full of a mysterious, dark blue lambency. There was something friendly in her look, or at least that's what Thomas had supposed, until, just as they were going out the door, he overheard her whisper, much to his distress, the word *"shutas"* in Romuald's ear, this vulgar Lithuanian epithet being obviously at his expense. The visit was spoiled. Even so, from that moment on, almost in defiance, out of a desire to repair something, he felt a strange attraction for Borkuny.

Romuald climbed into the britska with them. It was only a stone's throw, he said, and his mother would be tickled. Borkuny: three farms without a name, situated so that Masiulis's property was wedged between Romuald's mother's property and his own. Built on a rise, the porch overlooked a small lake at the bottom of a marshy basin. Catherine Bukowski was profusely polite and apologetic. But what a face! Bristly, tuftlike warts, shaggy brows of a faded ash-gray—it made Squeaky's look positively ravishing by comparison. Her voice was a deep masculine bass. Her physiognomy, he was quick to notice, was quite congenial to her reign. The farming was supervised by her son Denis, a bachelor, now well into his prime. Servile to his mother's every command, he had a habit of cringing every

time she barked at him. A nondescript man—at least in Thomas's eyes—except in one detail: a pair of boots that reached not to the knees but higher, with soft leather shanks laced with buckskin and sheathing the thighs cuplike. A third son, Victor, an adolescent going on young manhood, had bulging eyes, rough-cut features, and stuttered so badly that even when he stammered out a sentence he partially swallowed the words, managing only the vowels, along with a guttural signifying this or that letter; so, for example, "The hay's been took in," might come out sounding like "Ge gay's geen gook gin."

Again the same table-setting ritual, the exhortations to eat, the hot homemade mead passed around. "You're man enough to drink, laddie." And: "Your health!" The raising of mugs, the clinking of glass. Thomas took a sip and the burning liquor made his eyes water; but Mrs. Bukowski emptied her mug in one gurgling gulp (she was back and forth to the demijohn, Thomas later discovered, rummaging in the cupboard on some pretext, when— gurgle-gurgle—she'd slam it shut, with face aglow). Denis poured round after round, with Aunt Helen keeping pace, squinting and sipping her drink in her own quiet way. The voices grew louder, the jokes more obscure; he was surrounded by adults and their adult silliness, and it bored him. They began to sing songs; Mrs. Bukowski broke off, ran over to the wall, and took down a guitar that hung on a tapestry embroidered with a kitten. Standing in the middle of the room, keeping time with her foot, in her deep masculine bass she began wailing:

> Oh, Annie, honey, sweet li'l Annie,
> Why did Mama spank your fanny?
> Was it for the coffee, was it for the food,
> Or was it for fear of your maidenhood?
>
> Not for the coffee, not for the food,

And not for fear of my maidenhood.
Mama gave me such a drubbin'
'Cause I can't help from lovin'.

Spurred on by the applause, she sat down and, strumming on the strings of her guitar and turning up the whites of her eyes in a surge of emotion, she sang of Wurcell. It was a song well known to Thomas—how often he had heard Antonina sing it—but one that strained credulity. How could someone loved for forty years still be "young as a berry"? Because the words went like this:

Oh, Wurcell, Wurcell, I loved you strong,
Forty long years, heartless and cruel,
My life, my life you had to rule.
Forty long years or more,
So many letters, buried in the drawer.

So marry, if you will.
May the knot be tied in hell,
And may a prince take my hand
Still young as the berry
That grows in the dell.

In Mrs. Bukowski's mouth such sentimentality sounded comical, reaching outright hilarity when she came to the song "Hitch up the team, I must find my love," with its refrain of "I must—I must—I must—I must." Bad as it was, Thomas preferred this sort of entertainment to the ritual of gorging and guzzling. If he resigned himself to it, it was because he understood the need for patience: adults never were able to concentrate on one thing for very long. Only once was his curiosity kindled—when Denis told of having sighted a wolf that evening, a full-grown one, at the edge of the swamp, a safe bet there was a den nearby; but the moment Thomas began probing him for more details, their conversation was lost in the clamor of voices, guffaws,

and clanking dishes. Still, there was a lot to be learned at Borkuny. He felt less inhibited here than he did, say, at other manors. Table manners were not something that required constant vigilance. What reassured him, no doubt, was the sight of black-rimmed fingernails and calloused palms, not to mention the deference with which both he and his aunt were treated.

Of the two Borkuny farmsteads, Romuald's held by far the greater interest. While at Romuald's mother's the talk was mostly of crop yields, plantings, and the market price of flax, at Romuald's it was all horses, hounds, and guns. Thomas could hardly wait to get back, the more because of some gnawing recollection. For what was wrong with one admiring glance—or was one obliged to pretend the attraction wasn't there?

They started back after sundown, his aunt working the horses with the reins, her spirits high, yet giving no outward sign of being in her cups. The sunset out here was distinguished by the myriad sounds assailing him from both sides of the trail, communing in a multitude of voices from out of the scrub and from off the dank marsh. That quacking there, that croaking—were those frogs, wild ducks, or some other species of bird? Some goatsuckers cut diagonally across their field of vision. He was awed by it—filled with reverential awe for this tumult in the dark, for this proliferation of creatures whose habits and routine tasks, now secret, demanded to be studied and tracked. Breaking up the land was the work of stupid men. To travel between open fields was to miss the beauty of it. If he'd had his way, he would have made plowing a criminal offense. Let there be wooded lands where animals could run wild! Immersed in such thoughts—in such dreams—he vowed that when he grew up he would found a kingdom—a forest kingdom, of course—to which only a select few would be admitted. Like who? People like Romuald, for example.

34

AN ENTERPRISE to which Thomas became passionately addicted at Borkuny—this after he had won consent to spend a few days there—might have seemed strange to some. There are creatures protected by the sort of fear to which humans are susceptible in their presence, a fear or revulsion not necessarily springing from any explicit danger, being rather the vestigial traces of ancient tacit conventions and rites. To challenge openly that word-defying sphere was commendable, or perhaps not altogether so, but it was done only on condition that there was no risk of some unforeseen reprisal. Thomas, having once mastered his fear, saw himself as a knight sworn to annihilating evil.

We have in mind adders. Borkuny abounded in them, so bold they came crawling right up to the front porch, even inside the house—Romuald had once jumped one under his bed. They had two habitats. By the trail leading down to the stream was a small copse of birch, thickly wooded and carpeted with dry leaves. The leafy bed provided excellent cover; once inside, there was no finding them. The trail was their sunning terrace, and most likely the route they used when they went out hunting for field mice. Their second city was on a strip of swamp, where they sequestered themselves in the mossy islands under the pine scrub. To get at these, Thomas had to slip into Romuald's long boots and venture into enemy territory, his heart clutching as he passed the mossy clumps that stood nearly face-high.

The adder, taxonomically known as *Vipera berus*, se-

creted a poison inflicting serious illness and sometimes death. The most popular cures against snakebite were incantations, cauterizing the wound with a red-hot iron, and alcohol consumed to the point of delirium, preferably all three at once. The Borkuny adders were gray in color, with a black wavy stripe down the back, though the woodland was inhabited by others, smaller in length, distinguishable by their tawny color and their dark-brown, zigzag stripe. Romuald explained how, instead of depositing her eggs like other reptiles, the adder bore her young suspended from a branch, her head poised and ready to devour her offspring, but how with their born sinuosity they always escaped into the grass in time. Although not tree climbers by nature, they were known to attack people from trees—one girl was bitten in the face while picking nuts. They were a real scourge in Borkuny, so it was not surprising that Thomas aspired to the role of exterminator.

From Romuald he heard talk of other snakes. Some twenty kilometers away, deep in the forest, stretched huge quagmires inaccessible to man (the snakes infesting them were enough of a deterrent). Black-bodied, with a red head, they were the first to attack, without warning, always going for the face or hands. Death came instantly, before one could gasp "Holy Jesus!" Thomas felt drawn to the place—if only to know what animals could survive out there. They say it was the favorite refuge of the elk when stalked.

When the weather turned hot, Romuald used to sleep in the barn, not to escape the heat so much—the house was amply shaded by shrubbery—as for the love of it, for the abundance of fresh air. It took Thomas a while, several nights of itching and scratching, before he got used to all the gnats and little bugs. To make up for it, there was the fragrance of newly mown hay, which quickly made him sleepy. And the mornings! To wake to a bright babble of birds, first invading his sleep, then growing stronger, the

sun blazing through shingles alive with the scratching of tiny claws, the flutter of feathers . . . And the guessing game: just swallows, he would wonder, or something bigger like . . . wild pigeons? Then up early in the morning and off to the well with Romuald. Ahead of him: the joy of a long summer day. After a breakfast of whole-meal bread washed down with fresh milk, after the pulling on of boots (for precaution's sake), he was ready, hazel stick in hand, for the hunt.

Snake hunting was an art, requiring a stealthy approach to keep the prey, once surprised, from slithering away into the birch wood. Usually he caught sight of a few from a distance—lying like stretched-out whips, sunning themselves—then it was attack, on the run, banging with the stick, aiming always for the head, their bodies leaping, twisting, squirming, straining for the salvation of the brush, and he trying to cut off their retreat. With another stick—forked at one end, a small branch wedged in the fork—he would bear down on the snake's head, then slip out the branch. Pronged thus, the snake was borne back to the house, writhing in contortions: snakes were known for their endurance. The snake was then hung out to dry on the same stick. The dried ones were greatly in demand as a remedy against various cow ailments, especially among the river dwellers, the adder not being indigenous to that region.

Hunting in the swamp, where every bilberry or rosemary bush might conceal a adder, required even greater stealth—and skill, because the soft mossy matting cushioned every blow of the stick. Later (not that summer, but the next), out alone with the shotgun, he jumped a snake coiled some eight feet away from where he stood. He fired a barrel and the strangest thing happened: the snake vanished into thin air, the more astonishing since, at close range, the buckshot barely scatters.

Thomas's war with the adders did not imply that he

was free from prejudice, from the hideous shuddering sensation provoked by that unpredictable display of energy. The ripple of energy convulsing their cordlike bodies, the slimy crenulation lining their underbellies, the vertical slant of pupil—what a strange aberration of the animal kingdom! If it was true that birds were paralyzed by something inherent in their advance, then it was easy to understand, for their power seemed to reside outside them, as if they were merely an appendage, an instrument of something else.

Next spring, in the woodland surrounding Borkuny, Thomas was privileged to witness a rare spectacle: the mating ritual of adders. He was stopped in his tracks not by the observation of anything in particular. No, it was more like a vibration, an electrical discharge, a dance of lightning streaks on the ground. By the time he realized what it was, they were gone.

That summer, the first summer of his friendship with Romuald, he became adept at more than just snake hunting. He was granted—under Romuald's supervision, of course—the privilege of firing the double-barreled shotgun. First at the side of the barn—to get accustomed to the gun's kick—then at a live target. A screeching jay, a silencing finger, a sneaking up on tiptoes. Young and reckless, the bird, instead of taking cover, had perched on an exposed branch. A shot. Thomas came on the run, yelling. But as he picked it up by the feet, as the wings unfurled and a drop of blood beaded the jay's beak, he experienced a letdown he was not eager to acknowledge. But one had to be manly, to stifle any squeamishness, if one was to earn the title of hunter and naturalist.

Soon he was initiated into the hunter's workshop. He weighed out the shot with a metal gauge whenever Romuald made cartridges, and cleaned the barrels with steel wool soaked in oil so that they took on a mirrorlike sheen when peered through—as through binoculars—

under the light. He mastered, too, the art of skinning birds.

The chickens were forever being menaced by goshawks, whose attacks were signaled by Barbarka's frantic cries of "A bird! A bird!" (her description for any flying predator). One hawk, after being chased away, retreated as far as the nearest alder, there to survey the yard: he was soon a dead hawk. On him, Thomas served his apprenticeship. First came the incision down the middle, over breast and belly; then the skin was separated from the sides, a penknife serving to part the tissue joining skin and flesh. So far, so good; the real challenge came first with the tail (the tail feathers had to be left intact), followed by the legs (the claws had to be peeled off together with the skin). Once these obstacles were overcome, the skin was slipped off like a stocking, the tiny skull emptied of eyes and brain —a painstaking operation because one slip of the knife, one jerky move, and the delicate eyelids were ruined. After it was rubbed with ash and stuffed with oakum, the skin was left to dry. Wire and glass eyes were needed to stuff the bird in a sitting position.

The first time Thomas was a spectator to the sort of cunning exercised by men in the stalking of wild game was when he came to Borkuny for a few days to help with the mushroom picking. Mild mornings, pale blue skies, patches of cold dew and early frost blanketing the grass. In the pine grove, the one adjacent to the house, there were enough saffron milk cups in the moss flooring to fill baskets. Romuald stood nearby, a basket draped over one arm, his other hand clutching his gun strap; and in the pocket of his dolman, a little bone birdcall on a string— "Never can tell," he said, "it might come in handy." Birdcalls were carved usually from an owl's wing, sometimes from rabbit bone, the latter being less pure in tone. The bone one was good at imitating the trill of a hazel grouse, otherwise indistinguishable from the bark of the pine, its favorite sanctuary in times of danger. At a given signal,

Thomas held perfectly still, his jackknife poised against a mushroom stem, while a tremulous whistle pierced the silence of falling pine needles. Slowly, noiselessly, they slipped into the shadowy undergrowth. Again Romuald put the birdcall to his lips; he blew softly, knowingly, his fingers playing on the pipe's holes. Silence. Thomas was afraid his pounding heart would give them away. Then a reply—a hazel grouse, and another, closer. A feathery flurry, and there, dead ahead of them in the auburn lighting, silhouetted on a spruce branch, Thomas discerned a shadow pivoting its head, searching for its companion. Then an upward shifting of the arm, but so quick the shot and the report seemed to coincide; and when the smoke had cleared (when it came to gunpowder, Romuald swore only by the smoking, rather than nonsmoking kind), the hazel grouse lay lifeless under a tree, scarcely distinguishable from the bedding of dry needles.

Romuald was worthy of being admitted to the Kingdom to which normal mortals were denied access. Was worthy because the presence of wild animals excited him, made his cheek muscles quiver, made him vigilance personified, wholly oblivious to everything else. His housekeeper, Barbarka, on the other hand, belonged to the world of grownups, the more regrettable because she was so pretty, so childlike in appearance. It pained him to think there were actually people who went about blind to the things that mattered most. How bored they must be. To be fair, Barbarka spent much of her time tending the flower garden—and what exquisite flowers they were; whole beds of fragrant reseda, giant mallows, and rue, which she knew how to keep green all winter long, pinning it in her hair, like the other girls, before going to church. But that lambent stare of hers, so full of curiosity and scrutiny and ulterior motive . . . No, that bespoke something foreign, grown-up. Oh, Thomas had long forgiven her the insult, shamming indifference ever since; yet it needled him, that condescend-

ing way of hers, the way she had of making everything he
touched—like cleaning rifle barrels—seem frivolous. If, just
once, he could have elicited from her some sign of admir-
ation, of respect . . . But no; to his trophies borne back from
his snake-hunting she reacted with a disgusted "Phooey!"
screwing up the corners of her mouth in a kind of sneer, as
if the whole enterprise bordered on the indecent.

35

ROMUALD HAD four dogs: three hounds and
a pointer. Zagray, smoky-hued, with yellow brows,
bayed in a deep bass. Full grown, he was prized for his
tenacity and endurance, virtues compensating for a sense
of smell barely above average. Losing the scent, he never
moiled aimlessly about, but moved in circles, deliberately,
according to a plan. Dunay, a tenor, a dead ringer for the
other, only leaner, was a dreamer, hence lacking in any
aura of respect. One day deserving of praise and the next
day worthless, he let his devotion be dictated by his mood,
often only faking fickleness, as if to say: "I can bay with
the best of them, but let the others track today—I have a
headache." The dog combining a great heart with an infal-
lible sense of smell was the yellow bitch Lutnia, descended
from a race of Kostroma bloodhounds. Her pure gold eyes
flashing violet-blue, she braced her handsome paws affec-
tionately on Romuald's chest when she licked his face. The
threesome was kept chained up for summer, because once
unleashed they were apt to stage their own hunt, running
the game between them. Gossamer on the trails promised
liberation, though for the pointer, Karo, autumn was a time

for meditation by the stove, a time for sticking one's nose under one's tail and taking stock of one's smell.

All week long, Thomas counted the days until Sunday. On Saturday, he rode out with his aunt, who headed back the same evening, leaving Thomas to spend the night at Borkuny. Tense with excitement, he twisted and turned, kicked off his covers, and kept being prickled by the straw, but he soon fell into a deep sleep, warmed by the weight of his sheepskin coat, which someone had draped over him. He was awakened in the dark, around dawn, by a rapping on the window. Two faces, those of Denis and Victor, were flattened against the pane. They came inside, yawning. A groggy Barbarka, her uncombed hair spilling down over her shoulders, brought in a lantern with a smudged chimney, got a fire going in the kitchen, and rustled up some potato pancakes. Through the fog outside came the sound of thick drops dripping from the branches brushing the porch.

The brothers each drank one round at breakfast. "Bagaga, go gus go gnee," Victor insisted, which translated as "Barbarka, show us your knee"—a sign of hunter's good luck—to which the housekeeper responded with a thumbed nose. The dogs went wild on their leashes. Thomas was given charge of Dunay, and had to strain backward with all his might to keep him from breaking into a trot. They took the trail down to the stream, filed across the footbridge, and stepped onto the preserve. The forester was Romuald's friend and let him—with one eye closed—do a fair amount of poaching.

An immense silence. The morning fog had begun to lift, and with the lifting emerged a forest floor rank with wet grass and laced with russet-matted trails. Romuald's horn echoed far and wide, his cheeks swelling and his eyes reddening from exertion. With effort, if he worked at it, Thomas could get it to make sounds, but never anything like a tune.

Autumnal smells, the origin of which, the blendings of which lay beyond his or any other man's power to describe: the rot of leaves and needles; the dank effluvium of fungi and white filaments embedded in black, beneath the slime of decaying, peeling debris. They were surrounded by good hunting grounds. Glades broken up by brushlike rows of pine, a lane skirting the forest flank, with another, moss-covered, path-lined, diagonally across from it. Wild game was a slave to old habits. Flushed out of hiding, it tried to ward off its attackers by describing a circle, aiming for more familiar trails and crossings, its direction betrayed by the baying of the hounds. A hunter had only to guess the right crossing and be there in time. Distracted by the dogs at its back, unsuspecting of any danger ahead, it would then charge straight into his sights.

Thomas was not carrying a gun; he was there as a lowly apprentice. His instructions were to stay close to Romuald. The moment they were unleashed, the whining dogs bolted into the brush. Zagray reemerged once, nose to the ground, and moiled about with an inquisitive look. "Denis, you take the lane," said Romuald. "Vick, you get up to Red Meadow. Tommy and I'll stay here." The men receded into the distance, the gun barrels strapped to their shoulders slowly fading behind the trees. "Watch Lutnia flush 'im," Romuald predicted.

A woodpecker racket overhead, a scraping against bark. Suddenly, from far off, a dog's voice, thin and high-pitched. *"Aï, aï!"* "Didn't I tell you? Lutnia!" A lull. Then once again: *"Aï, aï!"* "She's picked it up, but it's a weak 'un, she's gonter have to work at it." It was then that Thomas, for the first time in his life, heard the music of the hounds. To the steady *"Arf, arf, arf, arf,"* was joined another voice. "Dunay!" Romuald shouted, shifting gun from shoulder. Zagray's powerful bass came at long intervals now. Thomas was amazed that such music could come from the throats of dogs, a choir muffled by distance, re-

verberating deep within the forest. "They jumped a hare. But he won't come out here. Come on, Tommy—run!" and Thomas chased after Romuald, at first keeping up with him, then falling back, panting his lungs out. They branched off from the lane, maneuvered through the hazel, dropped down into a ravine, and scrambled up a bank. "There—" Romuald pointed out Thomas's stand, a young spruce, as, taut of neck, shotgun in hand, he himself waited motionlessly out in the middle. The ridge, brown with needles, tapered down into a green gully, commanding a perfect view of it, along with a tawny strip framed by forest walls. The baying rose to the left of them, full of desire and courage and wildness—and then abated. *"Aï, aï,"* Lutnia wailed, still trying to pick up the scent.

Nothing coming their way . . . Wait—there it was! It looked mammoth, almost red against the green, as it slipped into the pocket opposite them. With mouth agape, glad in that instant to be without a gun, Thomas was gripped by hunter's fever as the animal, growing in stature, advanced; with eyes transfixed, his mouth still wide open, he was jolted by a shot. The hare went straight up, twisted in the air, and then it was over except for a convulsive twitching of the paws. Thomas was the first to get there. His gun back on his shoulder, Romuald strode up leisurely, grinning all the way. But the dogs had beaten him to it. Dunay looked up at the boy with a mouth full of fur. Romuald took out his knife, sliced off the hind paws, and tossed them to the hounds, giving Dunay a pat or two of approval; then he lit up. "That Dunay! He'd eat the wounded ones alive."

Thomas tried to get Romuald to explain how he knew where to get into position. Romuald laughed. "Got to play it smart. If they jumped him over there"—he pointed to the hazel ravine—"and he came back around this way"— he pointed to the left—"then he had to come out here. He'll always backtrack to where he lives."

He called in Denis and Victor with the horn, and he and the boy sat down on a couple of stumps. A pale November sun was burning a path through the mist. Thomas was curious to know what other game they were likely to meet.

"A buck. A fox maybe, but don't count on it. Got too much sense, a fox has."

As soon as the others came out of the brush, parting the damp pine branches, they held council, then moved out along the ridge, winding through the terraced, steplike trails braced by rocks. As they were making their way, leisurely, shooting the breeze, the dogs let out a powerful wail full of wounded pride. *"Aï, aï . . ."* They went for their guns. "They got it on the run," Denis yelled. Just then Thomas saw a hare's tail flit across the slope, the elongated shapes of the dogs right behind it. "Out of range!" Romuald said. "No sense runnin' now." And he told of some hunters who, seeing their dogs were so far out they were no longer within earshot, spread out under a tree for a game of cards, and of how the hare came bounding right down the middle, scattering their hands. The anecdote made Thomas indignant, as it bespoke an irreverent attitude toward the best, the most essential of tasks. He was gnawed by a suspicion, not without foundation, that for some people hunting meant not much more than vodka and cards, that it was just another idle pastime.

The ferocious whining subsided to a normal baying. The men spread out on the stands, taking their time about it, and the screeching of jays testified to the intrusion. Thomas had his gaze fixed to the line made by the trail in front of him, when a couple of shots rang out, echoing in the trees' whispering murmur. "Denis"—Thomas surmised. Two shots meant a double-barrel, and Victor was toting a single-barreled Berdan.

Around a bend in the trail, from behind some trunks, loomed a spectacle in miniature: Denis, a hare at his feet,

surrounded by moiling dogs. It was evident, from Romuald's gentle needling, that Denis's first shot had gone wide, that he'd hit it only on the second. Romuald pulled out a felt-covered flask, jokingly offered Thomas a swig, who declined, secretly wondering whether the liquid stuff was befitting the honor of Romuald the Magnificent.

"Aw, Tommy, those shoes of yours are goners." As a matter of fact, the shoes he had on—they happened to be his Sunday shoes—were not the best for hiking in the wet grass. Now that he was almost initiated, he was entitled to wear boots, the long-shanked kind, preferably a pair that laced all the way up to the knees, if there was no chance of his owning a pair like Denis's hip boots. The one person likely to be moved by such a request was Grandpa, as neither his grandmother nor his aunt would be very sympathetic—for reasons of frugality alone.

36

GRANDFATHER, having never really explored the library before now—before his grandson began rifling the bookshelves—browsed through the tomes of Narbutt's *The History of Lithuania*. On the advice of his grandfather, Thomas brought the volumes over to Joseph the Black's place, whence they passed into the hands of Father Monkiewicz. No doubt both, each according to his interests, were rewarded for their efforts. The pastor gruffly cleared his throat and sat up in his chair as he read of the sheer abundance of gods and goddesses once worshipped in the land; of the familiar superstitions at whose extirpa-

tion he had so diligently worked. There was no telling how injurious such books could be to the soul. A person might close the book, take off his glasses, and turn to other tasks, when suddenly, out of nowhere, the image of Ragutis sprang to mind, as vividly as if freshly unearthed from forest sands—Ragutis, that corpulent idol of liquor and lusty living, hewn from oak, leering mischievously, his giant feet clad in clogs, standing there unsupported in all his assiduously carved indecency—*in naturalibus.* And once conceived, there was no getting rid of him.

Some chapters like those dealing with the goddess Liethua, guardian protector of freedom, compared by the author to Freya of the Scandinavians, seemed expressly written for Joseph. But not a trace, not a single grain of dust remained of Lejčis, impaled or hung by the lords, even though independence had, centuries later, been restored to his native land. Nor would any trace remain, if not for a name mentioned in a scrap of parchment, a royal charter dating from A.D. 1483. By said charter, the nobleman Rynwid had been granted land "in reward for suppressing an insurrection of serfs claiming more freedom than that accorded them by law, and for taking captive their leader, the one called Lejčis, who, in wanton disregard for the royal majesty and sovereignty, did brazenly flout the King in the name of Liethua's pagan freedom."

In 1805, the historian Narbutt, a nobleman like Rynwid and Surkont, gave his timepiece to a man who, at a country fair, aroused his curiosity by reciting for him the words of an ancient dirge addressed to the goddess Liethua. "Little Liethua," it ran, "precious freedom! Hidden in the sky, where are you? Is death our only refuge? Wherever a poor man turns—to the east or to the west— naught but misery, duress, and slavery. The great earth is flooded with sweat, with the blood of wounds. Little Liethua, precious freedom, step down from heaven, take

pity on us." Clearly, this was music for Joseph's ears. And so, brooking no quarter, they went on debating the merits of that book in a room at the rectory, to the ticking of a clock and in full view of the dahlias spying through the window. The dahlias were from a lovely garden planted once upon a time by Magdalena, a garden now sorely in need of pruning.

One autumnal afternoon, Joseph, less given to nostalgia since becoming privy to certain libelous facts in the town, was reciting the litany of his grievances while the pastor, his arms folded on his paunch, his eyes half shut, sat and listened. There was nothing remarkable or unusual in this recitation, which belonged to the ritual of their regular confabulations, but this time Joseph was assailed by doubts, these having to do with the manner of reprisal.

Joseph finished calculating the acreage of Surkont's farmland and briefed him on what he had heard in the town. If the man considered to be a model of virtue was not above such trickery, well, that was worth at least a shrug. "What's he need it for? He can't take it with him to the grave, can he? And if they all find loopholes, who'll get the land? Don't they see their days are over? The Latvians were wise in leaving them only a hundred acres."

The priest muttered that it was not the number of acres as much as the corruption, the way officials kowtowed to the rich. Joseph: It's up to the villages to decide whose and how much land to confiscate. The priest: That would be to invite anarchy. Maybe so, but *something* had to be done.

Joseph could not condone the practice of informing, nor any other method that might have gone by a different name but which amounted to the same thing in the end—and if, then only as a last resort. So the choice was between sinning through indifference and doing one's duty, however bad the consequences. Nor could one ignore the

effects on the next of kin. But, then, there was no talk of confiscating the whole estate, much less of killing or jailing him; he would just own a little less, that was all.

This being the general gist of his words, Joseph asked the priest for his opinion.

Father Monkiewicz reflected, stroked his bald patch, then hit on a solution. "Didn't Surkont promise to donate some lumber for the school?"

"He did, but not until the first frost."

"If he and the other farm owners live up to their promise, how much wood will you still be short?"

"Thirty cords, more or less."

"Hm . . ."

It was a "hm" rife with implications. Such a solution had never occurred to Joseph, and he was quick to seize on it. He had only to sit down with Surkont, insinuate that he was wise to him, make him see that he was cornered. That would put the old man in a bargaining mood, force him to make certain concessions, and the thirty cords would be as good as delivered.

He asked no more questions, and they moved on to politics; that is, to the age-old debate of whether, given the choice of siding with the Poles against the Knights, or with the Knights against the Poles, the Grand Duke could have saved the country. A controversy not without relevance when one stopped to ponder the consequences of the first alternative. Take only the case of Misia, who would have died rather than admit to being a Lithuanian. Or Grandfather Surkont and the thousands of others like him. Such were the ripples of history, still spreading outward centuries later.

"Any news of the boy's father?" asked the priest.

"What's there to report? He's not coming back. And if he does, he's sure to land in prison for serving in their army. No, he'll settle there and send for the boy."

The priest sighed. "They're ashamed of belonging to such a small country. They're too in love with culture, big cities. But Narbutt wasn't ashamed—except that in those days people didn't think of their nationality the way we do . . ."

"People are crazy, if you ask me."

The priest shook his head. "Things are so mixed up today. Old lady Dilbin, Thomas's grandmother, now she's a German by descent. But in Prussia you find both Polish and Lithuanian names, and yet they're Germans. As long as it doesn't spell disaster."

Several months passed before Joseph returned Narbutt's *History*, the discussions prompted by it leaving nary a trace, neither on the leather binding nor in any of the margins of its stiff pages. Restored to its bookcase, the work was again left at the mercy of creeping mildew, to the scurrying of insects that exult in inhabiting dank and dark places.

Joseph never did sit Surkont down and offer him silence in exchange for the lumber, though he long entertained such a notion. It had not been an easy decision: at one end of the scale was the school, a more immediate goal; at the other, the principle of the thing, that and the welfare of the cottagers, who stood to benefit most from the redistribution. Principle had prevailed. Not that this had prescribed the proper course of action. The first course: to tell Surkont right to his face and threaten exposing him to the authorities, because what was wrong was wrong. All-out war, in other words. The second: to stool on him. And the third: to wait and see what came of all the sleight-of-hand maneuvering. This last course was most to his liking, since haste was the enemy of reason and patience had a way of rectifying many wrongs.

37

THOMAS HAD a kingdom all his own—a
paper kingdom, admittedly, but one that could be assem-
bled and reassembled at will. The inspiration for it came
from the rolls of paper which Grandfather and Aunt Helen
(now a frequent visitor at the manor) periodically un-
rolled on the table—sheets embellished with watercolor
designs, rectangles of all sizes, and boundary lines making
up the property map of Gine. The bright, smoothly ex-
ecuted color planes showed through the paper.

Thomas's kingdom, ringed by quagmires inhabited by
the red-hooded snake, was absolutely impenetrable. Orig-
inally, it was to have been entirely forest, but on second
thought he decided to relieve the landscape with meadows
painted a bright green. No roads cut through the forest—
how could a virgin forest be traversed by a road?—leaving
the riverways, laced with blue strips of canals, and lakes as
the only arteries. Those who were allowed access—by spe-
cial invitation, of course—entered by way of secret pas-
sages marked through the swamps. All the kingdom's
inhabitants—a handful at most, the land being primarily at
the disposal of such animals as the bison, the elk, and the
bear—lived exclusively off the land.

The arrival of the autumnal chill deprived him of his
table, which was shifted to the wing from that part of the
house closed off for the winter. But the various family
conferences held around the table, where people huddled
over maps and the word "reform" was a constant refrain,
coupled with the anxiety aroused by Aunt Helen's nosy
intrusions, soon forced him to transfer his mapmaking and

other activities to a little table in Grandmother Dilbin's room. There he was not disturbed by anyone, least of all by his grandmother, who was mostly bedridden, though he had to pay the price of being made a captive of her incessant bellyaching: she was neglected, alone among strangers, wasting away in some godforsaken hole, never to see her sons again . . . Nor did she spare the Lithuanians for their black ingratitude. Just let Constantine and Theodore and the Polish army stop fighting the Bolsheviks—ha, then they'd see what was left of their Lithuania! And how had they been rewarded, Thomas's father and uncle? By being denied a few days' furlough in their native land, like a couple of common criminals! Their letters reached them by way of Latvia—late, naturally—all personal correspondence being banned between Poland and Lithuania. The song-and-dance routines that went into getting those letters! The cunning she had used in getting someone to ride to the post office if she had no way of going to town herself. Nor was she above shamming some fatal illness to have Dr. Kohn summoned to the house, no matter how miserable the weather. And later, her eyes blinking and her cheeks burning, he watched her fingers tremble as they tore open the letters.

Thomas was unable to take her seriously, he paid little attention to her whining, being somehow rankled by her constant brooding over Constantine—the "black sheep," as Grandmother Misia and his aunt used to call him. Fresh out of Officers' Training School, Constantine was now a career officer, a lieutenant in a Uhlan regiment, though no doubt he had enrolled under false pretenses, having completed only three years of the mandatory secondary education. Her exaltation of her son bordered on the comical, as did her imprecations at being stuck in Gine, at having to live off the charity of the Surkonts, the irregular meals, the lack of companionship, the way Antonina ruled the household . . . She even com-

plained about the homegrown tobacco, which Thomas took great pleasure in rolling and cutting—the cigarettes achieved a pleasing shape the moment the loose ends sticking out of the cartridge were trimmed with scissors—and neatly arranging for her in a little box. If he was attentive, it was only when she spoke of his mother, of how when she returned, Grandmother would take them both away, and how wonderful that would be.

Two or three days out of the week, Thomas traipsed into the village for his lessons with Joseph. He exerted himself especially at handwriting, the praise of his teacher being of greater consequence than the deprecation heaped on him by his grandmother and aunt. Joseph, sitting with his elbows propped on the table, his shoulders hunched together, the Adam's apple in his sinewy throat bobbing up and down, had a fixity about him, an aura of dependability. Perhaps this was what Thomas needed most—someone to say this was right and that was wrong, and knowing it had to be so.

Whenever they were visited by Lithuanians on official business, Grandmother Misia and Aunt Helen ran for cover: to show them too much hospitality would have been a breach of decorum, would have been to risk social opprobrium by associating with those yokels—one of their favorite epithets—masquerading as officials. Thomas used to watch through the half-open door as his grandfather, seemingly for the sake of diplomacy, drank just to whet their appetite. Later, Grandfather and the officials would ride out to the granary, where Pakenas loaded their britska with one or two sacks of oats for the horses.

The more frequent the visits, the more intense became the "business talks," from which not even Misia, rocking sideways in front of the tiled stove, remained aloof. It was "business," too, which sent Grandfather on frequent trips to the city. Before leaving, he cached some money and documents in a little canvas pouch, strung it around

his neck, and, just to be safe, pinned it to his warm under-shirt. Over this went a waistcoat and woolen jacket. A knotted cravat, looped with an elastic neckband, was then wedged between the corners of his stiff shirt collar. A watch chain spanned the pockets of his waistcoat.

Inspired by his trips to Borkuny, Thomas, after re-treating to his grandmother's room or, when he could bear her lamentations no more, to the dining-room lamp, began compiling a notebook, or rather a scrapbook, having the shape and feel of an actual book. Cutting sheets of paper to size, he glued the margins together and bound them with a cardboard cover inscribed with the word *Birds.* Anyone taking the liberty to pry (which no one ever did, not want-ing to risk Thomas's contempt, since confidentiality was the very heart and soul of the enterprise) would have found a series of headings, capitalized and underlined, fol-lowed by ornithological descriptions in small-case letters. Mastering his tendency to scribble—tongue out, pen la-boriously at work—was no small feat. But in the end his efforts were rewarded: the execution, as a whole, was flaw-less.

Take the section on woodpeckers. Naturally, the one that held him in the greatest thrall was the large, speckled woodpecker, frequently sighted in the park in winter. This large, redheaded woodpecker was a lone species, hence:

"The dappled woodpecker—*Picus leucotos L.*" And underneath: "Inhabits deciduous forests with lots of rot-ting trees and ancient coniferous forests. Winters near human habitations."

Or:

"The black woodpecker—*Picus martius L.* Largest of the woodpecker family. Black with a red patch on the head. Nests in pine or birch forests."

Thomas had spotted a black woodpecker at Borkuny —not close up, since it was impossible to view at close

range, but as it streaked among the birch trunks, its shrill
kri-kri-kri carrying.

He had no way of knowing, of course, that the *L.*, or
Latinized "Linni," was in honor of the Swedish naturalist
Linnaeus, the first bird taxonomist. Yet he scrupulously
guarded against allowing any discrepancies between other
taxonomies and his own, the Latin names appealing to him
because of their sonority: *Emberiza citrinella* for yellow-
hammer, *Turdus pilaris* for fieldfare, *Garrulus glandarius*
for jay, and so on. Some of the names were conspicuous
for their proliferation of letters, forcing his eyes to jump
continuously from his notebook to the antiquated orni-
thology at his elbow. Even the longer names, if repeated
often enough, acquired a pleasant lilt, one of them, that of
the common nutcracker, being absolutely magical: *Nuci-
fraga caryocatactes.*

The notebook proved that Thomas had the gift of
concentrating on things that excited him. To name a
bird, to cage it in letters, was tantamount to owning it
forever. The endless multiplicity of colors, shadings, mat-
ing calls, trills, wing sounds . . . Turning the pages, he had
them all before him, at his command, affecting and order-
ing the plenitude of things that were. In reality, everything
about birds gave rise to unease. Was it enough, he won-
dered, to verify their existence? The way the light modu-
lated their feathers in flight, the warm, yellow flesh lining
the bills of the young feeding in deeply sequestered nests,
suffused him with a feeling of communion. Yet, for many,
they were little more than a mobile decoration, scarcely
worthy of scrutiny, whereas, surrounded by such wonders
on earth, people should have consecrated their whole lives
to contemplating only one thing: felicity.

Such, roughly speaking, were Thomas's thoughts, and
neither the "Reform" nor any "business matters" could
compete, even though the passion aroused by their con-
stant iteration gave him pause: "Pogirai," "Balthazar,"

"the meadowland" . . . He was big enough and bright enough to grasp what was happening, but his heart just wasn't in it. He surely wished his grandfather luck, but he was decidedly not in favor of his holding council with Aunt Helen.

38

BALTHAZAR WAS gaining weight, the afflictions of the soul giving rise to this condition being sometimes more acute than those that cause a man to lose weight. When he first heard about the famous Rabbi of Šilelai, he had sneered, but his laughter soon hardened into fear: who was he to refuse help that might have been heaven-sent? He waited until the roads were fit for traveling by sleigh. Then the first snowfall turned to ice. Numb with cold, Balthazar stopped off at a pothouse, got stone drunk, and slept it off on a bench. Came morning, a hangover, back on the road, and telegraph poles—so stark and stiff they pained the eye—aswirl with billowing snow all the way to Šilelai. The Rabbi's house was sprawling, had a sagging wooden roof, and was situated a little below street level and fronted by a sloping yard. In the hallway he was immediately beset by three or four men—the whole place swarmed with men, both young and old. Where from, what brought him here? He dumped his whip in the corner, undid his sheepskin, dug into his pockets for some money, and counted out the amount he had been told was fitting. That done, he was whisked into a room where a bearded man in a skullcap sat facing him from behind a desk, inscribing something in a large book. He informed Balthazar that he was not the Rabbi but that he, Balthazar, was to lay

bare the reasons for his visit, and that he, the Rabbi's assistant, would convey them to the Rabbi, because that was how it was done. Balthazar balked. Gestures of confusion, a scratching of a scruffy forelock, a look of helplessness. He still believed, in spite of everything, in that ray of light, transfixing and illuminating him. But *speak*? The moment he opened his mouth, the mere sound of his voice would ring false, and how to find the words, how to unburden his soul before some stranger, a Jew, who never let up with his pen, and who even took his sweet time offering him a seat? Then Balthazar began to babble, and this babbling only made manifest that he was without a place to call his own, alive yet not alive, doomed without the counsel of a saintly man. The Jew put aside his pen and fingered his beard.

"You have a farm?" he asked. "A wife, children?" And: "Your sins, they make life difficult, no? What kind of sins? Big sins?"

Balthazar, though he would have been hard put to state whence his unease came—from sins, or fear, or something else—assented.

"You pray to God?" The Jew went on with the interrogation.

This last question gave him pause. If someone ached, he wanted to get better, and it was up to God to heal. But what if He wasn't in the mood? If He was too far out of reach? Balthazar went to church, so he nodded: yes, he prayed.

He later waited in the hallway, his back against the wall, a bystander to all the comings and goings, to the continual shaking of snow from boots. Soon the pandemonium swelled, thickening with incomprehensible palaver and frantic gesticulations. Suddenly a shriek from the back, a stampede into the reception room—the same one —an opening of doors, a squeezing of bodies; and Balthazar, caught up in the crush, was flung into a long chamber

converging toward a black table at the far end. Over the clamor and commotion and wild vociferations came a commanding "Shh!" which was taken up by one and all: "Shh! Shh!"

The Rabbi, trailed by his bearded secretary, entered through a side door. An elfin figure with girlish features—a double for St. Catherine's face in the picture that hung in the church in Gine. His cheeks were adorned with fleecy blond curls; his apparel, dark and somber. The collar stud of his undershirt glinted underneath and his head was covered by a silken skullcap. Demure of mien, eyes downcast. The moment his assistant motioned for Balthazar to come forward, the eyelids rose, the gaze turned piercing. He fixed him with a long stare, cocked his head, and stroked the lapel of his frock coat. In the Rabbi's presence, Balthazar felt the full weight of his impotent mass.

His eyes still fixed on Balthazar, the Rabbi uttered a few words in their language, unleashing a fury of whispers, a rocking and reeling at Balthazar's back, until they were silenced with a "Shh! Shh!"

"He says, 'No—man—is—good,'" the Rabbi's secretary translated into Lithuanian.

The Rabbi's voice again purled softly behind the table.

"He says, 'Whatever—wrong—you—have—committed—man—that—and—only—that—is—your—fate.'"

Balthazar felt a surging at his back as he attended, in a shushing silence fraught with expectation, to the bearded man's words.

"He says, 'Do—not—curse—your—fate—man—for—whoever—thinks—he—has—another—and—not—his—own—is—lost—and—will—be—damned—forever. Think—not—of—the—life—that—might—have—been—for—such—a—life—would—not—have—been—yours.'" He stopped speaking.

Balthazar knew that the audience was over; someone else stood before the Rabbi and his words were now addressed to him. Jostling his way through the crowd, Bal-

thazar stormed out of the house in a rage. Was this what he had traveled twenty kilometers through the freezing cold for? Damn these Jews. And damn his own gullibility. But by the time his boot was slung over the lower crossbar and furrowing a groove through the white, anger had given way to disappointment. An hour-long sermon or a few words—what was the difference? It was the emptiness of it all, the absence that made a man want to howl: no angels' trumpets, no fiery tongues, no swords forked like fangs . . . All right, he was homeward bound, a livid blue forest in the distance, clouds overhead . . . What else was there to say? He had been born, he would die, and he would have to bear his burden. Priest or rabbi—it was the same old rigmarole, never getting to the heart of it . . . Now, if a giant head were to peer out from behind the horizon and huff and puff and suck up everything in one furious rush of air . . . But nothing doing. So why should he be sore at the Jew? He was just a man, no better and no worse . . . But show me the man who *could* do something. A man could have his guts torn apart, could ache like hell, and here they'd come, preaching their words of comfort, blah-blah-blah, the same with all their machines, inventions . . . But they didn't know anything except "he was born and he died."

Gradually he was willing to admit to having gained some wisdom at Šilelai. The Rabbi's first utterance had even filled him with hope. Maybe everybody was troubled and repentant but was afraid to admit it. Wouldn't it be easier if people confessed to one another? No man is good? What about those with small sins? Was it enough to be without sin? Ooo, that Jew wasn't so dumb . . .

He took off his gloves and rolled a cigarette. The horse moved briskly along, the harness bells tinkled in the emptiness of space. A hare sprang out from behind a bed of willows, bounded along a frozen brook. Dusk fell, overtaking him in the forest, but not so abruptly that his eyes

couldn't make out the notches on the pine trunks. Trees marked for cutting. He had read about the big government sale to England. There was a pine with no notch. Too crooked. It had a good straight trunk before lurching to one side and shooting up like a ship's mast. Maybe that was the sort of fate the Rabbi had in mind. A pine couldn't start over; it had to start from what it was, what it had become, bent and all. Then it could grow tall and straight. No more than a man could start again from scratch.

He bore down with the whip, somehow unconsoled. A man was not a tree; a tree knew at least what it had to have—light. The trouble is, you think you're growing straight, but you're not. Life going one way, and you going back and forth, trying to change it. Straight as a bullet, you think; not until it's too late do you see it's not climbing straight but curving. So much for that Jewish wisdom of theirs.

Firmly resolved not to stop along the way, Balthazar began pulling on the reins as soon as he saw snowy clumps sparkling in the light of the tavern windows. The horses hitched to the corner of the building worked their feed bags up and down, their harness bells tinkling with every toss of the head. No one's fate but his own. So be it. He clutched the door handle. Did he go inside? He went inside.

39

IF ONE accepted the thesis that the preference shown by devils for frock coats and knee stockings was an expression of their eighteenth-century sympathies, then the Land Reform, that taking of land from some and

the giving of it to others, must have lain beyond the com-
pass of their expertise. The devil having custody of Bal-
thazar—a crow circling a wounded rabbit—must have felt
duty-bound to take inventory. The demands of accuracy,
therefore, compel us to give an exact rendering.

An inventory of Surkont's landholdings would have
looked as follows:

Arable land	271.2 acres
Pasturage along the Issa, fallow land, etc.	19.7 "
Disputed pasturage adjoining Pogirai	75.0 "
Timberland, grassland, and land cleared by Balthazar	105.0 "
Total	470.9 "

The newly instituted Land Reform meant that all
lands in excess of 200 acres were to be distributed among
the landless peasants—at a rate of indemnity so low as to
be almost negligible. Surkont—or rather his daughter,
mindful of her own interests—had found a loophole:
under the law, farm properties could be divided among
family members, up to 200 acres per household head, pro-
vided the estates were independently managed and sup-
ported structures. Surkont decided to pacify the govern-
ment with the seventy-five acres of disputed land, dividing
the remaining 395.9 acres between Helen and himself. But
what about the deadline? The statute expressly prohibited
any land divisions after the stipulated deadline. One need
only solicit the cooperation of certain civil servants, not
immune to blandishments of one sort or another, to have
an older title "mistakenly" recorded in the books. And
soliciting it he was.

There was one hitch: the forest. Under the terms of
the Reform, all timberland was to become state property.
So what did Surkont do? He had the forest land recorded
as grassland. It all depended on how the assessors looked

at it, on whether they kept their eyes to the ground or glanced up at the unusual blades of grass. Not much was left of the oak forest, anyway—a few dark-shaded groves of young hornbeam, a sprinkling of fir saplings, and a lot of swamp clearings. Still, the land bordered on a state for est, stretching dozens of kilometers, and that made it all the riskier . . .

Two farms: his own and Helen's. But if another farm —where? It was Balthazar who, quite unexpectedly, came to their assistance. In indulging Balthazar his lifelong dream, Surkont was guided less by self-interest than by a weakness for the boy—Balthazar, whether at thirty or forty, was still boyish-looking. The forester's cottage would be the loophole.

This, in outline, was the situation and the principal strategy. The best beer, along with that aromatic home-made brew laced with nine varieties of forest herbs, now graced Balthazar's table every time Helen Juchniewicz came to call. But Balthazar knew her well enough to keep a vigilant eye on her, all the while grinning that good-natured smile of his. Coyly, in her own sweet way, she was prying—into the barn, the crib. Women of her kind were the trickiest to handle.

There are those who believe the devil to be nothing more than a hallucination, a manifestation of inner tur-moil. If that is so, then the world must appear to them an even more incomprehensible place, since hallucinations are the province of humans. Even if we were to grant, for the sake of argument, that the affectionate little creature promenading about the table, jauntily sidestepping the streaks of brew described by Balthazar's finger, owed its existence to an alcoholic stupor, what would that prove?

There were days when the old gaiety returned, when a whistling Balthazar came up behind the plow—when suddenly a wrenching of the gut announced some immi-nent terror. It was always like this: one, two steps out of

bounds, and some external force was there to repel him, drive him back. Yes, external: the pain he felt was not, could not have been a part of himself; deep down, he was still the same happy-go-lucky Balthazar; whatever had him on the run was attacking from the outside. And the terror came from the certitude that it was not his own doing, that it was not he who was summoning a subtlety of reasoning in times of despair, but it was the work of an otherworldly clairvoyance. Even his foolishness was a part of the jinx, and his tormentor knew how to make the most of it.

"So there you have it, Balthazar," he said. "One life. Millions of people with millions of worries. And you? Surkont, Helen Juchniewicz, the property, that shooting accident . . . A drop in the bucket. Why you? You could have landed anywhere, like a falling star. But you had to land here. And you won't be born a second time."

"The Rabbi was speaking the truth."

"The truth? Look at you, you're chewing your knuckles over that Juchniewicz woman; you're worried sick she's going to chuck you out . . . and you're worried just because you're so worried. If only you could accept your fate—but you can't. The Rabbi, though, he had you pegged. A wise and experienced man, that Rabbi. But, then, were you really so hard to figure out? The dirty Balthazar feels sorry for the clean Balthazar. Only there's no such person."

His fingers dug into the table. Oh, he was just aching to swing away, to tear the place apart, to become fire or stone!

"Okay, so knock the table over. Then what? That's not what you really want; you've got questions. Go ahead —ask them, get it off your chest. You drink it away; it takes your mind off things—but only for so long, for as long as the stuff burns your throat. Do you want to know, or don't you?"

Balthazar slumped down onto the table, both elbows

spread out wide, at the mercy of some weak but predacious weasel.

"If you've done something, was it because you couldn't do otherwise? That's what's hounding you, isn't it? I am what I am because of what I did. At such and such a time, in such and such a way. But why did I act that way? Was it because I was always what I am now? Is that it?"

In the presence scrutinizing him from afar, assuming a multitude of faces yet itself remaining constant, he assented.

"What are you moping about? That you're bad seed? That a stalk of wheat didn't sprout from nettles?"

"That must be it."

"Take an oak. Any oak in the forest. You look at it standing there, and what do you think? That it's where it ought to be, that place and no other. Right?"

"Right."

"But supposing the acorn was dug up and eaten by a wild pig. Would you still look down at the ground and say an oak tree belonged there?"

Balthazar played with the loose strands of his unruly hair, winding them around his finger.

"No. Why not? Because once a thing is, it's like it had to be that way always, always and forever. Same as with a man. Later you'll swear you just couldn't have gone into town to squeal on him . . ."

"I won't turn informer."

"The good Balthazar loves Surkont. Not really, you're just scared it could backfire—you know he's been greasing their palms—he might find out, and leave you at the mercy of his daughter . . . And you're scared that if you win, they'll annex the forest. Okay, they might make you a forester, but they're bound to ask, 'Why so much land, Balthazar?' Don't try to lie. And don't think cursing your fate will get you off the hook."

"I never know why I do anything. Not even why I sent the matchmakers that time. Or that Russian. I didn't have to kill him; I could have given him a good scare. Can't remember why."

"Ahhh . . . !"

Balthazar's cry was the cry that wells up from inside and that nothing can ever suppress or overcome or contend with. And the crime of it is, we go on tearing leaves from the calendar, pulling on our boots, testing our arm muscles, living . . . And that gnawing recollection of past deeds, but without recollection of the reasons. Either these deeds are ours, issuing from our very being, immutable, signifying a sickening burden, a stench in the skin, or they are the work of some masked perpetrator, the more terrifying since that means they are beyond getting rid of, that they are part of a hideous malediction.

Balthazar foresaw that Surkont would succeed. Out of fatigue, distrusting his own nature and all those subterranean forces impersonating us, he chose apathy. Inertia gave fewer causes for regret later on. If his own life had gone foul, why shouldn't everything go foul. For a while he took to beating his wife, then stopped, withdrawing into a heavy, brooding silence. The most sensible thing would have been to leave home, apply for a homestead somewhere else—which the Land Reform now made possible—but was it really worth starting all over from scratch, roughing it in a log cabin, putting up buildings? Better to leave well enough alone. Dividing up the land didn't mean the Juchniewiczes were about to set up house in the woods. And if anything ever happened to Surkont, she was bound to take charge, anyway.

Then a third child, a daughter, was born to Balthazar. But when the village midwife from Pogirai brought the baby over for his inspection, he couldn't remember how it was done, which night, or whether he had even taken pleasure in it. She looked so like a little kitten, the spitting

image of her father. Not until the day after the christening party, as he was getting out of bed, was he told—it had been sloughed off as a joke at the time—that he had gone after someone with a knife.

40

TINKLING BELLS, a snorting horse, the sleigh runners' noiseless glide, and a white landscape embroidered with tracks. The wobbly square denoted a hare; the elongated one, a hare on the run. A fox track—neatly aligned, one paw behind the other—ran straight up a knoll, up to where the snow scintillated in the sun, before disappearing in a birch wood bathed in violet. Bird tracks were the easiest to spot: three overlapping dashes, often accompanied by a tail smudge or the faint imprint of pinion feathers.

The cold brought out the veins on Aunt Helen's nose —dark red against her pink-flushed face—beetling above the collar of her sheepskin. Her sheepskin's original color had faded, but Thomas's was new, still preserving its tawny sheen reminiscent of a squirrel's summer coat, and just because it was so tawny and soft, he loved to rub his cheek against the sleeve, patiently pushing back his grandfather's cap with earflaps every time it threatened to flop down over his eyes. Helen wore a round cap of gray astrakhan.

The snow trails around the house at Borkuny were tarnished yellow from tramping, the grounds pocked with frozen water patches and little piles of horse manure a-swarm with sparrows. Inside, a hurrying Barbarka brushed past them in woolen stockings and wooden clogs. Refreshments were served, and the three of them sat down at table; but Thomas, tiring quickly of the table talk, got up

and browsed among the hunting gear mounted on the wall. A sort of compact had arisen between Romuald and Helen, and it rankled him. This was a different Romuald he was seeing now, one unworthy of the real Romuald—an accomplice of adults, lacing his talk with cracks that incited his aunt to fits of tee-heeing. Another incentive for clearing out as soon as was politely possible was the sulking Barbarka, whose biting lips betrayed a curious rancor. When forced to remain at table, he became so ruefully introspective that his aunt's commanding "Eat!" had a jolting, almost waking effect on him. But she never divined his real thoughts—those thoughts of a somewhat indelicate nature.

The smiles, the constant cajoling to eat and drink, were for him a sign of affectation. Why all the posturing, the pretending to be something other than what one was? Not a sign, never a hint of their true selves. In private, one thing; in company, another. Romuald, the real Romuald, would say, "Time for a crap," crouch down beside a tree, and afterward wipe himself with a leaf, without inhibition, without concealment; but in the presence of Thomas's aunt, he was all gentility and courtly manners. Nor was Aunt Helen above squatting and dribbling through her legs, yet how ladylike, how primly proper was her bearing now, almost as if she was without any privy part, or had left it behind somewhere. Even Barbarka. Why "even"? Because how could someone so uncannily beautiful squat down and, with flushed cheeks, make a puddle with her hairy part? As he looked at her and tried to imagine her in this pose, he quivered: miles separated the smoothness of her brow, the blue lambency of her gaze from that other region below. If each knew the other's business, why pretend ignorance? He had always been contemptuous of the decorum of the visit, of those social occasions when he was forced to be a spectator to their tedious proprieties, but never so much as during those winter visits to Borkuny. Meanwhile, he entertained visions of them squatting naked,

attending to their bodily needs, each in full view of the other. Would they, in that position, still have felt obliged to blab the same banalities, the same platitudes that, alone, they were too ashamed to utter? The perverse pleasure he took in conjuring up such visions was tinged with one desire: to triumph over their disguises, to strip them of pretense. He swore never to become like them. Yet it was Helen who bore the brunt of his silent protestations—for her having infected Romuald, for implicating him in all this ceremonial silliness.

At dusk, when the sky was suffused from below with a stark red, when the thin tree branches seemed to inflict an icy cold, blackcocks flocked to the birch by the brook. Thomas would observe their tail feathers in flight, the white lining of their wings. At sufficiently close range, the metal black of feathers took on a shimmering iridescence; at a distance, the birds became silhouetted among the crowns of trees. From the cupboard Romuald removed a wooden decoy, as faithful a replica of a real blackcock as ever was carved. Fastening it to the end of a long pole, with the decoy propped up to look like a roosting cock, he stood the pole against the trunk of a birch; taking it for one of their companions, the blackcocks would swoop down out of the sky to within shooting range. Romuald promised to take him along on one of his trips, but the promise, for one reason or another, was never kept. A bad cold spell kept them indoors that winter, the result being they made only one leisurely stroll into the forest—in the company, alas, of Helen. Romuald pointed out a track in the snow—a wolf's, he said, after giving it careful scrutiny. How could he tell it was a wolf's and not a dog's? Hm, would have had to be a pretty big dog, said Romuald, adding that the pads on a wolf's paw, because they were more spread out, made for a deeper, cleaner print.

Romuald was not much of a churchgoer, though he aways stopped off at the manor when he went. But Bar-

barka was at church every Sunday, and with her head bowed over a thick missal, her kerchief's triangular fold falling between her bent shoulders, her presence was not nearly so intimidating. Church had a way of mitigating what was otherwise fearful; even Dominic, whose unkempt hair made him stand out among the men, seemed tamer, less belligerent. For Thomas, although he was reconciled to it, church attendance was a cause of some frustration. During Mass, a person's inner feelings had to ascend straight up to God; otherwise, he thought, he was guilty of cheating. Not wanting to cheat, he would clamp his eyes shut and try—without success—to let his mind soar up through the roof and into heaven. But it never worked; God was like air, dissolving into nothing, no matter how the mind conceived of Him. Then back it came, that irresistible earthly curiosity about who was seated next to him, who wore what, the facial expressions . . . And even when he was able to break loose and hurl himself into space, it was always to take the place of God, to gaze down on the church and on all those assembled. Through roofs and clothes made miraculously transparent, he would contemplate them. Their shameful parts, while hidden from others, were now fully exposed; their minds laid bare. With his giant fingers he would reach down and pluck one at random, cradle him in his palm, and study his movements. However much he fought against such fantasies, they reasserted themselves with every flight to heavenly spheres.

One book affected him deeply: a book about the first Christians and the Emperor Nero (the one shown making living torches of people in the print that hung in Grandfather's room). To it must be attributed his dream about purity. The dream: a group of Christians, with Thomas among them, stood singing in the arena of a Roman amphitheater. Tears streamed down his face, but they were tears of joy, the joy of a martyrdom willingly endured, bringing with it a cleansing of spirit that transformed him

live into a flowing river. Once—and it happened only once
—on his grandfather's orders, he'd had his hide tanned
for some more serious transgression. Antonina had held
him, while one of the farm boys whipped his bare behind
with a switch. Painful as the punishment had been, the
recollection of it somehow remained precious: a lightness
of spirit, an exhilaration, a joyful expiation—the same
tears of exultation and plenitude that had attended his
dream about death.

The lions advanced, their serrated jaws coming closer
and closer; the sinking of fangs into raw flesh, the gushing
of blood, and the sensation of luminous exoneration, of
eternal reconciliation with the Good.

But this was just a dream. In reality, that same week
—the week of his dream—he created an awful scene when
the black-bound book from whose pages he diligently
transcribed the Latin names of his birds was missing. He
searched high and low, exasperated the grownups with his
pestering, but the book was nowhere to be found. What
had happened to it? He discovered it by chance—in the
same room where, among drying seeds strewn on canvas
sheets and stacks of wool yarn, Aunt Helen slept. One of
her turned bedposts had a foot missing; the bird book was
there in place of it. He screeched, yelled, clenched his fists
menacingly while his aunt, in a state of shock, demanded
to know the reason for this tantrum. Damn fool woman! A
book or a brick, what did she care! What were birds and
animals to her—she who couldn't tell the difference be-
tween a sparrow and a yellowhammer! The owl, yes, the
owl had mattered, but only because of the money it fetched.
She was no more interested than she was in what Romuald
had to say about hunting; it was all an act, a hoax, part of
her flirtatious designs. Such malevolence was unworthy of
a Christian. But Thomas wasn't bothered by such qualms.
His contempt sought revenge; it inspired visions of punish-
ment, both for this latest crime and for the crass stupidity

she embodied. Visions, for example, of lacing her soup with belladonna berries. But the berries now lay under the deep winter snows, and a few days later his hatred abated. Anyone that blind to things deserving of love wasn't even worthy of being poisoned.

Thomas built his snowman on the front lawn, rolling the balls of snow in the winding sheet of down stirred up by his momentum. Three clumps, one on top of the other, the smallest—the head—fixed with coal eyes and a twig pipe. But by the time it stood erect, the hands were frozen and the fun already over: there was only so much one could do with a snowman. On winter mornings he gave Antonina a hand with lighting the fires. From the hallway her footfalls resounded crisply in the house—so hushed it seemed bedded in cotton—as she entered, trailing the cold and dumping the glazed firewood on the floor with a clatter. It was then up to him to lay the birch bark and erect a little tent of kindling—debris dried in the gap between tiled stove and wall. The bark, licked by the flame, would curl into trumpets. A moment of suspense:,would it catch or wouldn't it? Next Antonina, her arms full of wood, with Thomas tagging behind, would march into Grandmother Dilbin's room, where everything was still a blur, and straightaway open the shutters, causing both Thomas and his grandmother, hunched in front of a pillow braced upright against the headboard, to blink from the sudden burst of light. On her bedstand, next to a thick prayer book, medicine bottles filled the room with their sickly odors. Having no inclination to linger, as he sometimes did in autumn, he resorted to any excuse to escape her weepy jeremiads. Poised on the edge of his chair by her bed, he felt conscience-bound to stay, but, unable to endure it for very long, he would invariably sneak out, his guilt made none the worse by his escape: his grandmother, because she was sick and weepy, belonged to those things that lent them-

selves to dispassionate observation, even annoyance, and from this detachment came both satisfaction and shame.

An important event: that winter Thomas got his boots, the ones he'd had his heart set on. Hand-sewn by a cobbler from Pogirai, they were a size too big (to allow for growth), but still a snug fit. To keep the foot from sliding, the soft shank could be tightened by a strap in the instep. Another strap, looped through eyelets, kept the shank tight around the knee.

41

THAT SPRING was unlike any Thomas had ever known. Not only because of the sudden thaw and the ferocity of sun. That year, instead of waiting passively for the leaves to appear, for the yellow keys of St. Peter to blossom, and for nightingales to trill in the bushes, he went out to meet it. The naked earth barely steamed in the cloudless light as, whistling and singing and flourishing his stick, he made his way to Borkuny. From the moment he slipped into the forest behind the farm that afternoon, he felt like losing himself in it, so painful was the swelling from within, so great the urge to proclaim his rapture. But he checked the urge, treading softly enough not to snap a twig, freezing in his tracks at the slightest rustle. This was the only way of gaining entrance to the kingdom, birds being panicked less by the sight of a man than by his movement. Dappled thrushes promenaded nearby, and he knew how to distinguish them from the fieldfare by their gray-brown, rather than bluish, head plummage. Circling a small spruce, he discovered a new hawfinch nest; and if not for their anxious screeching, he would have missed a jay's

nest, so well camouflaged that it was hardly to be detected from below. The young spruce, its branches hugging the ground, was easy climbing at first; but the higher he climbed, the thicker became the needles, and it was a scratched and sweaty Thomas who finally surfaced at the top, his head adjacent to the nest. He swayed, clinging with both arms to the thin trunk, while the frantic jays threatened attack from higher up, clearly intent on spearing him with their beaks, only to recoil in panic, resume their places, and renew the attack. He refrained from touching the eggs—there were four, all light blue and russet-flecked. Why were mottled eggs so common among forest birds? No one had been able to give him a satisfactory answer. Nature's way, he guessed. But why? He slid back down, extremely content with his accomplishment.

He returned, flushed with his impressions of the forest spring, whose beauty derived not from any one thing in particular but from a myriad of voices comprising a chorus of promise. From the treetops, now black against the western sky, came the long-drawn melodies of thrushes—the *Turdus musicus*, which only an ignoramus could have mistaken for the *Turdus pilaris* or *Turdus viscivorus*; from overhead, the winnowing of snipe in flight, like a bleating of lambs in the distance, somewhere beyond the rose-green swath of silk. Antonina pretended these sounds were the work of the witch Ragana, spurring her mount, the devil, transformed by her into a flying goat; but Thomas knew that it was only the wind whistling in their feathers.

To Barbarka he made a present of a bouquet of rose-petaled daphne, hyacinthlike in their fragrance, and they were graciously accepted. Romuald sat in the twilight, holding the barrel of his shotgun up to the lamplight for inspection. He asked a question that left Thomas momentarily speechless, even made him pale a little. Whether from pity or respect for Thomas's ability to incarnate the forest spirits, he inquired: "Want to come?"

His happiness was marred only by the burden imposed on him. The stalking of wood grouse, guided only by their song, was a recognized feat. One careless step, and the hunt was over; yet Romuald had trusted enough in his abilities to invite him along. His honor compelled him not to betray that confidence.

Thomas, no stranger to the ways of the wood grouse, had never seen a live one before, as it kept to the interior, away from human habitations—bird symbol of the wilderness. It was stalked two or three steps at a time, at the end of each song, when the bird was deaf to any movement in the dim light—it hooted only at daybreak, in the interlude between winter's thaw and the first greening.

Thomas's exultation over the lore of the wilderness, over anything having to do with nature, was deceiving. Was it the image of the bird itself—turkey-sized, long-necked, fan-tailed—that fired his imagination, or visions of himself stalking in the penumbra? The thrill of adventure, the prospect of participation as a genuine hunter, moving stealthily in the forest, mute and vigilant, his ears on the baying of the hounds? For he was capable of picturing not only the details, not only the trappings, but himself in the act of registering them; he exulted, in other words, in the role as much as in the thing itself. The arching of foot while stalking, for example, was a sign of his own proficiency, all too consciously perceived. And grownups were deluded if they supposed they didn't indulge in similar games. If they were honest, they would admit to a greater fascination with the role of lover than with the object of that love; to their wanting to savor the situation, the source of their pride. No wonder their words and gestures were artificial; they were performed, under censorship, on behalf of some ideal. Their affections had to be commensurate with their own ideal; when lacking, they had to be invented and their sincerity constantly reaffirmed. Acting was their stock and trade: one half impersonated someone the other

half knew to be false. Thus, much can be said in Thomas's defense.

The fanaticism with which he divided people into worthy and unworthy, depending on whether he sensed in them the presence or absence of some passion, testified to his heart's exorbitant demands. Once he acknowledged birds as the supreme beauty, he vowed to remain faithful both to them and to his chosen vocation. His tenacity could be read in his exemplary conduct, in the steady grinding of teeth: "I will be what I choose to be."

The following afternoon, they set off in Romuald's one-horse britska. The sandy, deep-rutted road cut straight through the forest before weaving through the moorland, the spare landscape being relieved by a few scattered pine left for seed and by clumps of seedlings so young they were nearly transparent, many of them already crumpled and broken, grasslike, by the snows and winter winds. The moor, its barren aspect in stark contrast to the lush verdure along the Issa or around Borkuny, evoked little sympathy in Thomas. In the mixed forest past the range, Romuald looked for the logging trail used as a shortcut. Here the ground was already dry enough not to risk a sunken axle; the shadows now and then reverberated with the thumping of hoofs on hardened snow. They came out on a highroad lined with ditches, and a half hour later a clearing, the sky above it wreathed with chimney smoke, rolled into view.

"Jaugele," said Romuald. "In that village, everyone's a poacher."

In the vesperal light, the brushwood, mantled with mist, looked gunmetal blue against the black timberline. After crossing a little bridge choked with alder, they headed up a levee that led to the forester's. A stork nest on the rooftop, its occupants freshly returned, seethed with beaks and feathers. A dog bayed and stretched his limbs in front of the door, where a big-boned woman, wearing a

dark green skirt, informed them that her husband was camped out in the woods. She invited them inside, but anxious to reach him before nightfall, they stayed only for some milk, served them in an earthenware jug. Following her directions—a right, then a left past the pine tree with the beehive, then another right by the peat bog—they picked up the trail, a horse track matted with wood chips and a bedding of pine branches. It was dark now; barkless logs shone by the trailside. Before long, they spotted a fire burning in the distance.

The lean-to of freshly cut pine took on a dark coppery glaze in the light of the campfire, around which a couple of peasants sat on their spread sheepskins. Thomas was quick to spot a pair of shotgun barrels leaning against the sloped pine shelter. The hooting was nearing its peak— they were told by the gamekeeper and his partner—and the sunrise promised good weather, with little chance of rain. "The boy"—the gamekeeper nodded at Thomas. "Out here for the grouse hunt?" He stroked his bushy mustache, a facetious grin playing underneath, shook his head, and eyed him up and down. Thomas felt uncomfortable under his scrutinizing gaze.

Sparks showered and shot up and scattered in the soft black. Thomas stretched out his legs toward the fire and felt the generous warmth through his boot soles. Lying flat on his bed of fir, he covered himself with his sheepskin and listened to the sighing in the fir crowns, to an owl screeching somewhere far off; to the drawling voices of the men, who sat up trading gossip: a wedding, a lawsuit, the case of a man who accidentally plowed someone else's property . . . Occasionally, one of them got up and disappeared, to reemerge from the dark, hauling a dry log, which he tossed onto the fire. Lulled by the campfire patter, Thomas turned over on his side and fell into a drowse, the voices and the crackling reaching him through that half sleep between dream and wakefulness.

He was awakened by a tugging on the arm. The camp-fire, now out, was ringed by ash. The firmament, slightly paler in one half of the sky, glittered overhead. He shivered, as much from anticipation as from the chill.

42

IT WAS pitch-dark—silent except for a boot colliding with a root, a barrel scraping a branch. A hunting party of three; the fourth, the friend of the game-keeper, had gone to try his luck on other stands. The path narrowed and the smell of pine needles slowly gave way to the smells of the swamp. Pools of water glimmered in the gray pre-dawn light. They waded into the water, circled around it, got stuck in the elders, and later balanced their way across slimy logs laid out bridge-fashion among the phantoms of dry reeds, forming something between an embankment and a levee. To the left, beyond a ditch resonant with a bullfrog's croaking, loomed a wall of pine scrub; to the right, a dark density of swamp forest, in whose interior Thomas made out here and there a light-barked trunk, the tangled underside of an uprooted tree, clumps of rushes, brake, and sedge. The sky ahead of them was saturated with rose; the longer the eye lingered on it, the blacker became the circumscribing darkness.

They stopped occasionally, ears perked. At one point, Romuald squeezed Thomas's arm. "There he is," he said in a whisper. But it took Thomas awhile to register the sound —a sort of muffled sigh, unlike any other creature sound he knew. At times it sounded vaguely like a hammering, an uncorking, but no—it eluded definition. They shook hands

with the gamekeeper, who immediately dropped out of sight.

"We'll keep on at the same pace for a while," murmured Romuald. "He's too far out of range now. But later on—watch your step."

Clutching his gun with one hand, keeping his balance with the other, Romuald waded into the brush. Thomas trailed behind, straining to maintain the silence. But how to avoid making any telltale sounds when the foot, even before it had touched the ground, met with a matting of dry stalks? He found a way: before setting his foot down, he first dug his boot into the matting, or else sought out the moss. The grouse did indeed have need of the wilderness as a protection. Barricades of fallen tree trunks occasionally blocked their way, and Romuald debated whether to crawl under or over. The hooting carried more distinctly now—a strenuous, quickening *tek-ap, tek-ap* . . .

Such scenes remain fixed forever in one's memory: giant aspen, made even more towering by the pearl-gray lighting between night and day, their boughs brushed with a radiance announcing the sunrise; roots like gigantic appendages fingering the dank dusk; the rush of naked stems, surging up to the light; and Romuald, no more than an ant beside them, cutting a path through the underbrush, his gun held high. And the song of the grouse. Thomas understood now why the grouse hunt was so celebrated. Nature could have invented no better song with which to convey the wildness of the spring. Neither a melody nor a graceful trill—more of a drumming, cadenced, causing a throbbing in the temples, a merging of grouse song and heartbeat.

Thomas imitated Romuald's every move and gesture. The moment Romuald turned and signaled, he halted in his tracks. The time had come. From now on, they had to take leaping steps. The bird broke off. Silence. Tiny birds, warbling shrilly, flocked overhead. Then it started up again. *Tek-ap* . . . faster and faster, until the hooting was

joined by another sound, rather like knife-grinding; that's when Romuald took his first hop, followed by a second, turning stock-still on the third. Thomas was afraid to budge before he was sure of his timing. But the instant the grouse began a new series, he was ready; taking his cue from the whetting, he jumped together with Romuald. One, two, three. He knew why the interval: the bird was momentarily deaf. They could risk a clamor now, so long as the body was prepared to become a statue on a moment's notice.

One, two, three. He concentrated entirely on the exercise, and prayed: "Please, God, make it work. Make it work." Once executed, there was no improving one's position—you stayed where you landed. But as his leg was probing for a mossy island, he lost his footing on the third hop and slid into the muck with a loud gurgle. He could have hoisted himself out by grabbing hold of a sapling at his back, but he was afraid the rustle might give him away. In despair he sank into the mud, while Romuald shook his fist at him.

He lost one sequence during the time it took to extricate his foot from the swamp. Soon he was jumping in tandem with Romuald, his anxiety steadily mounting at the prospect of flushing the bird, so close was the hooting now. He found safe footing for the next series, poised, but nothing happened. Minutes passed. It was over. It had escaped. Terrified, Thomas implored Romuald with his eyes to bring it back.

Then the grouse started up again, exactly as before, only a little higher up. Had he merely shifted his perch? From Romuald's repeated crouching and scouting, Thomas surmised that he was plotting the most surreptitious approach. The sky above the forest roof had brightened; ahead of them, a clump of aspen was tinted red by the sun's rays. Romuald, taking huge strides, steered in that direction, motioning for Thomas to follow.

The grouse sat high up in a gap among the spruce. Kneeling and craning his head, Thomas observed it from behind a tree trunk. It seemed small enough to be a blackbird. Wings lowered, tail feathers beetling at an angle, buff-gray against its black spruce perch. Romuald, bent low, ducked under a needle curtain: he was trying to outflank it.

A shot. Thomas watched as the grouse, wings arrested, was pulled from the branch; saw the long path of descent, heard the thump, the shot's rippling echo. He licked his lips—joyous and grateful to God.

When he grabbed the bird by the head—a metallic sheen, a crimson brow, an ivorylike beak—and hoisted it shoulder-high, it hung down to his feet. It did not know the world of humans; once or twice, it may have heard men's voices from afar. It was oblivious to Aunt Helen, books, boots, the shape of a gun; oblivious to Romuald's and Thomas's existence, too. Nor would it ever know. Struck by a thunderbolt, it had died instantly. But he, Thomas, still resided on this side of the thunderbolt; they had met in the only way possible, and he felt a twinge of remorse that it could never be otherwise. The truth was that Thomas hungered for a sort of impossible communion with living creatures. Why this barrier, and why become a hunter if one loved nature? It had been the same with the owl: he had secretly dreamed of the day when the owl, by some word or deed, would cease to be an owl, if only for an instant. But the dream never came true; hence what was to be gained by keeping it locked in a cage? Since it was not within his power to assume another form—that of a grouse, say—all that was left was to bring the dead bird back, inhaling its smell, the smell of the forest's savage interior.

The sun was up. The tree craters and swampy patches congested with rushes now took on a more mundane aspect. Soon they were back alongside the ditch, which, to his astonishment, seemed closer in the daylight. He had a

liking for this walk by the ditch: a ruthless dawn caught in a chaos of leaning, overlapping pine; this man with his black strip of a gun; a blue wreath of cigarette smoke, and himself, bearer of the trophy.

43

THOSE WHO have never stepped out of the house at the break of day and heard the babble of black-cock must lead sorry lives indeed, because such have never known spring. Nor will they be able, in times of despair, to conjure those weddings celebrated in places far from what afflicts them. But did it really matter if they could not experience such ecstasy, if someone else could? That time when lilac-hued flowers, powdery yellow on the inside, their stems coated with velvety down, were born among the needles; when cocks danced in the glades, trailing their wings along the ground and brandishing their tail feathers, ink-colored on the outside, white on the inside, their throats so surfeited with song they could only swell from the excess.

Romuald never hunted blackcock at Borkuny, taking care to preserve the wildlife there. The same birch wood that provided sanctuary for the adders bordered on a young pine forest; it was here that the blackcocks had chosen as the place for their mating rituals. Though sparsely wooded, the trees there were luxurious, their boughs bent to the ground, the floor beneath them like a mosaic: islands of close-cropped moss, patches of gray lichen, and clusters of red whortleberry. Blinds, fashioned to look like bushes, were favored for hunting; the hunter hid in them just before daybreak and waited, commanding a view of the

blackcocks' ballroom. Thomas regarded it as a matter of honor to rely only on his naturalist's cunning; that is, he hunted without a gun, the challenge being to get close enough so that, if he had been armed, he would not have missed.

A milk-white mist, a child's pastel-pink sky. Such mists were not uncommon at any season, but none so breathtakingly serene as this. In the mist, against the white dew or frost, the luminous blackcocks resembled metal-plated scarabs. The mating grounds, the site they had selected for their love games, was for Thomas an enchanted garden. Crawling up on all fours, he would spy on them, though only once at close range. Another time he was startled by the mating call of a blackcock perched in a young pine. *Choo-shee!* Translucent drops glistened and sparkled on the needle tips, yet the bird was the focal point of space, equal in size to a planet. The bird flew away on its own, unprompted by any careless move on his part. How he longed for the cap of invisibility from the fairy tale, though there were times when he knew indeed how to make himself invisible.

The spring was gaining in strength: bird cherries along the Issa, overpowering the senses with their bitter perfume; young girls tiptoeing to pluck sprays of flowers so fragile they scattered at the slightest jostle; and those evenings on the village green, where a little drum and horn played accompaniment to the monotonous village reel known as the *suktinis*. And the house in Gine, now suddenly buried in clouds of lilac.

That year, Thomas's hand never once touched the four-pronged spear that he used to take pike-fishing, either with Pakenas or Akulonis, and the line on his pole was corroded by their rusty hooks. This neglect of a boyhood passion left him with a guilty conscience; but he now had other, more urgent things to occupy him, both at Romuald's and at old lady Bukowski's at Borkuny. What drew

him there was neither the old woman nor Denis nor Victor, but a lake.

It was a small lake, secluded from both fields and roads, which made it all the more appealing. It was surrounded by marshland, and though a trail gave access, one had to slosh ankle-deep in water before reaching the shoreline. The lake was thickly ringed by tall rushes, but Thomas had discovered a small cove with a panoramic view, and an alder stump, where he would sit for hours in rigid contemplation. A perfect placidity, a sheet of another sky traversed by water birds trailing long creases. The lake had its permanent residents, and Thomas was perennially on the lookout for them. The ducks came whirring down out of the sky, skimmed long and low over the surface, their triangular wing tips at first brushing the water, then ruffling it and sending ripples back to the shoreline. The ducks were preyed on by wailing hawks from above, and he once witnessed an attack in midair; the drake escaped by taking cover in the reeds. But the habits of the grebe engaged him most of all. Sometimes they surfaced close by: red-billed, crested, rufous side-whiskers on a white neck. He was mystified by their bizarre ceremonies, always performed out in the middle of the lake. Their snakelike necks suddenly elongated, they streaked across the water's surface with prodigious speed, the snake-necks now arched and their heads lowered. Their forward thrust was all the more astounding in that they barely touched the water and didn't fly. Like the motorboats in Grandmother Dilbin's illustrated magazines. How did they do it, he once asked Victor. "Gey gage geag goger guz ger gugid"—that is, "They chase each other because they're stupid," an explanation not likely to satisfy a naturalist.

Victor, because of his lumbering, stuttering ways, was not really the best company. He plowed, harrowed, tended the feed troughs, and even milked the cows with the servant girl. Always busy with menial chores, something of a

hired hand. His stuttering, no doubt, had its origin in maternal terror. The old woman had a habit of sitting with her legs apart, huge of belly, fists clenched on her knees, and this brooding pose was of a decidedly different order from the crooning and the upturned eyes that went with the guitar playing. Thomas was always shocked to hear her sing, much as if a bull were imitating a nightingale.

Mrs. Bukowski bred many ducks, and one aspect of their behavior gave Thomas pause. The ducks waddled about the house, nibbling on the grass, or dabbled in a hollow, which, except after a rainfall when water collected at the bottom, was either a mudhole or, during drought season, a cracked basin. "Why don't they go down to the lake?" he asked. Victor sneered, and his response, or at least what could be salvaged from it was: "Ha! If they only knew!" They were unaware that close by was a diver's paradise, offering warm water, algae, sprawling pads adrift on somnolent depths, and sanctuaries among the reeds. As he contemplated their flattened, lapping bills and billowy cheeks, Thomas took pity on this strange debility of theirs. What could have been easier than to migrate over to the lake? A ten minute's journey, at most. Not until some years later was Thomas to pursue this philosophical insight, now only vaguely formulated, to its logical conclusion. Mankind was a pitiable lot. Not unlike those ducks.

The beauty of that spring—his twelfth—did not spare Thomas certain anxieties, and may have even contributed to them. For the first time he perceived that he had two selves, and that they were not altogether commensurate: the one he felt inside, and the outside one, his bodily self, the one he was born with, and nothing of which was really his. Barbarka, had she known of his admiration for her, would never have wounded him by calling him a "*shutas.*" She had judged him by his exterior, and this allegiance to his own face ("Tommy has a face like a Tartar's ass"), to his own gestures, for which he was held responsible,

weighed heavily on him. And what if he was fashioned differently from others, not as well proportioned? Romuald, for example, was sinewy, lean in the hips, and had tapered knees. Thomas, measuring with his hands, found his thighs too big around; standing sideways before the mirror, he would examine his prominent backside, pretending, the moment he heard footsteps approaching, to be merely passing by. Others were able to part their hair down the middle, but no matter how often he combed or brushed, it was like trying to groom a dog's hide against the grain.

We live inside ourselves as in a prison. If people make fun of us, it's because they can't see through to our true selves. We carry inside images of our physical selves closely bound to our souls, though all it takes is another person's glance to dissolve that bond, to show us that we are not at all what we flatter ourselves to be. Chastened, we go around, existing inside ourselves, all too painfully aware of ourselves from the outside. This discrepancy made him yearn all the more for his Kingdom of the Forest, the map to which lay locked in a drawer. After due thought, he decided that women should be barred from the Kingdom, whether they were like Helen, Mrs. Bukowski, or Barbarka. Men, too, were adept at posing, but women were somehow to blame for their cold, squinting glances. Men whose minds were fixed on more noble aims did not have to bother with their appearance.

The linden leaves around the manor house in Gine had unfurled to become green hands concealing a little bell that hung in a worm-eaten shelter in a tree fork. Thomas could not recall anyone ever having used this bell; no cord was attached, and it was situated too high up for anyone to reach. During the month-of-May devotions to the Blessed Virgin, a yellow afternoon light fell through the windows into the church, heavy with the scent of flowers clustered at the foot of the blue Virgin.

Warm rains. The rains left the trails awash with

shoals of silt, laced with rivulets tunneling through the loam. If you stepped barefoot in the mud, your toes secreted a squishy paste. Then came the water, seeping back into the impression and filling the print left by the naked sole.

44

THE WINDOW of Grandmother Dilbin's room was open and, though it was still light outside, a nightingale trilled in the brake by the pond. Waking from a sleep heavy with premonition, she felt someone standing by her bedside. "Arthur!" she cried out. But there was no one, and then she remembered where she was, and she remembered that years had passed, and that the gold lettering on the gravestone had probably been washed away by the rains.

Bronislawa Ritter, a little girl with two blond braids who had just caught and freed a butterfly stranded on the windowpane, stared up at the evening shadows inscribed on the ceiling, two strands of gray hair now stuck fast to her down-filled pillow. The walls of her family home in Riga had been a protection from evil and the encroachment of time. A too happy childhood, followed by life's rapid descent, had left her unwilling to admit to the reality of it, to admit that laughter would never again resound—a bright and sunny laughter to dispel the irreversible. What was the meaning of it all? The little spoon used for serving jam; the iridescent silk gown belonging to her mother; the sister who used to tie her ribbon; the ringing at the front door; and Father, back from his patients, placing his checkered medical bag on the pier table . . . ? Of all the possible

roads, why this one? Hard to accept that it had happened, hard but irrefutable, even without the reasoning of it, like a tearful novel that could be put down at will, no, that could *not* be put down ... Why me?

The descent. It began the day she and Arthur rode back from the church, with the snow melting on her eyelashes. The flickering candlelight of the candelabra, the creaking floor, the house that was to become hers from that day forward. "No, no!" It was like the discovery of death. The paper chains used to decorate the Christmas tree, and the caroling, and the flowers, and the hoop-spinning in the garden—all scattered, dispersed, leaving cruelty as the only reality. "No, no!" *Consummatio* forever. Arthur had been a good man. And she had ceded to it, to that monstrous order of the world with which he was at home. The smell of tobacco and leather stirrups had introduced her to a land where a person counted for nothing more than an object, a land where the cultivation of gracious customs was revealed as an affectation, a feeble mask covering the severity of law. And always the same bewildering question: "Was this it?" A land where nobody rebelled, where everything was sanctified and acknowledged, where no word could reconcile, where nothing could be changed.

She had hardly known the man, not even when his mustache had stood out in relief against his waxlike face, when, tending to the wicks by the coffin, she had yielded to the thought: "A thing." A man who could suppress his impetuous nature merely by sucking on a pipestem. A discreet man, reticent about the past. A man whose back bore the scars of Russian knouts—"for leading a revolt in the camp," he once muttered, grudgingly. A man who had traveled by reindeer in the land of eternal night and eternal day—in the Siberian tundra; taken cover in the forests during the Uprising, tall and lanky in his Polish overcoat and buckled belt. And the pride he took in his marksman-

ship . . . Like the time he knocked a Russian officer out of the saddle with a boar gun. And all the notes and IOU's left behind: "Fifty rubles to Matyda Zidonis." "To T.K.—twenty rubles." Although she suspected him of having betrayed her, he never gave any outward indication of it. Only later, in his will, there were those mysterious legacies to boys in the neighboring villages: his sons.

A whirl of dates, winters, springtimes, minor incidents, illnesses, guests . . . Theodore was born in the year 1884—yes, she was barely nineteen at the time. Had she wept the day she got the news that Constantine had drowned in a swimming accident—Constantine, a man she could have been happy with? She couldn't remember. Staring fixedly, she probed deep into the past, transfixed the way one's gaze can be arrested by an eddy or a flame. The sketchbook containing his drawings still lay in her trunk, preserved there to this day.

The nightingale cried out, was answered. Dampness seeped through the window. Whatever has been cannot endure; it fades, flickers, scatters; a man, doubting that he has been, can only pray. If a star ablaze in the bluish-green firmament was millions of miles away, and beyond it other stars, other suns; if all that was born passed without leaving a trace, then only God could rescue the past from insignificance. Even a past full of pain. Oh, if only one could say with certainty that it was not a dream.

"Shut the window, Tommy; it's cold."

Her voice now grated like a rusty-hinged door. He registered the change. He had been studying her for a good long while: the fingers intertwined, the once-full cheeks sagging, the deep furrows dividing them from the chin, the thin neck doubly creased. She turned her face toward him, her eyes, as usual, partially distracted by something.

Her grandson. Good or bad blood? Had he inherited Arthur's manliness, passion—or her own fear of everything that assailed us on this earth? Or did he have the

blood of those—savages? It was her fault that Theodore was not like his father, that he was soft and even weak. She was also to blame for Constantine. If the boy took after her, he might well turn out like Constantine.

"Shatybelko brought back a letter. Look, Thomas, there it is."

Lying on one corner of the medicine table were several sheets of stationery, partially concealing an envelope. The slanted, jerky, practically illegible handwriting belonged to his father. The other, in which some letters had been doubly inscribed, as if to ensure their legibility, was his mother's.

"Mommy writes that she'll be home soon, in a few months at the most."

"Which way is she coming?"

"Everything's planned. You know the border's closed, there's no way to cross legally. But she writes that she knows of a little town where it's easy to cross."

"Will we go back the same way, or by way of Riga?"

His grandmother looked around for her rosary beads. He bent down and picked them up from the floor.

"You two will go. That's all I care about."

"Why do you say such things, Grandmother?" Secretly he registered no emotion, and he reproached himself for it.

She said nothing in reply. Groaning, she tried to raise herself up in bed. He leaned over and helped her, her sloping shoulders wrapped in a fustian morning jacket, a band of wrinkles running from the back of her neck to under her earlobe.

"These pillows. Look how they sink. Maybe you can straighten them a little."

Thomas's pity was somehow deficient; he wished it could have been more sincere, but that would have meant forcing himself, and he winced at this inability to feel genuine emotion. At the moment his grandmother seemed less

irritating than usual, for what reason he didn't know—
more open, perhaps, free of her usual craftiness.

"Lots of nightingales this year—eh, Thomas?"

"Lots, Grandmother."

As she began fingering her rosary beads, he couldn't
decide whether to leave or to stay.

"With all the cats around," she said at last, "it's a
wonder the birds aren't afraid to sing."

45

WHO SAID there were no witnesses? The
lush grass, crushed underfoot, had not yet recovered as the
booted feet went on trampling more weeds, rough stalks
rustled against leather shanks, and a frightened thrush re-
sumed its caterpillar hunting. A couple were sitting at the
bottom of a small, leafy-walled hollow, under a sky of drift-
ing clouds. A dark arm was wrapped around shoulders
sheathed in a white blouse. An ant, suddenly encumbered,
was trying to free itself from its unwanted burden.

This was the time when the cuckoo's song trailed more
and more into laughter, before lapsing into silence until
the next spring. But no one was counting the trills now—
the number of which were a portent of how many years a
person had left on earth. Whispering was heard on the
green floor below, along with the soft jangling of spurs.

Treading lightly, the wizard Masiulis strayed closer, a
small gunnysack, used for collecting herbs, slung over his
shoulder. Stooping, he put down his walking stick and dug
out a plant root with his knife. The sound of a human
voice. He took a few steps, parted the leafy curtain, and,
unobserved by anyone, squinted wryly. The woman's ges-

ture—he had just caught her in the act of straightening her dress—said that what had happened never happened. The deed irrevocably severed, she had begun talking of mundane matters, somehow relieved, as if just returned from adventures encountered in the kingdom of the night. The wizard let go of the branches, made his way back to the edge of the forest, sat down, and lit his pipe.

Masiulis was not without his passions. His wisdom, so far as one could tell, was the sort nurtured by mockery and contempt. Contempt for human nature in general, and for his own in particular. Wasn't it he who told someone (for what reason, it was difficult to say): "Man is like a sheep. But on top of this sheep God built another sheep, this one of air, and the live sheep wants never to be itself but the other"? Contained in this fable was the whole secret of Masiulis's magic. Given such a vision of human nature, nothing was more natural than wanting to help those sheep which could not sustain themselves in air.

There was no reason for Masiulis to think kindly of the couple in the woods. The sight of any couple somehow offended him—how they distanced themselves from others, the privileged air they assumed . . . Not so much offended as amused, to the point of provoking his sarcasm, for the same reason people threw sticks at dogs for making a public spectacle of their lust: their drooping tongues and lovesick glances communicated a recklessness, a disregard for their own silly exhibition, for everything but the savoring of their pleasure, seemingly given only to them. "Eh, you old jade," Masiulis grumped, his anger having been aroused by Helen's modest gesture.

Several days later, by coincidence, Barbarka came to call on Masiulis for advice, there being no one else to whom she could appeal for advice and medicine. At least Masiulis didn't ask, as the priest did in the confessional, "How many times, my child?" To be fair, Father Monkiewicz, after hearing the confessions of his parishioners,

required of them only sincere repentance. Repentance means pleading to God to take note of our ardent desire to be rid of all sinful desire—so that He will be lenient with us the next time around. Since He is All-seeing, surely He must see that we are angels, that we surrender to temptations of the flesh against our wills, without our consent, even with grief for having been made thus and not otherwise. No sooner was she out of the confessional, no sooner relieved of one burden, than Barbarka knew, as did all who went to confession, that she was ready to assume another.

There were time-honored remedies for dealing with Barbarka's dilemma. It was enough, for example, to add a portion of menses to a man's food to make him feel bound by invisible threads. But either this remedy had failed her or she was simply seized with a desire to confide in someone. The wizard, receiving her cordially, spoke at length, until her tears fell one by one onto her fingers. They were tears of remorse, but also tears of shame. Because if Romuald had learned of her coming, he would have beaten her, and rightfully so. For Masiulis was inciting her against him—his festering grudge against the Pole had been aggravated by the couple in the woods. And instead of giving her a portion of lovage—the prescribed remedy, a liquid extract which was added to a man's food in small doses—he advised her to stop wasting her charms on an old lecher, on that traitor of a nobleman who had eyes only for ladies.

Puffy-eyed, Barbarka made her way home. She lingered for a while on the forest path, pensively blurring the horse tracks with her bare foot. "Eh, what does he know?" Did he know Romuald? Not the way she did. Old? But what man his age . . . ? Crooking her big toe, she scooped up the sand and needles. No, it would have to be done her way.

Barbarka was twenty-two years old. Her skirt flut-

tered and grazed her thighs and her steps gradually gained in surety. She strutted now with her head held high, her lips pursed in a smile of confidence. At the spot where the farm buildings came into view, she stopped and surveyed the rooftops, the well crane, and the orchard, as if noticing them all for the first time.

Her way. But how? Give it time, it would come. For now, it was enough that she had in her head the vague outline of a decision. Nothing like a good cry to change one's outlook on things, to make one see the fallacy of humbly submitting to one's fate. Leave Borkuny? Never.

Her visit with the wizard had not been in vain, though its effects were not exactly those anticipated by Masiulis. He had yielded to his passions, which were of benefit only when they fostered wisdom, not when they took command. No, he had acted contrary to his vocation.

Romuald stood in front of the barn, mending the plow with a hammer. In the kitchen, Barbarka scooped some water from a pail, wiped her face, and looked into the mirror. Mustn't let it show. A woman's cunning—yes, but unawares. And she licked her lips to make them look less chapped.

46

Luke Juchniewicz, a man as easily given to sulking as to effusiveness, sat whimpering on one end of the couch. "But, Lukey"—Grandmother Misia tried to console him—"maybe the land won't be parceled. Nothing's happened yet, has it?"

"Not yet, but it will," he whined. "It's for sure now. The crooks, they'll make beggars of us all." He wiped his

eyes with the back of his hand. "What's to become of us, anyway?"

It was hard to contradict him; the Juchniewicz estate was one of those scheduled for redistribution under the Land Reform Act. Aunt Helen sat beside him, her gaze fogged with mild resignation. Grandfather, seated opposite them, cleared his throat. "You'll move in with us, of course. It'll be better all the way around. You can help us run the farm, and Helen can take up residence here."

"Imagine Joseph turning informer," sighed Helen.

"The skunk. I warned you, didn't I? So much for your Lithuanians!" Grandmother turned to her husband and said, mimicking him: "They're so nice and loyal and innocent. Leave it to me, I'd teach them a lesson—with the whip, the whip!"

Grandfather fidgeted with his cuff-links, something he did when he felt uncomfortable. "The official gave me his word. Joseph won't give us any trouble, so long as we keep greasing their palms."

"If you ask me," said Helen, "we should move out to the cottage. That way they'd see Daddy on his property and me on mine," she said, placing undue emphasis on the word "mine." "Home is home, after all."

Thomas looked up from his book and listened until the voices suddenly merged into a meaningless patter. He was seated on the couch, having warmed a little hollow in the cold leather upholstery. The dining-room window was atwitter with sparrows clinging to the wild vine that wound its tendrils about the window frame. The leaves of the agave on the lawn stood upright, bronzed by the late-afternoon sun.

"The poor thing," said Grandmother mockingly, "he'll never survive. Ugh, what a seedy, good-for-nothing lummox, a moonshiner, a bootlegger, a damn fool drunkard. Besides, he's so fat it's disgusting. Good riddance, I say!"

"Well, well . . . hm . . . he did build himself a house," said Grandfather in Balthazar's defense. "And he does look after the forest. No, no, that's not the way to treat a man."

"A man! But he's no ordinary man—that's our darling Balthazar, the apple of our eye, dearer than our own daughter!"

"God forbid," said Helen, raising her hands in horror. "I would never dream of bringing harm to anyone. Why, he could be put up at the manor; Shatybelko's getting old, and he could help out around the farm. Or what about one of the cottages in the commune?"

Thomas perked up his ears, curious to see how Grandfather would respond.

"Yes, that's a possibility," he conceded. "It even makes sense. Only you see, Helen . . . hm . . . the way things are, if you offend them, get them riled up . . . You'll have to admit that right now . . . I mean, it's just a matter of getting the divisions approved . . . No, now is not the time for making enemies. And he does know the forest . . . As it is, we have enough trouble on our hands with Joseph."

The vision of danger evoked by Grandfather had a silencing effect on the women. Luke clutched his head. "What awful times we're living in! Don't rile them, treat them with kid gloves . . . Oh, deep down I feel so sick."

"Poor Lukey. He could use some drops." Grandmother's suggestion went unheeded by Helen.

For Thomas, Luke was an enigma, a man who acted like none of the other grownups and the very sight of whom was enough to provoke a snicker. But no one ever laughed, and that made Thomas distrustful of his own instincts. On the other hand, Luke was someone who wore long pants, was married to Helen, and who knew when and where to sow and harvest. Thomas suspected that behind the rubberlike face—a face that could alternately stretch

from an excess of sympathy and shrink in times of despair —there was hidden the real Luke, a man not half as stupid as he looked. Yet he never found any evidence of that other, more intelligent Luke. Still, there had to be more to him than that. Thomas was forced to conclude that he was an exceedingly cunning man, that he was only shamming. Even his manner of dress was different, was supportive of the comic role he had adopted: he wore a pair of tight-fitting checkered knickers, straps under the soles of his shoes, and a hat identical to those pre-war hats that, sprinkled with naphthaline, lay stored in a huge trunk in the attic.

Aunt Helen was always amiable but, as Thomas could not help noticing, also patronizing toward her husband. Luke had a knack of never volunteering his opinion about anything.

"Well now, one room would do it. Just one little room. Enough for the officials to see—" It was Helen speaking now.

Grandmother groused in disgust. "Helen, how could you? All alone in the forest, at the mercy of that . . . that bumpkin? Ugh!"

"Well, it wouldn't have to be forever, just once every few days, enough to let the news get around that the Juchniewiczes were running their own farm. That wouldn't be too much to ask, would it, Papa?"

"Hm, I suppose I could have a chat with him. No harm in talking to him, I guess," Grandfather answered evasively.

Thomas went back to his book, but was soon distracted when the grownups turned their invective on Joseph. He was a chauvinist, a fanatic; he would have killed if he could; he was the sly type; he had been showered with wood for teaching the boy a little arithmetic, and with so many other blessings. Grandfather held his peace, and not

until after a long pause did he shyly mumble: "If you look at it his way, he might be—well—justified."

Grandmother Misia clasped her hands and raised her eyes to the ceiling, calling on heaven as her witness. "Oh, good Lord!"

47

THE DAY was at hand. Back at Borkuny, they had decided to stay clear of the flood waters around Joniškiai: the place was so thick with sweet flag as to be almost unnavigable by boat, and so crowded with the local peasants during opening season as to be a shooting gallery. Their choice had fallen on Lake Alunta, a little out of the way, but worth traveling the extra distance. "Wait'll you see all the ducks, Tommy!" The guns: Thomas was to use Victor's Berdan; Victor, the muzzle-loader. With the muzzle-loader went a bag full of accessories: powder in one pouch, shot in another, firing caps in still a third, along with a good supply of hemp. To load it: a powder gauge measured the right amount into the barrel, a long wooden ramrod being used to drive home the hemp; then came the shot and another wad of hemp. Uncocking a Berdan was tricky, but Thomas soon got the hang of it, squeezing the trigger with his index finger, gently lowering the hammer with his thumb. But the muzzle-loader was trickier; the sight of the little round cap exposed was enough to evoke visions of the hammer slipping and firing.

The choice of dogs was carefully weighed. Karo was left behind; duck hunting was bad for pointers, ruining their stance. Dunay was not to be trusted because of his flightiness; any moment, he could bolt into the brush.

Lutnia was out, too—no challenge in it; besides, she was in pup. That left Zagray—serious, systematic Zagray—for flushing the ducks.

A rack wagon, littered with straw, with Romuald, Thomas, Denis, Victor, and Zagray aboard. A cracking whip, dust swirling up from behind the wheels, and Thomas lying on his back, watching the recession of rock, trees, and settlement fences. Romuald whistled, and Thomas chimed in; they were traveling, spirits were high. A half hour later the food sack was raided, the kielbasa passed around, and there was a lot of gnawing and chewing and lurching with the bumps.

The plan was to get there before nightfall, spend the night, and head for the water at daybreak. Would they manage to get their hands on a boat, Thomas wondered. What're you worried about; a village on a lake was bound to have its share of boats and dugouts.

Water loomed in the distance, bluish-red from the western glow. They took the high bank, the lake clearly outlined below. Oval-shaped, one end sharply tapered; the near shore bordered by hillside meadows; the far shore, starting from about midway around the oval, by a blackish mass in which here and there, silhouetted against the sky, stood the perpendicular feather of a pine. Over there were the big swamps in which they would be hunting. By the roadside, on a mound so round it could have been man-made, they passed the ruins of a castle, then dipped down into the fenced lane that was the entrance to the village of Alunta.

At the cottage, they ate curdled milk from huge earthenware bowls. Later, at twilight, Thomas scaled the castle slope. A full moon was on the rise; crickets chirruped in the hushed grass, still warm from the afternoon sun. Tiny waves shimmered at his feet, scalelike. His hand touched slabs of rock—remnants of the castle wall. Was it from here that she had plunged to her death, he wondered.

For Romuald had initiated him into the lore of the castle
—how following its conquest by the Teutonic Knights, the
pagan priestess had chosen death rather than surrender.
He had visions of a woman's figure, arms outstretched,
wailing, a white cloak fluttering. Then the same scene,
only in a slightly different version: a slow descent, a waist
girded with cloth, a head crowned with a green wreath, a
woman's voice intoning chants to her god, and a body,
gradually arching over the shoreline. Her soul—where was
it now? Had it been damned for refusing baptism? The
Knights had been enemies; they had burned and killed and
pillaged in the name of Christ and bestowed baptism as a
protection against hell. Maybe her soul inhabited neither
heaven nor hell but these ruins . . . Something rustled
behind him; he flinched. A field mouse, probably. And even
though he had come up in search of some thrill, he bolted
back down the slope, taking refuge among cottage roofs,
human voices, cows, and chickens.

Zagray, curled beside them in the hay, sighed in his
sleep; Thomas, being the lightest, kept sliding down into
the hole Victor had burrowed in the hay. Someone came
crawling up the ladder and began stepping over them.
"Who's that?" asked Romuald. "A friend," came the an-
swer. Then silence, and Thomas fell asleep with his eyes
fixed on a star peeking through a slit in the barn roof.

When you wake up in the hay, you always find your-
self shifted around. Thomas woke to find himself danger-
ously close to the edge of the hayloft, a snoring, wheezing
Victor no longer beside him but huddled at his feet. His
unoccupied horse blanket lay creased and crumpled in the
gray dawn, Romuald and Denis buried in the hay, with
Zagray sprawled on top. Thomas yawned restlessly, was
about to wake the others, when the barn door creaked
open, there was a burst of light, of cold air, and a voice
sounded from below: "Mr. Bukowski! Time to get up!"

They assembled their gear on a bench in front of the

cottage. Romuald and Denis buckled on their cartridge belts while Thomas stuffed his pockets with shotgun shells, breakfasting on a little milk so as not to have to awaken the women from their Sunday sleep. Their host and his son, who were to accompany them, their pants legs rolled up nearly to their calves, lowered the poles and oars from hooks under the eaves.

The lake was mantled with winding strands of mist. From high up on the steep path, they spotted the boats, one end beached on the shingle, the other in a mist revealing here and there a flawless smoothness, with their ribbed interiors seemingly immobilized forever. By the time they reached the boats, patches of water were already agleam with sky.

48

DUTIES AND pleasures are never evenly divided. Handsomely feathered, the drake prefers solitude to the tedium of sitting on eggs and the guardianship of the young. A duck is either nesting during the best months of the year—May, June, and July—or trailing a string of quacking creatures, her freedom of movement always checked by the last, graceless link in the chain. The first and most urgent exercise the young are taught is the art of taking cover under the leaves of water lilies, totally submerged except for their bill tips. Next comes flying, the hardest part being not the flapping as much as the breaking away. They are a long time in mastering it—beating the air, kicking up a spray, straining for flight, but never quite achieving it . . . The opening of the hunting season invariably finds them in this latter stage.

The boats smelled of tar. In one of them sat Thomas, crouched in the bow, with Romuald and the dog at his back, then their guide, rhythmically transferring the paddle from one hand to the other. They glided, pushing deeper into virgin territory, as rippling waves slapped against the sides. The other boat, along with the heads of the men, loomed up out of the shimmery mist as if suspended. They were steering straight for the opposite shore. As soon as they made out the gaunt shapes of bulrushes, their guide, laying down his paddle, switched to the pole, each thrust against the bottom pitching his body forward.

A flock of ducks: a floating city, a concentration of smudges wrapped in mist. The skiff picked up speed, cutting off their escape route into the rushes; the ducklings, lined up behind their mother, broke in panic, their shrill cries denoting helplessness and desperation. Laughing, Romuald yelled: "Steady, or you'll be taking a bath." Thomas braced himself in the bow, ready to fire. They were nearly alongside when the ducks took wing; there was a frenzy of flapping, water spray. Thomas fired first—bang —then Romuald—bang, bang—the surface was pelted with shot, leaving little circular pools, along with three oblong shapes, immobile, and a fourth, spinning in one spot.

It's hard to explain to someone who's never done it what it's like to retrieve a duck killed by one's own hand. Either you strip and swim out from the shore, in which case the bird will rise to eye level on the swell of your approach; or you maneuver your boat alongside it and stick out your arm. In both cases, it's the interval between seeing it up close and touching it that counts. In the beginning it's no more than a floating object to which you're drawn by curiosity. When touched, it becomes a dead bird. But at the very moment it lies within reach, barely an arm's length away, when its speckled belly lies bobbing up and down in the water, there is always the promise of a

surprise. For we never know whom we may have killed—a duck-philosopher perhaps, or a duck-explorer—and we half expect, without seriously believing it, that we will find a diary on it. And with waterfowl there is always the hope, seldom but occasionally rewarded, of finding an identification tag, inscribed with numbers and the markings of some research station located in a faraway land.

They picked up the four mallards and, skirting the reeds along the shore, searched the coves. Thomas spotted a duck under a tangle of stalks and fired: there was a flapping of wings, a toppled bird. "Good spotting!" Romuald commended him. Just then there was a clamor of wings on water; a column of birds, all well advanced in flying, surged upward, and Romuald brought down two with one shot. Denis and Victor responded with a barrage nearby.

The shoreline separating land from water was blurred by a hide of matted grass. They turned Zagray loose. Going under with every step, half treading and half paddling, he splashed resolutely forward, barking all the way. The younger ducks scurried ratlike in all directions, but with such speed there was barely time to take aim. Bulrushes scraped against the hull as their guide pushed them through to a clearing rank with plant roots. It was in one of these little lagoons that it happened. As he was searching for a new target, Thomas discovered—a tribute to his keen eye—that what had looked to be a slight bulge in a pad was a bird's head. Its presence was betrayed by an inability to keep still. With gun already to shoulder, he decided to grant it a reprieve: how could he shoot something so scared to death, so confident of its camouflage? By not killing it, he assumed greater power over it than if he had killed it. Later, as they were working their way out of the marshes, pulling on the stalks to help the rower, he consoled himself with the thought that the bird was still there, alive; that it would never know its life had been

spared by a man, would never know that he had contemplated it; that he had reckoned what he could do but had willed otherwise. From that day on, they were forever joined in a pact.

Thomas gave up shooting at ducks in flight, having tried once and failed miserably. Nonetheless, he marveled at Romuald, whose aim was so sure that not even the rocking of the boat could disturb him. Especially with garganeys. So swift they made the air whistle, they were much smaller than mallards; but Romuald never missed—three already lay stretched out beneath the rower's bank.

"How'd you make out, fellas?" Romuald asked of the two Bukowski brothers. Victor started stuttering, while Denis kidded at his brother's expense. "Aw hell, by the time he loaded up, they coulda been nestin' on his head!"

Thomas felt a twinge of discomfort for having deprived Victor of his Berdan.

A light breeze creased the lake, which now matched perfectly the color of the sky. A bell in the village was announcing Sunday Mass. Terns cried as they circled the channel poles sticking out of the water at an angle. A buzzard, aiming for the forest, lazily flapped its wings under a cloud.

Their guides suggested making a detour by way of the river. The river ran off the lake behind the castle; the village of Alunta, hugging the tip of the promontory, was wedged between the old fortress on the hill and the river. At the mouth of a tunnel cutting through the reeds, they flushed some birds, which fluttered upward, eddylike. Romuald brought down one of them—a teal, the smallest of the species.

Lagoonlike, sheltered from winds and storms, the region recalled that African interior where Thomas had once built settlements inaccessible to humans. Protruding black poles, bearded with algae rocked by the current, marked the place where a bridge had once stood. Peasant cottages

bordered on the sweet flag; the imprints and depressions left by their beached boats were visible up and down the shoreline. There were apple trees in every garden, the backdrop for fishing nets and laundry strung out to dry. White ducks and geese splashed by the footbridges where the laundry was washed. Viewed from such a tranquil river, a village assumed the dimensions of a country or a kingdom, the details of which escaped notice or were shrugged off as commonplace when observed from the street.

Victor and Denis, their boat now in the lead, had just flushed some mallards, but they held their fire—tame or wild ducks, they couldn't be sure; their ungainly flight triggered three barrels at once, killing one of the birds. The hunting over, they turned back and added up their kill. Romuald and Thomas had twenty-three between them, seven of them Thomas's. The other two boasted fifteen, including one white-eyed duck, and one merganser, gray, with a ruddy head and a hooked bill.

Now facing in the direction of the fortress on the hill, they squinted from the glare. The castle ruins shimmered in the luminescent haze. The pagan priestess who had once lived within those walls, and who was still very present at night, had disappeared forever, taking her place among ghosts and fairy tales. Zagray, suddenly restless, put his paws up onto the side of the skiff. Thomas turned around and held him back by his collar. With the butt of his gun resting on the bank and the barrel against his chest, he had the look of a hunter. But his duck, the one he had left behind, was still hugging the shore. What was it doing? Preening its feathers? Flapping its wings and quacking joyously, now that the danger had passed? Was it God who had decreed that its life should be spared? If it was God's decision, then He must have whispered to Thomas not to shoot. But if that was so, why this feeling that he alone was the arbiter of the bird's fate?

49

SAULÈ, THE SUN, wanders in bright raiment through the sky above the earth where all that lives must perish. Those who would endow her with masculine powers can only cause consternation. Her face is the face of earth's mother. Her time is not our time, and of her doings we know only what a mind prey to the terror of its own solitude can fathom. Immutable in her rhythms, she nonetheless has a history of her own, as narrated in the song of antiquity. Long, long ago, during the first spring, before which there was only chaos, she was wedded to the Moon, Ménuo. When she awoke in the morning, her spouse was gone. During his solitary wanderings, he had fallen in love with Aurora, Aušra. Seeing this, Perkunas, god of thunder and lightning, cleaved the Moon with his sword. A just punishment, perhaps, since Aurora was the Sun's daughter by birth. The memory of Aurora's acquiescence to her stepfather's advances may explain Perkunas's later vengeance. The songs, composed by those in whose memories these events were preserved, are mute as to the reasons, testifying only that on Aurora's wedding day Perkunas drove through the gate and struck a green oak, shattering it. Blood gushed from the oak, spattering Aurora's dress and her maiden's wreath. Sun's daughter wept and asked her mother: "Where, Mama dear, shall I wash out the blood?" "Go, daughter dear, to the lake fed by nine rivers." "Where shall I lay my dress out to dry?" asked Aurora. "In the garden, O daughter, where nine roses are in bloom." And the last, most fearful question of all: "When shall I wear my white dress at the wedding?"

"Not until nine suns shine, O daughter, will you wear it."

Of the customs and cares of those who stir in realms above us, we know very little. To this day the nuptials have never been celebrated, but, then, the passage of a thousand years need last no longer than a second. We owe what information we have to a girl who once lost a sheep—this at a time when mortals were still in communion with deities of the sky. "I went to Aurora," the girl sang, "and Aurora said: 'Every morning I must build a fire for Saulè'" (hence the belief that Aurora is unmarried and lives in the house of her mother). "I went to the Evening Star," she continued, recounting her futile efforts, "who said: 'At night I must make up Saulè's bed.'" And the Moon also refused to help her: "Look at my pitiable face cut in half by a sword." (Thanks at last to a sign from Saulè, she discovered her sheep bleating in the distance, somewhere in the polar regions of northern Finland.)

Was Father Monkiewicz a planet? For a butterfly fluttering over the nasturtium and reseda beds, he surely was. Refracted in the butterfly's many eyes, who knows what charm was exerted by the summit of that shiny bald pate? An insect's lifespan of only a few days, but who's to say whether its ephemeral existence didn't find compensation in the ecstasy of shape and color denied us humans?

Father Monkiewicz. And beneath the surface: the toiling of planetary machines, the circulation of blood, the vibrations of a billion nerves. There were those who regarded him as little more than an ant, who would have been provoked to laughter by the sight of his drawers and of something once suggestive of a bathrobe (his cassock was never worn at home, to save on wear and tear). Breviary in hand, he rocked as he paced the yard, this man who, if his mother had not decided to spare at least one of her sons the life of a peasant, might now have been swinging a scythe. Circumstances more compelling than his wanting or not wanting had destined him to become a

faithful servant of the Church. Yet it was this man who went about the daily exercise of his duties aimed at reassuring people they were worth more than a mountain, a planet, or the universe itself. Conceived in lust, infants slobbered and wailed as he administered the pinch of salt signifying a life of bitterness; as with the baptismal water he imparted the seal of the Word, elevating these products of Nature to dwelling places of the Holy Spirit. From that moment on, wrenched from the order of the immutable, they were justified in seeing themselves in opposition to Nature. And later, when the body's house began to crumble and the heart to slacken, Father Monkiewicz—or someone else invested with the very same power—would describe crosses in oil on limbs about to be turned to dust: thus was the contract between matter and breath dissolved.

Not all of Father Monkiewicz's time was devoted to pondering his duties. Just now, for example, he was flushing a butterfly from the grass to observe its flight; attending to a bee hovering above the chalice of a white lily; and, with one finger stuck in his breviary, was thinking: "The cheapskates!" The insult sprang from a recollection of the last christening. Hard-strapped, eh? A likely story. And he kicked himself for having settled for less than what was customary.

Thomas took off his cap as he squeezed the gate latch. He stood before the priest, fully conscious of the gravity of his mission. The tone of his words was suitably solemn, tragic. "It's Grandmother Dilbin, Father—she's in a bad way. The doctor said she won't pull through."

"Ah . . . !" uttered the priest at the news. "Right—I'll be there in a jiffy."

He was already tripping toward the stairs.

"I have a britska hitched down below."

"Fine, fine. You wait right here."

Though the rectory was practically next door, send-

ing the britska was obligatory. Grandmother Misia's expression, her hushed consultations with Grandfather and Helen, their changed behavior in the proximity of the Unspoken—swelled Thomas with pride, the pride that came of participating in the most solemn, most grown-up event of all. With all hands out in the fields—it was the start of the harvest season—the task of fetching the priest had fallen to Thomas. Though he knew how to hitch a horse, the straps were always getting tangled, so as usual Grandfather had to lend him a helping hand. There was no road through the Swedish Ramparts, which meant going down the hill and past the shrine—reins tight, feet braced against the front, making a gradual descent toward the bend at the bottom. Once past the crucifix, you could let up on the reins—first, because there was no holding back the horses; and second, because custom allowed it.

The presence of Grandmother Dilbin, who lay motionless in the dark, somehow smaller, was enough to make Thomas, utterly consumed by his role of grandson and man of the house, tiptoe. He pictured the return trip home: the ringing of the bell, the faces peering out from behind fences, the piously bowed heads, himself in the driver's seat.

It was as he had imagined. The priest yelled over to the nearest hut, a small boy climbed aboard, sat down next to Thomas on the front seat, and shook the bell. Thomas drove cautiously (such a responsibility!), glancing furtively to the left and right. Unfortunately, most of the houses stood empty—their occupants were out in the fields—and their progress was observed only by an occasional old man or woman emerging from the yard, where, making the sign of the cross, elbows propped on fence, they followed with their eyes the most important traveler of all.

The warm afternoon sun drew beads of perspiration on the priest's bald pate. Neither the Sun nor the Moon nor

the Dawn was any match for Father Monkiewicz. He was
a Man, and if that did not suffice, there was always the
object he held in his hands to tip the scale, for the planets
and stars weighed no more than the sand on the road. His
homespun shirt was stained under the armpits and gave off
an animal smell, yet it was through such as he that the
promise would be fulfilled: "It is sown in corruption; it is
raised in incorruption: It is sown in dishonor; it is raised in
glory: It is sown in weakness; it is raised in power: It is
sown a natural body; it is raised a spiritual body."

50

"A LETTER!"

A barely audible squeak from out of the dark relieved
only by a luminous crack in the shutter.

"No, Grandmother, there's no letter."

He was lying; a letter lay on Grandmother Surkont's
nightstand. The censoring had begun some time ago—and
not without cause, as it turned out. Thomas had eaves-
dropped on the conversations provoked by this last letter
bearing a German stamp and reaching them by way of
Königsberg instead of Latvia. God forbid she should ever
lay eyes on it! The letter, in the gentlest way possible, had
confirmed what Thomas's mother had written privately to
her parents. Charged with embezzling army funds, Con-
stantine had been sentenced, given a dishonorable dis-
charge, and was presently applying for a job as a police-
man. Theodore must not have taken the news of his
mother's illness too seriously if he could be so indiscreet
about his brother's misconduct.

The news was never to be divulged. It happened and

at the same time did not happen, reaching only those who were apt to slough it off as just another misdeed. A bullet lethal enough to pierce the human heart, forever buried in wood.

"I'm dying. Call the priest."

How often during her illness had she said she was dying, exaggerating every pain like the fairy-tale princess who complained of being pricked by a pea through seven layers of eiderdown. And perhaps just because they were so natural, so routinely familiar, these sighs—the sighs of hypochondria—actually did bring her some relief. The more we can show by our words that we are in control of our demise, the surer we are it will never come to pass.

"My dear, you will outlive us all," Grandmother Misia hastened to reassure her. "But a priest can't do any harm, can he? Why, if we'd sent for him right away, by now you'd be up and around the garden."

Reassurances. Sick people, refusing to accept what the mind knows to be true, are grateful for the sound of human speech, for that inflection of voice that precludes passage into the realm where there are no voices. Thomas was somehow irritated by Grandmother Misia's saccharine bedside manner. Why exaggerate so much?

That same day the priest climbed the steps framed by vine-covered porch columns. The changes wrought by the forty or fifty years since infancy had not been enough to efface the rustic cattle boy. His feet, now shod, had once borne the red and blue traces of autumnal frosts. Bracing himself with his crop, he contemplated, with the sort of curiosity evoked by rare animals, the procession of gentry arriving either on horseback or in glittering carriages driven by liveried coachmen. And now, as he entered the low-ceilinged rooms, it was not as a vicar of Christ: trailing him by the hand was the person he was once, the one almost too shy to cross the manorial threshold. The respect paid

him did not exempt him from the fear of humiliation. He took refuge, therefore, in his surplice and stole: they gave him support, lent a dignified air to his gestures—if a roly-poly figure on short legs is capable of any dignity.

Then the door closed, and Grandmother Dilbin found herself alone with the priest. Despite Misia's false assurances, she could have few illusions now, not when a rustling descended, when the blurs of faces parted to reveal a flickering of white, a violet luster. That premonition of the end, an end so evident to those persisting in the external world, was gradually taking hold, as it must all of us, although it is difficult, if not impossible, to admit to the deprivation of our own private sphere, and that all must submit to the inescapable: the cipher that defies our imagination.

"Are you up to confessing, my daughter?"

"My daughter": thus did this squat Lithuanian shepherd address Bronislawa Ritter from the Hanseatic city of Riga.

"In the name of the Father, and of the Son, and of the Holy Spirit. Amen. Don't worry, my child, just repent your sins and God'll be satisfied."

But Broncia Ritter was wandering through a fog, frantically parting it with her hands, struggling toward some unattainable realm of clarity. "I sinned," she whispered.

"Sinned? How?" He brought his ear up close to her lips.

"I doubted in God . . . that He is, that He hears me."

Her fingers clutched his sleeve. "I sinned."

"Go on, I'm listening."

"I never loved my husband . . . I beg his forgiveness."

Groping through the fog was hard, very hard. Then a soft rustling of leaves: "My son . . . I must tell—"

The priest raised his hand and said out loud: *"Ego te absolvo."* The white disk of the Host descended in the pale light filtering through the partially open shutter.

A ball bounces off the gravel path into a waiting hand, grass glistens with dew, birds sing, generations of birds come and go . . . Grandmother Mohl, the one now buried in the family grave at Imbrody, sits unraveling some wool: "Broncia, spread out your hands like this," and slowly winds a soft strand around her wrists. The coral crucifix given her by her grandmother, the one with the tiny window in the center, through which the peeking eye can see the Last Supper being celebrated. Jesus breaks the bread, His brow swarming with rays translucent against the room's cracked wall. All becomes equal, great and small: a peek inside brightly veined coral, a woman's voice in the worn-out dawn of childbirth ("A son!"), the scraping of sleigh runners, the fear of spaces, the gestures made by Christ that were not but are now, time foreshortened, where nothing can be measured by a clock or by the sand in an hourglass . . . Mouth too weak to open . . . help is coming from outside, from out there . . . the Host clings to the tongue . . . the coral opens . . . she enters, diminished in size, goes up to the table, and receives a piece of the bread broken by Christ . . . the legs already far away, in another land, far from the touch of Father Monkiewicz's spatula-like hand, the swollen finger of a plowman's son and grandson, descendant of reapers, now smearing her skin with oil.

Whenever he stood by the bedside of the dying, the priest felt the presence of the Invisible Ones—squatting in a row on the floor, fanning the air, always to a noisy ferment, to a clanging of swords. Those enticed by mental anguish reveled in the effluvia of despair haunting that place where the future had been abolished. Their whispered exhortations were aimed at abetting the self-obsessions of the dying, at trapping them in their own snares;

even as they were conjuring images of past happiness, they showed a Necessity impossible to breach. No wonder they sat in vigil of the blasphemy, the cursing of life's cheat, of the promise betrayed.

By making the sign of the cross, Father Monkiewicz drove them away, those who call for the demanding of proof, always proof, and in that way ensure victory for themselves when the hidden God is put to the test. Just reveal a fraction of your power and I will believe I am not dissolving into nothingness, into the rot of the earth: they crawl alongside, trying to sustain the idea amid the dissolution of all ideas.

But lying on Michalina Surkont's nightstand was a letter, a letter bearing news that prayers are rarely answered. If her having begotten bad fruit was interpreted by her as an affirmation of her baseness, then the letter could only worsen her grief. Was there any wisdom in keeping it from her? Perhaps she was being put to the supreme test: the necessity of trusting when all reason for trusting had been refused. By taking pity on her, by sparing her the blow, people were helping her the only way they knew how: through the sharing of illusions. For those verdicts delivered from on high were judged to be excessively severe.

"Asleep yet?"

"Barely."

Dr. Kohn left behind some morphine and told them how to use a syringe. At first, when he was asked about her illness, it was "probable cancer," then simply "cancer," meaning there was little he could do. Not so Father Monkiewicz, for no sooner did he leave than her chest began to heave and her breathing became more regular.

Gathering the folds of his cassock, the priest, always more sure of himself when seated at table, sat down in the dining room. After uttering a few appropriate remarks, he commented on this season's exceptionally good crop.

"The mercury is falling." Grandfather sighed. "I hope they can get in the harvest before it rains." He offered him some sweetmeats.

The priest was itching for the latest political and domestic gossip.

"Poor Mrs. Dilbin. All alone without her sons. They're so far away."

More he didn't learn.

"Far, far away," Grandfather repeated. "Ah well, a man's home is where he finds work."

"Not everywhere are things the way they are here." Grandmother could not let go an opportunity to vent her sarcasm.

"Duty first."

The priest attributed the flour sacks in his britska (a welcome gift, coming as it did just before the harvest) to the man of the house, as Surkont's wife, that miserly skinflint of a woman, would have taken advantage of his timidity in laying claim to any worldly compensation. Thomas slipped the harness over the horse's head and forced the bit between lips stained a yellow-green. The lindens gave off a honey smell; the bees, clinging to their humming flowers, went about their work as Bronislawa Ritter slowly meandered on the outskirts of time.

51

❧❦❧❦❧❦❧

STACKING A rack wagon is like putting up a house: both require skill. Once the structure is up, a rope, one end looped around a log laid lengthwise on top, is fastened to the platform; the beam, round and smooth

from years of hauling, is used to brace the load, to keep it from spilling every time the wagon lurches. Another rope is strung at the back and two men are needed to cinch it, the risk being that the beam, if it ever slipped out, could fracture the horses' necks. When the driver climbs up on top, he looks down on horses not much bigger than squirrels and has to lie flat to clear the barn door. All day long, these rectangular yellow ricks wobble down the lane, blades of straw among the branches marking where a wagon has brushed a hazel bush. A sultry air, swelling clouds, and by evening it begins to rain—a light drizzle that gradually becomes a downpour lasting until daybreak.

Thomas sensed an air of impatience around the house. Misia and Antonina took turns at Grandmother's bedside, but privately they bore her a grudge. Pity combined with sleepiness often makes one impatient for the end. But then the weather turned sunny, the air shimmered from the heat, and the patient was given a shot of morphine. Thomas thought of Borkuny; no telling how long before he could make another trip out there. To air the room, they opened the shutters and window, letting in a swallow, which described a circle around the room.

On the afternoon of the third day following the priest's visit, Antonina barked out Thomas's name from the porch. He jumped up from the lawn, annoyed at having been discovered there: it gave the impression of keeping a deathwatch. Semidarkness. He found Misia struggling with the trunk lid—the same trunk from which Grandmother Broncia had produced so many trinkets. Packed inside the lid was a funeral candle. "When it's time for me to die, remember where it is."

There was a wavering and remitting in the sick woman's eyes that somehow complemented the grating voice of recent days. Antonina knelt down and, reading from a book, began reciting a litany in Lithuanian, while

Grandmother Surkont, her nose—the nose of a big mouse —beetling over the head of the bed, fussed about, turning the wax candle in her hand.

Thomas, more acutely aware than ever of his physical self, stood by the window, rubbing one bare foot against the other in the warm patch of sunshine on the wood-stained flooring. His heart was ticking, his gaze taking in every detail; he was aching to stretch, lift his arms, take a deep breath. His grandmother's fading swelled him with a triumph odious even to himself. It was cut short by a sob. He looked at her, her chest fighting for one more breath, so small and defenseless against the monstrosity bearing blindly down on her; and full of remorse for all his past injustices toward her, he collapsed at the foot of the bed, crying "Grandmother, Grandmother . . . !"

Though apparently still conscious, she was oblivious of their presence. He rose to his feet and, swallowing his tears, endeavored to fix her every gesture, her every twitch; her fingers opening and closing on the bedcover, the rasping sound escaping from her mouth. She was resisting the flight of language.

"Con-stan-tine . . ."

A match was struck, the wick took, burning low; the deathwatch had begun.

"Jesus!" she said in a distinct voice.

And then, in a low whisper, one which trailed into silence but which was still overheard by Thomas: "Save me."

Father Monkiewicz, had he been present, would have said that the Invisible Ones had been defeated. For the law which says that whatever dies must scatter into ashes and fade into oblivion had been defied by a single hope: by Him who has the power to break the law. Without demanding any proof, despite all arguments to the contrary, she believed.

The whites of her eyes were motionless; a hush except

for the sputtering candle. But no: her breast heaved. A deep breath, an interval lasting several seconds, and the body which had appeared dead exhaled—a startling, fitful, unrecognizable rattle. Thomas shuddered at this surrendering of one's humanity. The woman lying there was no longer Grandmother Dilbin, but death itself; neither the shape of her head nor the complexion of her skin denoted anything anymore; even the terror conveyed by her "Oyey, oyey" was gone. In the space of a half hour (it might have consumed a lifetime), her mouth became fixed, parted in the act of inhaling.

"May eternal light shine upon her, amen," whispered Misia, and she gently lowered the dead woman's eyelids with one finger. Slowly, solemnly, Grandfather crossed himself. They debated where to move her. The bed sagged so much they were afraid the body would stiffen in its half-crouched position. They decided to bring in the long table, and Thomas helped them to get it through the door. The table was covered with a dark blanket.

He helped move Grandmother Dilbin onto the table. As he wrapped his arm around her torso, her nightie shifted and he quickly averted his gaze. Glancing down at the bed sheet when they had her in the air, he in front and Antonina in back, he saw a blotch of feces excreted during the death spasm.

He came back after the washing and dressing. Hands folded on breast, heels touching, soles spread apart, jaw bound with a handkerchief. The open window let in the sounds of evening: the quacking of ducks, the slow rumbling of a cart, a horse's whinny. The world outside was so different, so serene, that it made what he had just witnessed seem unreal.

They sent him to get the cartwright, easing the pain. The cartwright, serving both the manor and the village, lived in the commune. Thomas brought him to the manor and helped him with the measurements. But that evening

he had trouble getting to sleep. How could he sleep if next door her body lay in repose, if she could read his shabby thoughts from the other world. Yes, he had derived pleasure from watching her die. A bitter pleasure, like the taste of berries, which, however much they may burn the tongue, keep tantalizing us to eat more. Candles were burning in two tall candle holders beside the table-catafalque, prayers were being recited, but she was all alone in the dark night.

Early the next morning—the wax in the candleholders was embedded with a moth's wings; his grandmother's eyelids had parted, revealing a thin strip of white —he went to see the cartwright go about the art of coffinmaking. The yard in front of the shop was littered with rimless wooden wheels stacked one against the other and with piles of cut lumber. Thomas was already familiar with the workbench, with its surface rough and scored with cuts and indentations, with its hand vises at the sides, whose threaded bolts screwed in and out with such ease, and with the constant smell of shavings underfoot. He could, as now, sit rapt on a stump, spellbound by the back-and-forth motion of the wood plane.

"Pine's no good; let's use oak," said the master carpenter. (Because of his beetling nose and bulging cheeks, Kelpšis bore a slight resemblance to Misia.) The backs of his hands were a tangle of veins, a landscape of mountains and valleys. A ribbon of shavings curled up from the chink in the plane, and Thomas rejoiced at this mastery over wooden matter; if a board could be planed, then anything could be planed, made smooth. Thus were Grandmother's cheeks to be graced forever by oak-grained filigree. The coffin made him relive his dream of Magdalena. He wondered about the worms, whether they could squeeze through the slits. A white skull, deep sockets for eyes, the durability of wood. His grandmother most certainly was

dead, not in a stupor or coma. The gruesome stories she had told of coffins that had been known to bang after being sealed and even after being lowered into the grave, and of how, after clearing away the dirt and raising the lid, they had found people suffocated inside, their bodies convulsed by the struggle to escape. Grandmother had been so afraid of waking to discover she had been buried alive that she insisted it was better to verify death as someone in her family had done: by shattering the skull with a hammer.

Oak was also chosen for the cross. The cartwright took a fat pencil from his pocket, wet it with spit, and drew the outline of a cross on a wood chip. He handed it to Thomas, seeking his opinion, and he again savored a grandson's prerogative. The sketch showed a sort of lean-to spanning the arms of the cross.

"What's that for?" he asked, pointing to the little shelter.

"Got to. Two boards nailed together—uh-uh, not very pretty. Anyway, it'll keep the rain off, keep it from rotting."

According to Antonina, the soul circles the shell it has just abandoned. It hovers about, examining its former self, amazed that it could have seen itself until now only in relation to a body. As the hours go by, the face, once the soul's mirror, begins more and more to resemble rock moss. That evening Thomas witnessed a change in his grandmother's appearance, but suddenly withdrew in panic: she had looked at him! He bolted for the door, all set to yell that she was waking from a coma. But she made not the slightest movement. It was an illusion, caused by a further parting of the eyelids and the play of candlelight in the whites of her eyes. A soul no longer lived inside. If Antonina was right, it was floating about the room, brushing familiar objects, biding its time until the funeral, when with a clear conscience it could finally abandon what, after all, had once been its own.

52

CLOUDS GATHER into big-bellied shapes; a dragon with a twisted tail, fins, and streaming jaws journeys across the sky; the jaws become more attenuated, frazzled, until a tiny cluster of white detaches itself and, propelled by the dragon's breath, is borne swiftly away. A slender cross traverses the dragon's flank; the cross is held by the sacristan, who is followed by the priest, then the coffin carried by Balthazar, Pakenas, Kelpšis, and the young Sypniewski. The procession files across the Swedish Ramparts, from the top of which the eye can make out diminutive figures moving between the peaked sheaves that line the steeply sloped fields on the opposite shore.

Luke Juchniewicz, who arrived yesterday with Helen, runs up to the coffin to relieve Pakenas, his coattails parting to reveal a pair of dark checkered pants. He shifts his head under the load, the coffin sags, wobbles as his mincing steps throw the others off stride. Thomas's hopes are again betrayed: Luke has lived up to his comic role. But Luke is stubborn and with face tearfully contorted he bears up. Shatybelko has on a dark blue capote; his wife, a silk scarf embroidered with black flowers.

They seat themselves in the church pews. Thomas tries to pray but can't help thinking of the freshly dug grave. The family plot has room for only two more graves —one for Misia, the other for Grandfather—so Grandmother Dilbin has to be interred nearby. In digging her grave, they struck an oak root that had to be cut with an ax, leaving white wounds in the clay. The roots will enfold,

possibly invade the coffin, and Grandmother will be trapped as in a bird's claws.

The others are still trailing toward the exit by the time he is threading his way through the tombstones. Here it is, on the outskirts of the cemetery, chosen for its proximity to the Surkonts, and where, only a few steps away, now partially eroded and tufted with weeds, stands another mound, that of Thomas's friend, Magdalena. Somehow they must meet, and he tries to imagine it, knowing that in reality there was no imagining it. They reach out to one another —Magdalena's head is now restored—and burst into tears.

"Why, oh, why did we punish ourselves so? Why were we strangers until now? Why did we have to suffer in solitude? You could have stayed with me. I could have found you a husband, and you, with your courage, could have helped me through life. Too bad people can't love each other until after they die. What's it like to poison yourself? I'm curious."

"Hard," Magdalena sighs. "I prayed for God's forgiveness, on my knees I swallowed the poison, but right away I got scared, cried out for help ... "

They look young—Grandmother exactly as in the old photographs showing her cinched snugly at the waist. They call each other by first name.

"Why did you spook people?" asks Grandmother.

Magdalena smiles. "Why ask when you already know?"

"Yes, now I know ... "

Thomas could not admit to their inhabiting separate worlds, no more than he could assent to Magdalena's soul being among the damned. Damned were those who failed to evoke pity or love. There, around the freshly dug grave, the others are already clustered as he begins a Hail Mary, digging his nails into his palm to add fervor to the recitation. He commends Magdalena to the Mother of God.

The coffin is lowered in a sling, seesawing, getting

snagged on a severed root before finally settling on the bottom. Thomas looks down while Father Monkiewicz delivers the graveside sermon. He thinks: For hundreds, thousands of years they have been burying the dead like this; if all were to rise at the same time, one beside the other, their millions would make a solid wall. Every living person knows he must die—Grandfather says they are waiting for him between the chains of the Surkont plot. They know, yet don't seem to care. Death—the passing from one life to another—is so terrifying, why aren't they screaming, tearing their hair out . . . ? But, no—nothing. Their calm, their shrugging it off with a "That's the way it is . . ."—baffled him. He believed there was a secret that God revealed to those who wanted Him to very much: that death was not inevitable, not what it was made out to be. Or did they know more than they were letting on, and was that why they took it so calmly? Thomas, in other words, gave them credit, just as he did Luke, who, if he did not possess another, more intelligent self, would have demolished an entire order; just so, grownups would have been nothing more than pathetic children in disguise. What looked to be simple could not be so simple.

One day he too would be lowered in a sling. Even if he became Pope? Even. But if the grenade had gone off that time, he would have died without knowing he was dying. The grouse brought down by Romuald had not had time to feel the terror. Oh, God, don't let me die a slow death like Grandmother.

"You throw first," Misia said, half aloud. Yes, as her grandson, he was the closest, indeed the only blood relative present. He picked up a yellowish clod of dirt and threw it, watching it shatter as it landed; others fell, drumming on the wooden coffin lid, and then came the shoveling, creating a narrow mound of earth along the top plank. They worked quickly, filling the cracks between the coffin walls and then the surrounding gaps until the brown-stained

boards assumed the tawny color of earth. If the coffin had aroused curiosity from the moment it was sealed, from the moment it contained a body, the urge was all the greater now: an empty space, a tiny pocket of air, a segment of tunnel.

Oaks overhead, some so old they must have sheltered Hieronymous Surkont on his horseback rides. At the foot of the close-cropped slope, a stream ran under a footbridge before emptying into the Issa. Orchards and huts on the other side of the canyon. Such was the view marking the end of the journey.

"We mustn't forget to order a plate," Thomas's grandfather said.

"It should read: *The widow of an 1863 insurgent,*" Thomas intruded, knowing how proud she was of the past.

"Thomas and I will plant some flowers," promised Antonina.

Kelpšis held steady his cross with the shelter and planted it in the ground, shoring it up with dirt and leveling the rectangular-shaped grave with his shovel. Here our chronicler rests his pen as he tries to visualize those who will come to this place many years hence. Who are they? What sort of trade? Parking their shiny car down by the bridge, they will hike the rest of the way on foot. "What a funny old cross. Look at those oaks—what a waste of good lumber!" It's obvious they do not like death; the mere thought of it diminishes their dignity; their feet squarely on the ground, they proclaim, "We are alive!" Yet each is endowed with a heart, a heart that is sometimes gripped by terror, and their feeling of superiority over those who have passed is scarcely a protection. Bluish-gray lichen will hang from Kelpšis's shelter, the name on the plate will have faded. And clouds will gather into big-bellied shapes, just as on that day, long ago.

53

IT WAS a sound unlike any the human throat could make, but Thomas soon got the hang of it. It was hard going at first, but he practiced it to perfection, to a point where he almost believed he could speak their language. In the forest near Borkuny there was a hollow, thick with alder, and in spring the hollow became a lake. It was just after sundown, the treetops stood black against the orange sky: the time was right. He stood facing a solid wall of young trees, immersed in slime and the effluvium of rotting leaves, and with calculated fury, avoiding any abrupt movements, he picked off the mosquitoes attacking his face and neck. The mosquitoes were so bloated with blood that his palms were streaked from swatting. Softly, he released the safety on his Berdan. The Berdan, borrowed from Victor for the summer, had somehow become a part of him.

"What you need it for, anyway?" Romuald had told his brother. "You're too busy to take it out. It just hangs there, don't it? So why not let Thomas do a little huntin'."

Victor had consented.

Goshawks nested deep in the forest, deep enough for the swampy ground to make access tricky. Once they had got their wings, the young spent the day circling the forest, high up in the air, in imitation of their parents; by evening, the family was homeward bound for the night. The day before yesterday, Thomas had tested his baiting call and was answered on several sides. The secret was to pick a time when not all were back yet, because that was the time of their mutual summoning. The shrieking was getting

closer; soon he spotted a pair of gray wings contoured among the leaves, heard the flutter as the hawk, oblivious of Thomas hidden in the shadows below, lighted on the slender treetop. He called and waited for an answer. Then ever so slowly he brought the barrel to eye level and squeezed the trigger. It fell! He spent a long time searching for it, afraid he might have to wait until dawn, when he practically tripped over it, its buff coloring almost bright against the dark-weeded swamp. And those flight feathers, stretching to full length as he picked the bird up by the wing . . . He nicked his finger while prying apart its tightly clenched claw. But one bird was hardly enough, not when he had gained the advantage. He waited a whole day before trying his luck a second time.

"*Eee-eee!*" The shrillness came from a constriction of the throat muscles, which, if done often enough, produced a painful cramping sensation. He could hear them deep in the forest. Would they fly back today, or not? Silence except for the buzzing of mosquitoes, a vertical column dancing up and down in the sunlight. He tried again: "*Eee-eee . . .*" What exactly this sound meant in their language he didn't know, though there was no mistaking the tone of longing, of urgency in it. They were coming, he could tell! He sent out another call; it carried in the silence that had already found other birds perched for the night or preening their feathers. Then it happened —that unremitting keening reaching him from several directions at once. They were out there, all right.

He savored his moment of triumph, trying not to make too much of it. The younger hawks were not yet trained to distinguish the real thing from an imitation, nor were there any jays to warn of a human presence. He called a third and final time, knowing that at close range he might give himself away.

Above the tree line—one bird shape, then another. In flight, but that still didn't mean anything. Heads up—a

shadow just flitted through the brush, in among those young alders. It was perched. Where? The mosquitoes lining Thomas's arms and forehead could now feel secure; he was paralyzed. He could hear it crying from another treetop, but the foliage blocked his view. If he moved closer, by as much as a few steps even, the bird would spot him and resort to that peculiar flight when flushed by a man: the flight of mystery.

He would have to risk another call. Intent on getting it right, losing all sense of himself, he incarnated the soul of a goshawk. *"Eee-eee . . ."* Suddenly alerted, the bird responded. A flutter of wings gave Thomas his target. He took aim, guessing more by instinct the location of the mouse-gray blotch against the black. A report: the bird lurched forward, bunched up into a ball, and fell, arresting its descent as it brushed the boughs. Thomas came on the run, the branches whipping his face. A second kill! a voice piped inside him. He found the bird lying on its back, still alive, its claws exposed in self-defense. Instead of a companion or its mother—whose keening had beckoned so unerringly—there now stood, leaning over its inert body, a giant. The goshawk was a predator—Thomas thought by way of justifying the act—one that fed on the meat and blood of pigeons and chickens. Holding the gun upright, he clubbed the bird's head with the stock and watched as it veiled its golden eyes with its lower eyelids. After the skinning, the meat would go to Lutnia and the stuffed skin would preserve indefinitely the appearance of a discrete being—until the moths set in.

If Thomas was troubled by a guilty conscience (as he frequently was), he told himself that a creature killed by one's hand would have had to die anyway, that it didn't really matter when or how. That these same animals might have had an urge to live could not distract him from a higher ambition: the need for a trophy. The sky was already a deep shade of blue as he emerged from the forest

and crossed the little footbridge over the stream. Through the bushes he saw the house lights burning. Barbarka was fixing supper. What would she say to this second kill?

But on the third try his luck ran out: the gunfire had scared them away. His bird-calling ability continued to bring him glory, until one morning (not that summer but another), as he went to test it, his voice broke. It had changed, become huskier, and he never recovered the purity of that signal that was something between a cat's meow and the whistle of a bullet.

54

BARBARKA slapped Romuald's face so hard it echoed in the orchard. "What's got into you?" he kept saying as he backed away. Taking the enemy by surprise was always the best tactic, and Romuald's surprise could not have been more genuine. A peaceful Sunday morning, unmarred by any squabbles or spats, when suddenly: "You cheater! You skirt chaser! Take that! That's what you get for cheating on me!" Romuald, no less stunned than if he'd sighted a comet, could have easily chased her off his property; but thinking she might have gone berserk, he quietly acquiesced. A moment later, a sobbing Barbarka was running down the forest path.

Though the tears were sincere, the slapping had come of a mixture of anger and premeditation. Her woman's instinct had told her that, win or lose, this was the only way, that moping and sulking would get her nowhere. The jump was best measured by the eye, not by any arithmetic. Romuald was the enemy, but not only. He was pleased with her service, and she knew it. Besides, he would have

been hard put to replace her, to find another housekeeper with her love of cleanliness and tidiness and her willingness to try her hand at any kind of work, even plowing (once, when Romuald had taken ill, she had plowed practically on her own after the hired farmhand lost his temper and walked off the job). She was also a better cook than most. Romuald was getting on in years, was rather set in his ways; breaking in someone else would not be easy. But there were other reasons for her self-assurance.

They led a secluded life, but were not in need of company. Spring and summer, a time of endless chores, passed quickly. Barbarka spent the autumn canning apples and pears; the rainy season, at her spinning wheel (she knew how to weave a tight weave). They raised their own flax and bought their wool from Masiulis. She made linen from homespun; on her loom, cloth. In winter the thump of the shifting foot pedal lasted until sunset; in the evening she could spin almost blindfolded—weaving required greater light and concentration. A wooden loom and a handful of skirts stored in a chest were her only dowry.

The busy work week ended with Saturday's bathing ceremony and a trip to Sunday Mass, either in the britska or on foot. Romuald, not a fervid churchgoer, often skipped several Sundays in a row for the sake of his hunting.

The bathhouse was built with Romuald's own hands, on the river, and it was built according to plan. There were two rooms. In one he installed clothes-pegs, even a hand-carved bench for dressing and undressing. It also housed a log fireplace, the flat stone on the other side reaching such temperatures that a pail of water tossed on it was immediately converted to steam. In the other room, three shelves, built steplike one on top of the other, stretched from wall to wall. To keep out the wind, the scourge of any bathhouse, the gaps between the logs were stuffed annually with moss.

The ceremony began with the washing of Romuald's back and shoulders, with Barbarka doing the scrubbing. Romuald then got up a good amount of steam—the thicker, the better—and took to the highest shelf, a bucket of cold water within easy reach (it was her job to see that it got there), a splash of cold water being one way of prolonging the thing. Standing below, besom in hand, Barbarka would then run the birch branches over his chest and belly, which took some know-how: exposure to the steam left the skin so sensitive that the slightest brush of the twigs, even more than a lash, burned like a red-hot poker, the trick being therefore to alternate the flicking and the whipping. Romuald would sigh and holler "Ahhh! More! More!" roll over on his belly, scoop water from the pail, yell "Come on! Harder! Harder!" then, red as a lobster, bolt outside and welter in the snow for as long as it took to numb the body against the cold. Then it was back to the shelf, because now it was Barbarka's turn, and he kept her up there, and how he did, and she groaning "Oyey, I cain't take it no more," and he saying "Sure you can; just turn over," working her with the switch, and she laughing and screeching "Cut it out, hear? That's enough!"

If he dismissed her, who would go to the bathhouse with him? Who would scrub his back and shoulders? He liked to look at her; she could tell. She was all health and youth, her breasts just the right size, sturdy in the haunches and shoulders. Skin a light pink, almost white alongside his. Yes, she satisfied his male pride in more ways than one.

In more ways than one. In submitting to the love ritual, Barbarka would invoke the most sacred Biblical names (which may not have been appropriate, but at such times who cares what is appropriate and what is not?), screaming in a whisper at the height of her panting: "Romuaaald!" Motionless, he would contemplate the wave

breaking on him, the wave he himself had set in motion. (In love, as in everything else, Romuald was a perfectionist.) He liked it when she caught her breath, and he again heard that incoherent litany of hers. Nor did she grumble if he went at it again and again and again . . . No, parting was out of the question. And if, despite time-honored methods, a kid was born? Well, so? And the next morning it was a new world, dew on the window, a trembling in the knees. And songs at the loom, joyous songs.

But at the moment she was crying as she pictured him in the orchard. His coming down the path, the sound of his footsteps, the creaking boards, and that voice—"Out!" *Let* him throw her out—he would be the one to suffer most. He didn't need this fling with Helen Juchniewicz. An aristocratic whim, so like a man, one of those male stupidities women had to put up with. Underneath all the masquerading, he was a man like any other. High time he saw how he was messing things up, chasing after highbred ladies just to prove he was no worse than other folk.

If not for old lady Bukowski . . . Now, there was the real enemy. While she did not oppose Barbarka's staying with Romuald—he needed company, same as any man—she kept a vigilant eye on them. The old lady would give him hell if he as much as sat her down next to him in the britska on the way to church: What would people say? A servant girl should know her place.

Yes, the old lady was an obstacle. An obstacle to her dream of becoming mistress of Borkuny, secure in the knowledge that she could never be evicted. But no Bukowski had ever married a peasant, not even a richly dowered one, much less one like herself. Sitting and staring into her lap, her knees spread wide apart, her skirt taut, Barbarka gave way to despair. Oh, if those were her only worries! When he came in, she would go down on her knees and beg forgiveness. Just let things be as they were.

The back of Romuald's neck—a robust neck, scored with tiny oblique rectangles—was red as a turkey's crest. Standing in rigid concentration, he suddenly made for the house, quickening his stride. He paused in front of the porch, then slowly mounted the wooden steps, went into his room, and took down the shotgun.

The forest, provided one attends to its whispering, can counsel a man what to do. Whether owing to the forest's counsel or the premise that men are tough only on the outside, that afternoon Romuald said nothing. But that evening, after the milking, his matter-of-fact voice rang out: "Barbarka!"

Quivering all over, she entered the room.

"On your belly!"

In his hand was the lash with the deer-hoof handle. He pulled back her skirt and, with measured but painful strokes, began whipping her bare buttocks. She winced and writhed and dug her teeth into the pillow; but she was happy. His punishing her could mean only one thing: She was *his*! And the punishment was deserved.

What came later was, in a way, a reward, the greater in that love mixed with tears and pain takes on a sweetness all its own. For it is one of man's stranger habits that even as he nears the moment of ecstasy, even as the body is surrendering, the mind continues to wander, more conscious than ever of the cleavage. The holy names that fell from Barbarka's lips proved that she was a faithful daughter of the Church, that the power of her emotions could be contained in no other language, all the while the mind was contemplating its triumph. For the same woman who a moment before would have been perfectly content with things as they were, that same woman was now plotting against old lady Bukowski. While the visible Barbarka hungered for the violation and the engorgement, the invis-

ible Barbarka was insinuating that there were far worse things than having a baby. Thus, a certain alliance was struck between them.

55

With the blackcock hunt only a week away, the incident with Aunt Helen thrust Thomas into perplexity. However great his dislike for her, he was bound by a sense of family loyalty. The incident: They were on their way to Borkuny (he couldn't resist tagging along when she decided to go), Thomas working the whip and reins, the two of them seated side by side, and the horse had just started climbing the wooded knoll when—it was hard to say which came first, the seeing or the hearing of it—out from behind a young spruce came a burst of white and a woman's shrieking, and both the screaming and the whiteness belonged to Barbarka, but now so strangely altered that Thomas was awestruck.

Flushed, eyebrows knitted, brandishing a hazel switch in one hand, she screeched: "Bitch! I'll teach you to do yer romancin' round here!" Then a stream of cuss words in two languages. "If I ever catch you around Borkuny again, you'll git such a whippin'—"

There was a *swish* and Helen cupped her cheek with both hands; then another, only this time she stuck out her arm for protection. Thomas, thoroughly overwhelmed, gave the horses the whip and there was a clatter of wheels.

"Back, Tommy! Back! Good Lord, what did I do, what did I do! Back, Tommy! I'll never set foot out here again, so help me!"

Turning around on a narrow trail was easier said

than done, but he managed it, wheel scraping against the side, crushing young scrub, and almost tipping over in the process. Big tears ran down his aunt's face; now it was she who was flushed, and her muted voice expressed shock. Prayerfully clasping both hands together, she turned up her blue eyes and implored heaven to exact revenge for the outrage she had so innocently endured.

"What a beastly thing to do. I don't understand. Why? How could she do such a thing? She must be deranged."

Thomas concealed his discomfort by gazing straight ahead, affecting concentration. Romancing was the word for it, all right. All those sugary looks and dewy-eyed, plum-eyed glances . . . But how did Barbarka fit in? That he couldn't quite understand. Maybe Romuald had tired of all the sweet-talk; maybe the ambush in the woods was his doing. But why plot against his aunt with the help of a servant girl?

Thomas had a hunting date with Romuald. Theirs was a friendship between men, far above the petty bickering of grownups. But what if his aunt was to stop visiting Borkuny, if she forbade him or anyone else to go for reason of decorum? Or would she? Although for Thomas such matters bordered on the inscrutable, he sensed in his aunt's behavior the residue of some shame. She said nothing, not a word, but her silence was the beginning of a pact between them. She sat beside him in the wagon, her mouth hemmed by deep creases, seesawing like an owl.

"What? Back already?" asked Grandmother Misia.

"Nobody home," Helen said, lying effortlessly.

Thomas thus emerged not only as a victor but as an accomplice. For his recollection of the avenging Barbarka was tainted with memories of a more private nature. Not long before, while out brush-breaking with the Berdan, he had walked out onto the forest apron skirting the hay fields of Pogirai. He was spotted by an old peasant, who stood

high up on a rack wagon, stacking the sheaves which an-
other man, this one younger, pitched up to him from
below. Thomas greeted him with the traditional *Padek*
Dèvu—Lithuanian for "God's help"—when the old man
broke off, stood up straight on the haystack, and began
reviling him with his shaking fist raised sunward. Thomas,
who hardly knew the man, and then only by sight, was
mortified by this show of contempt, especially since he had
done nothing to deserve it. Anger provoked by anger was
understandable; but he had been polite, and his civility had
met with the old man's fury and for one reason only: he
was a Polish *pan*. Stranded out in the open, Thomas
shuffled off at a deliberately slow pace—so as not to give
the impression of running—his cheeks on fire, his horse-
shoe-shaped mouth (though he would have been the last to
admit it) quivering.

Something about Barbarka's ambush reminded him
of that day. Only here it was he and Helen in the britska,
and Barbarka . . . But if Romuald was behind the con-
spiracy— And inexplicably, inexorably, the image of
Dominic came to mind—idolized, sacrilegious Dominic,
who more than once had appeared in his dreams in the
guise of Barbarka. "Nice company, this Mr. Bukowski"—
Misia used to say, laying undue emphasis on the "Mister."
"Honestly, the riffraff we let into this house!"

Romuald smelled of tobacco and masculine strength
and Thomas had no desire to lose him. When he suddenly
realized what was at stake—the hunt, the gun, everything
—he was aghast at having had such thoughts.

He managed to pry out of his grandmother some
cloth scraps for leggings and fixed himself a pair of moc-
casins from bast: for where he was going, the marshland,
nothing else would do.

56

⚜ 🙰*🙰*🙰*🙰*⚜

BALTHAZAR's distillery was located in the forest, far from the beaten track, and if the police came at all, it was to sample Balthazar's homemade brew up at the cottage, a couple of bottles sufficing to ensure the right kind of report. The liquor served not only Balthazar's own private use (he couldn't get drunk on beer), and not only as bootleg. Ever since the Commission's inspection of the forest—under his supervision—the village of Pogirai had borne him a grudge. Surkont's hospitality toward the three officials, their high spirits and flushed faces as they climbed aboard the britska, how they had sung most of the way, how one almost fell out—none of it had gone unnoticed. (Spirits later got so high they really couldn't tell the grass from the trees.) There were reasons, all carefully elaborated, why Pogirai was anxious for the forest to become state property, even at the expense of giving up certain privileges, such as poaching. Although no one except Joseph knew the real story behind the filing date of the Surkont land division, people's instincts told them that the timberland would be crucial to negotiations with the manor over the disputed pasturage. They were sore at Balthazar for conniving with Surkont, and the moonshine was used to quiet the most vociferous throats. One refusal and they were liable to take revenge by leading the police straight to the distillery in the woods.

Now when the men huddled after Sunday Mass by the church wall in Gine, the talk was mostly of the forest.

"That Surkont's a weasel." It was the young Wackonis, no longer wearing his military tunic but dressed like

Joseph the Black in a high-necked homespun jacket. The episode with the grenade had never been broached again; it was a thing of the past, buried and forgotten.

"You can bet," he said, running the tip of his tongue along the seam of his hand-rolled cigarette, "you can bet *he* ain't gonter give up what's his."

A poker face, without so much as a stare or facial twitch to give away the man's intent. But the mockery—a mockery aimed at the gullible—was not lost on Joseph.

"Maybe not now he won't," he conceded. "But give him a year or two."

"Balthazar's coverin' for him."

"He's tying his own noose."

"And it's gettin' tighter all the time. They say that Juchniewicz woman is gonter give him the boot."

"Who said?"

"Today, in the commune. Came lookin' for a house for him. He moves out, she moves in."

Joseph spat as a sign of his disgust. "A hired hand, eh? Uh-uh, he ain't that dumb."

"Think he won't?"

"Ain't nobody goin' to make him quit the forest. He'll fight it all the way. Take him to court and you can wait another ten years ..."

"No more. He's runnin' scared. Down comes a pine cone and he thinks it's the sky fallin'."

"What drink won't do to a man."

Wackonis's attitude, thus expressed, proof that one's judgment of others should always be based on strict observation, spoke for the majority of the villagers: plenty of bad blood and plenty of revulsion. Where another man would take a hundred steps in stride, Balthazar was the sort who ran in circles, panting his lungs out, banging his fists against imaginary walls. But Balthazar was ignorant of their feelings, of that mixture of disgust and pity. The prison in which he was wrestling was real, and if anyone

had told him he was imagining things he would have sloughed it off as the speech of blind and stupid men. And the liquoring was just to see their faces momentarily brighten, to hear a word of praise, to prove to himself that he was "a good man." So far, the liquor had done the trick; a little envy maybe, but that's as far as it went. Now there was this damned Commission, all these shady dealings of the manor . . . Wasn't it bad enough they'd made him an outcast, why had Surkont to go and mention his daughter —true, only one sentence, roundaboutlike, but enough to stand as a warning.

A batch of brew seething in a kettle, a big-cheeked face coppered by a blazing wood fire. Balthazar sat on the edge of the ditch staring down at the distillery below him, the darkness unrelieved except for the hazel leaves shimmering at his back. A hand blotting out the stars, aiming for the forests, guided by moonbeams over the waves of the Baltic . . . oh, why didn't someone's hand reach down and seize this tiny speck on the rotating earth, pick it up, and whisk old Balthazar away? Anywhere, didn't matter where, into the orchestra pit in the middle of a big-city concert, music stands flying, audience in an uproar, and he, Balthazar, sprawled on all fours, a fury of motion in long-legged boots, would rise to his feet, rocking, wild: "Yell!"

And obedient to the command of his tormentor, he would proclaim his secret affliction, that illness affecting so many of us born along the shores of the Issa: "It's not enough!"

"Not enough!"

"It was not enough just to live!"

"Yell!"

And then a savage howl: "It's wrong! All wrong!"

A cry protesting the fact that the earth was the earth; the sky, the sky. Against Nature's boundaries. Against the law which says every "I" must be itself and nothing more.

But instead of being borne away by a hand, Balthazar
got the hiccups. He scratched his chest through his open
shirt and wrapped himself in his sheepskin against the
chilly, transparent night.

The villagers of Pogirai were revulsed by the sight
of a man who didn't know what he wanted, who made life
hard for himself, embroiling himself in order not to be
alone with his fear, that nameless, faceless terror. But who
knew whether another fate did not await him, one which
had been there all along, since the beginning of the world,
that only he could fulfill but which had not been fulfilled,
so that in the place where an oak should have stood there
was now only empty space containing the barest outline of a
branch.

Balthazar slid down from the edge of the pit, squatted,
and stuck a tin cup under the spout. A long swig. From
deep within the forest came the keening of a bird being
torn apart. Dead silence except for the crackling fire. The
sky was getting paler; a falling star traced a perfect line
across the darker half.

"Kill somebody."

"Who?"

"I don't know."

57

A SNIPE is a gray bolt of lightning, taking
wing, then zigzagging low above the ground before straight-
ening its course. Why this particular pattern is hard to say,
almost as if the invention of the gun was foreseen in the
primeval scheme. A quivering Karo stood with forepaw

raised, and Romuald brought down a bird even before Thomas had time to shoulder his Berdan.

The above took place in a marshy meadow agleam with rust-stained patches. He was wearing his snug-fitting moccasins and leggings—a protection against stalks and adders—and the water felt pleasantly cool. They marched single-file behind the dog through sun-dappled dew. It was to have been a party of four, but Denis had backed out at the last minute, leaving only Romuald, Thomas, and Victor.

Once a lake, its former basin was now a sprawling meadowland covered with sharp sedge and, up ahead, with moss, thick with pine scrub and clumps of tangled withes. As they crossed the scrub line, Thomas inhaled its familiar fragrance. The moorland was a kingdom of fragrance. The moss sprouted bushes of marsh tea (*Ledum palustre*) with narrow leathery leaves, and blue bog bilberries the size of pigeon eggs thrived on the warm, vaporous air. The berries were invigorating to the taste, but too many could put a man in a trance (whether from eating or smelling was unclear). The moor made a good feeding ground for the young blackcocks, still under their mother's guardianship —the older cocks, spending the summer in solitude, took refuge in the brush in the molting season and during that time became too lethargic to fly.

"Flush 'im, Karo, flush 'im!"

Karo kept circling around, flashing his white and yellow-spotted hide, wagging his tail, now and then throwing an inquisitive backward glance. Romuald pointed out the direction. He wore his high-necked dolman, a cartridge belt around his waist, and the strap of his game bag spanned his shoulder blades. Victor hoisted the leather pouch with the muzzle-loader accessories.

Thomas had kept his hunting date, arriving at Borkuny as if nothing had happened, greeting Barbarka as if he had never been aboard the britska that afternoon.

Later, as they were hiking along and had a moment to themselves, Romuald asked nonchalantly: "Will your aunt be dropping by one of these days?"

Thomas gulped. Why pretend ignorance? But if I meddle—he thought—I'm sure to make a mess of it. "I— she has lots of errands, I think."

That was all that was said of her. His barrel leveled straight ahead, Thomas fixed on the moiling Karo in anxious concentration. It rankled him that he had yet to bring down a bird on the wing—he didn't count the slew of wild ducks he and Romuald had bagged on Alunta. It was time he got one; the blackcock would be as good a test as any. The first kill of the day—Romuald's snipe—had only quickened his anxiety. The ability to track a bird in flight, to know how many meters to anticipate, and all that in the space of a split second, seemed to him a feat beyond mastery. If only he'd had time to get a bead on that snipe, but the spasm in his throat had barely subsided when Karo was already retrieving.

"They're lyin' low," said Romuald. "Dog's gonter nose 'em out into the open. Eyes to the ground, Tommy."

They waded knee-deep through the moss.

"They're over there, I betcha!"

But Romuald had guessed wrong, and so they kept plowing through the moss and Karo pulled in his tongue and went back to work.

The worst was not knowing when to expect it. You went along, concentrating for a while, bearing down on every bush, then bit by bit you let up, lulled by the rhythm of your own footsteps, until pretty soon a bed of reeds, like those up ahead, became just another obstacle, something that had to be circumvented. And that's when it happened, out of meanness.

For a moment they lost sight of Karo. Suddenly Thomas was pelted by a loud fragmentation, an explosion in midair, a violent sundering of the world: panic—gun

bursts—blood rushing to the face—a blurring of vision—
hands trembling. There they were! But so close he could
see their elongated necks, their chickenlike bills beetling
through a frenzy of flapping wings. He took aim—no, he
merely pulled the trigger, hurriedly, pulling blindly and
praying for a miracle. And there was Victor right beside
him, all hunched up, shouldering his gun any old way, not
a hint of any grace or style; and Thomas heard him fire,
heard the report; and he saw his own bird in the distance,
and the other one—Victor's—falling, and the dog jumping
back and forth, not knowing if he was to sink his teeth into
Victor's or Romuald's . . .

Ejecting the empty shell, Thomas, even though the
sunny sky had become a funeral pall and his heart was
racing something awful the way it does after some terrific
scare, tried to bear his defeat courageously. He had
counted—assuming he had had time to think at all—on a
miracle. It was his own fault; next time he would be
smarter.

Victor was reloading his blunderbuss of a gun, pack-
ing the charge with the ramrod.

"Gel gack em"—meaning, "We'll catch 'em," a tact-
ful way of telling the boy not to take it too much to heart.

Thomas's gloom, the more painful for having to be
concealed, soon began to lift: there was always the future.
Just keep calm—above all, calm. The gray blight of
stunted pine, their desiccated undersides hung with beard
lichen, loomed everywhere. Romuald raised his finger, his
eye constantly on the pointer's movements. "He's got it,
he's got it."

The dog froze in its tracks, its tail perfectly rigid. The
men closed in, lengthening their strides, guns at the ready.
Thomas's insides implored the heavens.

"Get 'em, Karo!"

Karo inched forward, then froze again, fixated on
some point.

"Get 'em!"

Others might have withstood it, but not Thomas. No sooner had he vowed to maintain his composure than there was an ear-splitting *wh-r-r-r*. It was unlike anything he had expected: a vibrating, a clapping of white wings low above the ground, then a shot—Romuald's.

"Ptarmigan! At 'em, Karo, at 'em!"

The ptarmigan was a beige-brown bird in spats, its snow-white wings in stark contrast to the rest of its body. Glancing furtively at Romuald's game bag, Thomas, instead of rejoicing at the discovery, at the prospect of recording a new species under its Latin name, felt only envy.

But he had contained himself, and that gave him heart; he had exercised restraint, thus absolving his hunter's conscience. He felt a surge of hope, one that somehow made up for the extricating of feet from slime, for the squishing of water from his bast shoes every time he took a step forward. Along the way they killed an adder—Karo had barked at it furiously, curling its upper lip and grimacing the way a human does at the taste of something sour. The dog slowed, as if to give them time to cultivate a proper vigilance, carefully moving one paw ahead of the other, glancing back to check their progress, to see if they were attending.

An explosion. Lord, how easy, how easy . . . Here it comes, take your time, get a good bead on him . . . Oh God, make it work! A shot, and Thomas, stunned, not conceding the worst, stood and watched as the cock kept on its leisurely course. This discrepancy between what was willed, between the incantation and the fact, utterly demoralized him. For at heart there had been the certitude, then as now, of some magical bond between himself and the animal, one that made of the leveling and the aiming something superfluous, the result of some special dispensation.

Two young cocks, winged by a blast from Romuald's

double-barreled shotgun, fell practically at his feet. It was one of those hits that paralyzes, grounding the bird but leaving life intact. Thomas picked them up, their necks twisting. It was a task he felt obliged to perform, now that the other had eluded him. Grabbing them by the feet, he banged their tiny skulls against the butt of his Berdan; it didn't work; shrilly, they cackled in protest. He took a bitter pleasure in unburdening his anger, an anger tinged with shame that he nonetheless suppressed by invoking necessity. Putting aside the gun, he swung and whacked them with all his might against a pine. Not hard enough, eh? Take that! The bludgeoning continued until the blood oozed from their bills.

"Snack time, fellas, the old stomach's growling. Must be pushin' noon."

They sat down on a clump of moss and Romuald broke out some dark bread and cheese from his game bag. Thomas, who had sat among these men so often in the past, never felt so apart, so far removed as he did now: a whole world divided them. Not even Victor—stuttering old Victor—had come back empty-handed. They were made of a different substance. What was it? He could stalk with the best of them. Hadn't they said so themselves? What was the secret that even Victor in his own clumsy way seemed to grasp but that he never would? A bright afternoon glare overhead, the soporific heat of the swamp, lizards scurrying to their arid islands among the lichen. He sat with eyes closed, seemingly bathing his face in the sun, but there was sadness inside, and it weighed him down like cold lead shot.

"Why don't you ever fire your gun, Tommy?"

How could he? If he had, it would have only magnified the dimensions of his failure. What a day! Soon it would be over, then back to Borkuny, by way of the roundabout trail skirting the hill with no trees, the same trail they were now steering for.

But just as they were hitting dry ground they flushed a flock, and Thomas—thinking he deserved some reward, some consolation at the very end, that he did not deserve the banishment—really let loose.

Romuald gazed wistfully down at Thomas's smoking barrel, then up at the escaping blackcock. "Not your day, Tommy. That happens."

His words did nothing to redeem the situation, and Thomas hated himself for having betrayed his confidence.

58

THE BLACKCOCK hunt was the more painful to recall in that it confirmed certain debilities, long suspected but never acknowledged. A hunter's hunter when it came to baiting, stalking, imitating a tree or rock, and even a fair shot from a blind, Thomas nonetheless panicked at the slightest stirring. If the blackcock hunt was to be the final test, then Thomas was up against something truly formidable; and unless he overcame it, he would never be a real man, and his self-image, so carefully nurtured, would be shattered. How he had hungered to become a citizen of the forest, had so accustomed himself to the idea, and now, by a supreme irony that would deny him the one thing he craved most, he was hearing: "No." So what was he really? Who? Was this the end—the map to his kingdom of the elect, his partnership with Romuald? Unable to part with his Berdan, he took to the forest, deeply aggrieved, and there found relief.

The flickering in the crowns, the sighing in the treetops calmed him, were a distraction. Here there were no tests to be passed, no expectations to be fulfilled, nothing

to be tracked, hunted down, only the joy taken in the halting and advancing, the aimless silent treading, the ability to avoid detection by various creatures. At such times he would admit to being happiest without a gun, that he could do without the killing. On the other hand, breaking brush empty-handed looked funny; people were nosy, wanted to know why, and there was no explaining to them; but just say you're "out hunting," and no more questions asked. Besides, a gun barrel slung over the shoulder lent an element of adventure; no telling what sort of bird or animal you might jump along the way.

No gun was needed the time he surprised some roe. He was on one of those smooth, needle-strewn trails that dropped down to the swamp and whose ice-packed surface in winter made it ideal for sledding, when his legs buckled. An undefined presence, but a presence nonetheless: red tree trunks engaged in a dance, columns of light prancing among fern quills. No, not trees—live creatures sheathed in reddish-brown bark, existing on the very periphery of the plant kingdom. Feeding on the grass in front of him, they glided on tiny hoofs, their necks rippling; one turned its head in his direction but failed to distinguish him from his stationary surroundings. He had only one urge now: to prolong it, to dissolve into air and, thus made invisible, become a part of it. But whether it was a twitch of his eyelids or his scent that alerted them, they bounded nimbly into the hazel scrub, while he was left behind, on the verge of not believing his senses.

On another occasion, he had a similar encounter with a young fox foraging under a stump. Not content to contemplate its snout and tail, he had felt duty-bound to kill it and bring it back to Romuald as a trophy, thus redeeming himself for past sins; but the moment he touched his gun strap, the fox vanished without a trace, without so much as a quivering leaf to remind of its presence.

One day he yielded to temptation, and forever re-

gretted it. In the crown of a hazel he observed a shimmering, coil-like movement, half in green and half in light. It was a squirrel, the horizontal advance making it appear more elongated, more magically iridescent. From the lower branches came the wailing of small birds: the squirrel was raiding a nest. Unable to restrain himself, driven by sheer love for the animal, he fired.

It was a young one, so slender that what he had taken for a squirrel was not a squirrel but the shimmer of color deposited in its wake. Its body bending and unbending on the moss, it clutched its chest with its tiny paws, at the bloody patch on its little white vest. It didn't know what death was; it was trying to remove it, as if it were a spike on which it had been impaled and around which it could only pivot.

Thomas, his face twisted with anguish, knelt beside it and wept. How to stop it, how to stop it. He would have given half a lifetime to save it, but he could only participate passively in the agony, the mere sight of which was a punishment. He bent down, and the paws, with their minuscule fingers, became joined as if imploring his help. He took it in his hands, and while he might otherwise have felt an urge to kiss and pet it, his lips were now clamped shut, because it was no longer the urge of possession that welled up in him but of self-sacrifice—for it, the squirrel—and that was clearly beyond his power.

The hardest thing to endure was the littleness of it, and the writhing, like quicksilver trying to defer the moment of congealment. And for a brief moment, so brief he immediately lost access to it, a mystery unfolded. Then the writhing turned to convulsive jerks; the fluffy down on its cheeks was permeated by a dark trickle. The spasms slackened. Dead.

He sat on the stump, the drone of the forest in his ears. A second ago it had been alive, playing, gathering nuts. Grandmother Dilbin's death, for reasons he could not

altogether fathom, affected him less than did this creature's. A being, unique, never to be repeated, never to be resurrected. Because it was itself and no other. But where had they gone—the warmth, the suppleness, and above all the feeling of being itself? Animals were without souls. When they were killed, it was for keeps. They could not be saved, not even by Christ. But Grandmother could; she could cry "Save me" and Christ was there to receive her, to show her the way. Why not a squirrel, then, if He was almighty? Maybe a squirrel *couldn't* pray, but this one had prayed, because wasn't praying the same as wanting to live? And it was all his, Thomas's, fault. How low.

Bury it? It would just rot away to nothing. Take it with him? He didn't have the nerve to look people in the eye. It was best just to turn around and head home. As he was backtracking, an anthill caught his eye. A tall one, well camouflaged with pine needles. Abandoned? Wait, what about those mobile trails converging on it. When Thomas peeled away the top and probed it with a stick, the whole began to heave. He dug deeper until the collapsing tunnels gave up a stampeding, panic-stricken horde. Retrieving the squirrel, he laid it inside the hive and covered it. It would be stripped clean, leaving nothing but a white skeleton. It would be waiting for him when he came back. What then? No telling. Put it in a box and ditch it somewhere; that way, it would last longer.

Yes, low. To miss those able to protect themselves through skill and grace and hit only the vulnerable, the unsuspecting . . . That squirrel hadn't even seen him, it had not had any warning. He could feel the necks of those young blackcocks twisting inside him, could hear their tiny skulls thumping against the tree. A vision so palpable he could feel the brittle pine bark, could see the flakes flying with every clubbing blow. And other things that weighed on his conscience. Grandmother Misia told of how as a child he used to fill his basket with snails and toss them into

the Issa out of pity (he was moved, perhaps, by the sight of them taking to the paths after a rainstorm), believing that he was doing them a favor, swelling with magnanimity even as they were drowning at the bottom. Then he remembered the duck whose life he had spared. But it was not a consolation.

If only he could have leaned on someone, cried his heart out, protested. He passed an oak on the edge of a clearing, and suddenly yearned for it to be alive, his stomach caving in, collapsing with the sort of suction and terror one feels on the swing's downward plunge. A roller—or, as it was recorded in his album, *Coracias garrulus*, one of those birds he was continually stalking but which always eluded, there being only one other bird, the kingfisher, arrayed in the same resplendent blue that was such pure color in motion—crowed from its perch on a dead branch, but Thomas passed below without raising his head.

And all the time they kept saying: Mommy is coming, Mommy will be taking you to the big city, to school . . . Always the same: next month, won't be long now, and—nothing, no sign of her. "Mommy, Mommy—please come!" he kept intoning as he strode along, hunter-fashion, his Berdan at the ready, his legs sheathed in knee-high boots, and the tears streaming down his face leaving a salty taste in his mouth. The incantation evoked no particular memories, only an aura of softness and light.

He had need of another luminosity now, not the mirrorlike glare of an August afternoon shimmering above the stubble. Recently he had been given to strange moods. Everything—people, dogs, the woods, Gine—was as before, only somehow different. To hollow out an egg, you puncture one end and suck out the insides with a straw, leaving only the shell, the outward appearance. The same with Thomas's world. Outwardly the same, but inwardly gutted.

And boring. When we bolt from bed in response to the joyful summons of work or play, the day hardly seems long enough to contain our expectations; but when the summons is absent, then all the purpose and planning are lost.

"What, Thomas still asleep?"

"What's the matter, Tommy, not feeling well?"

"Naah, I'm okay."

He would stand on the banks of the Issa, not comprehending his former infatuation. Leaves covered with a thick coat of roadside dust, a midsummer heat, a lazy current adrift with the oily film of floating debris . . . He even dug out his poles, got the rust off his hooks, held the squirming earthworm between his fingers, and started to bury a hook's tip in the little pink opening when—the heck with it, he'd bait up with bread crumbs instead. He would watch the float, not really caring whether it jiggled and went under, the fishing being merely the repetition of a ritual that had once connoted something else. As much as he tried to rekindle the passion, he soon gave up.

He pulled out his arithmetic notebooks, neglected ever since his lessons were interrupted by Joseph's denunciation. His plan to devote one hour daily to his exercises lasted only as long as he began to founder, and then was abandoned. He took to rummaging in the library again, finding among other things a translation of the Koran, which he knew to be the sacred book of the Mohammedans—someone, evidently Thomas's great- or great-great-grandfather, had taken an interest in Islam. Despite the inscrutability of certain passages, Thomas took pleasure in reading it, delighting as much in the moral strictures as in the sonority of its phrases.

The Berdan hung idly on the wall and made him ashamed of his neglect. He planned a trip out to Borkuny but kept putting it off. Romuald, meanwhile, had stopped

calling at the manor. Thomas's aunt, who must have known from Misia that Thomas had joined Romuald on the blackcock hunt, affected indifference.

"Thomas, go help bring in the apples."

He helped. Lugging the baskets for Antonina, though exhausting, afforded some satisfaction. The apples were freighted on a carrying pole, the baskets being attached to hazel hooks. The orchard now had a new tenant, a relative of Chaim. The cavernous barn cellars were lined with shelves for the choicest apples and smelled acrimoniously of stone and packed earth. He bit into a rennet, delighting as always in the firmness of its pulp: so he *hadn't* changed, after all.

Almost a month had passed before he remembered the skeleton, and even then he had to force himself to make the trip back. He found the anthill in the forest, all right, but the squirrel was gone. He never did find out what happened to it.

59

THE SELF-IMPOSED fast observed by Thomas was a strict one: two days on water only. He was driven to it less by the hope of having the stigma removed than by a need for self-mortification. Such self-punishment, he sensed, was only right, proper, justified.

He had his reasons. As if to prove that he was different, not the same as ordinary people, he came down with a strange affliction. In the morning he sneaked a mugful of water and tried to rinse out the spots on his bed sheet. There were nightmares; Barbarka, naked, would wrap him in her arms and whip him with a birch switch. Melancholy thoughts. How to breach the curtain. For the things

around him seemed hollowed out, or veiled, their shapes no longer full but flat. And behind the curtain was the secret he kept pursuing, dreamlike—gaining steadily on it, the legs weighing like lead, only to lose it . . . God: why had He created a world where there was only death and death and death. If He was good, why was there no sticking out one's hand without killing, why no moving down a trail without crushing caterpillars or beetles no matter how one tried to avoid them? God might have created a different world, but He hadn't; He chose this one.

In this way his failure as a hunter, along with his shameful abnormality, by barring him from human company, thrust him into lonely, solitary contemplation. The fast was meant to cleanse, to bring a restoration of normality, and to permit of understanding. He who punishes himself shows disgust for his baseness and invokes God with his punishing part.

It was, he ascertained, an effective remedy. An empty stomach early in the morning, like fasting for Holy Communion. Then a few hours later the hunger, a sudden and terrific urge to eat, and the resisting of temptation: aw, come on, just a bite of apple . . . But the longer it went, the easier it got. Most of the time he lay on his back and drowsed, inwardly ennobling himself. Of greater importance was what it did to the objects in his proximity, to the sky and trees, when he went outside and stood by the porch. He made the discovery that the weaker the body, the more he got outside it, elevating himself—condensed, specklike—to a point just above his head. The look of this other self was intense, embracing the part left behind, as the latter shrank, withdrew below, taking the earth along with it, whole and unaltered in all its surface details, down to the very bottom. The melancholy lifted, a new vista unfurled. Antonina used to tell of the goddess Varpeia, who sat in heaven, spinning the threads of fate, and of how a star dangled at the end of each. When a star fell, it meant

she had cut the thread, that someone somewhere had died. But Thomas, instead of sinking, drifted skyward, like those tiny spiders that, hoisting themselves by means of an invisible thread, ascend nimbly to a higher branch.

What he set his mind to, he did, though by the afternoon of the second day he felt woozy and dizzy every time he got up. At supper he ate a plate of curdled milk and potatoes. Their fragrance—they were drenched in butter—never seemed so lovely.

By way of consolation, God rewarded him with hitherto unknown thoughts. One of his favorite pastimes had been to stand on the front lawn, bend over, and, through the arch of outstretched legs, survey the park on the other side: seen upside down, it came as a revelation. So, too, the fast transfigured not only him but everything the eye met. Not that the world ceased to be what it had been previously. No; both the old and the new converged. So maybe it was wrong to impugn God for the way He ran things; who knew, maybe one day we would wake to a new surprise. Maybe God looked down at the earth through straddled legs, or did so after a fast infinitely longer than Thomas's.

But the squirrel had suffered pain. Was there another angle from which to view it, from which to say the squirrel had suffered only in our imagination? That, no one, not even God, could say.

Thomas's fast had opened a chink admitting illumination. Touching the trunk of a maple, he wondered at its density. For inside was a realm where, made smaller, he would have roamed indefinitely, pushing to the very core, to those wood-locked villages and towns beyond the border of bark. Only figuratively, of course. For there were no towns inside, only in the imagination, though a maple was a colossus that, no less than the one looking on, contained the possibility of endless permutation.

Thomas was burdened by his loneliness, yet more

than anything he aspired to self-dissolution and a communion without words. He was quite demanding. Grandmother Misia—yes, but there was no confiding in her, not in Grandmother Misia. Nor was he much for confession; the examining of one's conscience according to a prayer book, according to questions requiring simple affirmation or denial, always omitting the most essential thing, repelled him. His guilt was inside him, a guilt too pervasive to be divided into sins.

God, let me be like the others—Thomas prayed, and the demons, plotting their next move, strained to listen. Make me a good shot with a gun, don't let me forget my hunter's, naturalist's vow. Cure me of that illness (a loud guffawing among the baser demons along the Issa, of which there were a great many). Let me understand your world when it pleases you to enlighten. The way it really is, not what I imagine it to be (here the demons fell to sulking, for the topic had turned grave).

If Thomas was subject to conflicting desires, they were not so for him. He brooded over pain and suffering, not for their own sake, but as attributes of the order of which he was a part. And since this order lay beyond the exercise of his will, he had to attend to his status, a status bestowed through the art of killing. Even though he wanted to keep up his friendship with Romuald and have access to the forest without the blood-spilling, he abdicated responsibility, without completely shirking it.

60

"Mama! Mama!"
Denis's whining supplications had little effect.
"Satan!" she ranted, banging her fist on the table.

"The Satan! Curse the day he was ever born! The scum!"

Her color—she was very flushed—worried him. She sat hunched over in her chair, breathing heavily, clutching her belly. "Oyey, what cramps!"

The lamentations went on: "He's disgraced us, dragged us through the mud. And him, he don't care if it kills his own mama. Oy, Denis, I feel so sick!"

Denis went to the cupboard, poured half a glass of vodka, and set it down in front of her. Emptying the glass in one gulp, she wiped her mouth, then gestured with the glass. Denis, pleased to see her not refuse this medicine, poured.

"Victor, keep me company awhile."

Denis stepped out onto the porch, where Romuald was sitting on a bench, smoking and brooding.

"Well?"

"Still rantin' and ailin'. Best not to show your face for a while."

"Got no mind to."

"What you have to do it that way for? Couldn't you have broke it to her more gentlelike?"

Romuald shrugged. "You know her better than that. Gentle or not gentle, she'd have taken it hard, either way."

They broke off. Hens clawed the ground under the apple trees; the earth was powdery and hollowed out and track-embroidered from the constant scratching. The cock, pursuing one of the hens, pounced on it, flapped its wings, then clumsily dismounting, let it go. The hen fluffed its feathers, dazed as usual by the whole procedure, oblivious even before it had time to be aware. A horse, its forelegs hobbled, bolted, heaving its mane. Denis took off on the run: the horse was trampling the poppies. He picked up a stick, flung it, and waved his arms. Ducks trailed through the grass, quacking plagently; it was a scorching, dry September day.

"What now?"

"Aw, she'll simmer down."

"She won't give her blessing—she said."

Romuald's face was drawn, stubbled, darkened by the ordeal. "If she don't, she don't. My tough luck. You— you're different, you obey. Don't marry, she says, and you don't. Can't do this, can't do that—there's no pleasin' her."

"Still and all, Rom, a farm girl ..."

"Yours was highbred and Mama was again' her."

Not against her, really. She had opposed it more for her son's sake, almost out of jealousy, out of a determination to keep him single. But this latest—as imperceptible in its unfolding as the stages by which a fly gets trapped in a spiderweb—was too horrifying to contemplate.

The family coat of arms. Buried in a large chest were the family records, lying there undisturbed since the death of old man Bukowski, the only one still capable of deciphering them. To mingle the blood of the Bukowskis with the blood of slaves, whose backs bore the scars of centuries, was to sully the family blazon. Never mind that the Bukowskis had worked the soil, that outwardly they were indistinguishable from peasants; their ancestors had once elected kings, and that made them the equal of kings. Not one of their forebears—not the father, his father, or even their great-great-grandfather—had ever bowed and scraped, and the Bukowski had yet to be born who would surrender to the dark impulses of servility, docility, or cunning, impulses more proper to those of baser stock. Marry a peasant and the recollection of who one was and all that was owing the family name would cease to be a protection, would be to debase the line and efface it in the slime of the crowd which neither knew nor cared to know anything of its lineage.

Old lady Bukowski, that guardian of the purity of the blood, had reason to despair. She also had herself to blame. She had never objected to Romuald's keeping Barbarka at Borkuny; she had counted on his good sense,

though certain signs—the woman's strutting self-confidence, the little liberties she took—should have been a warning.

Romuald had the banns published. Father Monkiewicz showed no surprise, though his heart ran with honey: what had been unchristian was now made Christian, and here at last was a nobleman with heart. One might question whether, for his own sake, it was wise of Romuald to have the banns announced. If it was to keep Barbarka on at his place, to have someone to scrub his back in the bathhouse, then he had acted wisely. Still, it would be hard to go on living the life to which he was accustomed; that was to be expected. It was a decision made not without certain qualms, a decision facilitated by the grudge he bore Helen Juchniewicz, who had dallied with him until by shunning him she had finally betrayed her genteel, aristocratic airs: hers was a threshold too tall for him.

Breaking the news to his mother had taken a feat of courage, and Romuald had sweated through the ordeal. He had gone on about the farm, about needing someone to help run it, about how it was high time he got married— Married? Who to? Well—uh—and then the name, followed by a belly laugh, and Romuald saying his mind was made up, and then a ranting, a throwing of chairs, a flailing with the cane ...

Denis, after going back inside, found his mother staring fixedly into space, her fists clenched on the table, the vodka bottle down. Victor looked on from the bed with mouth agape.

"A disgrace." She wagged her head.

Then again—softer, to herself: "What a disgrace."

Denis loved his mother greatly and felt sorry for her. But he had run out of things to say. From his stool he gawked up at St. Aloysius, whose hand, the one bearing the palm branch, was speckled with flies. The glass fly trap

on the sill was also blackened with specks that still stirred in the buttermilk. The stronger ones were crawling over their mired comrades, gracelessly dragging their wet wings.

61

GRANDMOTHER MISIA was the epitome of serenity. Rocked by the waves of a mighty river, she lived in a perpetual hush of timeless waters. If birth was a passage from the protection of the maternal womb into a world of sharp, wounding objects, then Grandmother Misia had never been born, having always existed, wrapped in the silk cocoon of that which Is.

A foot, delighting in itself, in the very gift of touch, feels the soft quilt and lifts it. A hand draws the fluffy material up to the sleeper's chin. A white mist outside, the babble of geese, an autumnal dawn streaking the window-pane with dewdrops. Still time to sleep, or rather to linger on the border, beyond the reach of that which can be formulated in words and thoughts, in a world as yet undifferentiated into blankets, earth, people, stars, leaving only this spaceless realm—and awe.

The experience of those mornings had taught Misia the relativity of names given to objects, the relativity of all things human. Not even the teachings of the Church, we may presume to tell, were a match for that truth of hers—instinctive, profound; and the only prayer she ever required was one that could be reduced to a single, incantatory: "Oh." Grandmother Dilbin always spoke of her as "that pagan," and she was right. For Misia was unencumbered by the sort of flaw that reveals itself in our human

striving. Incapable of exerting her will on behalf of some goal, disdainful of all goals, she relinquished. No wonder she was mystified by the cares and needs of others. Desires, needs? What for?

Fully awake, lying in bed with her eyes wide open, she dwells on details of a mundane nature, never exaggerating their importance, never racing out of bed to perform some errand she neglected the day before or which urgently demands her attention. Mindful of her place in the infinite, caressed by a giant hand, she is content to purr. The worries of others belonged to the sphere of things that happened, nothing more. Luke's, for example (what a couple they made!), or Helen's (thank goodness that's the end of her dalliance with Romuald!), or the Reform . . . Or Tekla, who had postponed her homecoming so often that people had ceased to give it any credence.

If Grandmother wasn't bothered by such things, the Invisible Ones, those spirits promenading about the parlor's squeaky flooring and furniture, *were* bothered by her indifference. Besides, they had long given up on her. There was no attacking the innocent, those never burdened by the awareness of sin. Even so, their experience came in handy in subjecting Thomas to a new brand of temptation.

Picking his nose, a habit favoring autumnal meditation, Thomas began, for the first time in his life, to pass judgment on Misia as a person. She was a horrible egoist, in love with no one but herself. But no sooner was the verdict pronounced than doubts were born. Granted, one had only to look at her to detect the pleasure she took in her own knees, her pillow's indentation, the way she sank into the eiderdown of her own interior (Thomas could feel—or imagined he could feel—Misia on the inside). But what made him think he was any different? He, too, loved to savor his own smell, to curl up and exult in his being *him*. Wasn't that cause for gratitude to God, for prayer? Or was it deceiving? His grandmother was pious,

churchgoing. True, but wasn't she the celebrant of her own private Mass to herself? We say: God. But couldn't the saying of it be our self-love in disguise, a way of ennobling what we really adore: our own warmth, our own heartbeat, the wrapping of ourselves in the snugness of a blanket.

There is no denying the cunning of demons. How ingenious of them to undermine Thomas's confidence in his own internal voice, to rob him of his peace of mind by appealing to his scrupulosity. No longer could he implore God for illumination; genuflecting, he would always have the feeling he was kneeling before himself. Thomas wanted to confide in the Real, not in a cloud that, nourished by what is inside us, hangs overhead. Hardly had he finished fasting, therefore, hardly had he freed himself somewhat from his self-torture and tasted a few mornings of felicity, than he again lost his footing. He wiped the fog from the window, his face trailing tears of solitude.

Meanwhile, every morning at dawn, Grandmother reveled in her delectations, never dreaming how corrupting she could be.

62

"SOON it'll be over."

The voice—a signal—vibrated above dry grass resonant with the chirruping of crickets. Swaying on his feet, Balthazar stood on the trail, struck by the derangement of everything. What was he doing out here? Objects, blurred and flat-surfaced, zigzagged before him, taunting him with their unfamiliarity. He was hovering at the center of a vast emptiness, made even worse by the absence of any

center, of any earthly support, the ground eluding, slipping away, senseless. He kept going, passing through a spray of sparks: insects, always the same, jumping without purpose.

"Soon it'll be over."

Creaking porch steps, an empty room—the wife and children were in Gine, visiting with the grandmother—a jug of beer on the table, a loaf of bread beside it. He tilted the jug, took a few swigs, then brought it down full-force on the floor. Streams of brownish-gold liquid fanned out starlike over the rough planks. He grabbed hold of the table, sickened by the smell of lye-coated wood, by the household rankness. His searching glance landed on the ax braced against the tile stove. He walked over, picked it up, and, dragging it along the floor with his free hand, went back to the table with a rocking motion. Taking deliberate aim, he swung and hit the table from above, not crosswise but lengthwise, collapsing it. The loaf of bread rolled along the floor until it came to a rest, upside down, exposing its smooth, mealy underbelly.

Balthazar then brought in a wicker-bound bottle from the other room, stood it on the floor, and kicked it. He leaned against the wall, and watched as the bubbling liquid spread out and encircled both the wreckage and the overturned loaf. He was captivated by it, by the spillage that, detached from its surroundings, now stood out in greater relief. The swollen peripheries lazily seeped under the bench, leaving little islands that momentarily were inundated. There was something inexorable about its movement, some element of necessity, and it was the only thing on Balthazar's mind as he took the matches from his pocket.

Then it came: the recognition of that moment at the border of what a second ago was not and what a second later was, once for all time, till the world's consummation. As one hand squeezed the box, the fingers of the other

approached the little stick with a darkened tip. Perhaps all along he had wanted to be only this: pure action, the sheer tension of doing, with no consequences to oppress him when, inaccessible to the past, he would be concentrated on a new action. He rubbed the match against the box and became fixated on the flame, as if it were a discovery, until the flame began to singe, and then the fingers parted and the match dropped to the floor, extinguished. He took out another, struck it hard, and tossed it in front of him. It went out. He lit a third, bent down, and slowly brought it up close to the spilled kerosene.

On his way out, he toppled the bench into the path of the creeping flame. His tunic, unbelted, was open; his pocket bulged with tobacco and a bottle of vodka.

"Soon it'll be over."

The future. What future? A voice calling in the distance; a pale, clear sky; crickets chirruping; day, night, day . . . Never to be again, superfluous. And the certitude, which came from somewhere, fortified itself. He walked with no destination in mind. Aimless wandering. Turned around once, and then came the horror of the aftereffect, of the irreversible provoked by the sight of the smoke seeping through the windows; and in protest—Balthazar's eternal protest—against the law which leaves nothing alone but chains us to its consequences, he clutched the bottle with trembling hand, weltered in the grass, got up on all fours, and let out a sound that we know to be a scream but which issues from the throat as a gurgling, rattling whisper.

Balthazar was sentient enough to run back and put out the fire. But such a course never occurred to him, the stifled scream coming not from the deed itself, not from what had been done, but from the necessity of its doing; and he sensed, possibly even as he had held the match, both that he was free and that he would do what had to be

done. Just as surely as he must have known, kneeling on all fours like an animal, that there was no going back to quell the flames.

A figure, describing straw-colored swirls in the air with a wooden sword, was bellying toward him like an adder. Balthazar could make out a pair of vertically set eyes, a body crouched furtively low. He leapt to his feet, tore out a large fence post, and took a deep breath: the grass was empty. Only some gossamer threads, signs of Indian summer, waved in the air: slightly arched lines of incandescence. A gilded forest, a midsummer hush. Neither friend nor foe; no one except for some ungraspable—and therefore menacing—presence. He spun around to fend off an attack from the rear. A magpie screeched up from a nearby gully. By now the smoke from the windows was intertwining, gathering into strands that trailed along the roof shingles and mantled the crowns of the hornbeam with a cloudy haze.

"Soon it will be over."

63

"THE FOREST."

"State preserve."

"No."

"Whose?"

"Balthazar's."

"It's Balthazar's place on fire."

The people of Pogirai began spilling out of the orchards, out onto the aprons and stubble, for a better view. They sounded the alarm, grabbed buckets, hook-tipped poles, axes, and started stampeding. Dogs and children ran

behind the men, a party of women, driven by curiosity, bringing up the rear.

In the next sequence of events, let us distinguish between appearances and reality. In the reconstruction of any past incident, no matter how logically consistent the facts, there are always some hidden gaps which, when filled, cast everything in a different light. If the effort is seldom made, it is because people are more content to rely on what is immediately taken for granted.

Balthazar, after setting fire to his house, lay in ambush out where the fence line ended on either side of the gangway. He was on the lookout because he knew that the fire would be visible from Pogirai and that they would come to put it out and that he couldn't allow it. Those were the appearances. In reality, he was innocent of any such motives, but sat in the grass, teeth chattering, menaced by reptilian shapes and supernatural magpies. A lot was due to the discordancy between body and soul. The soul was given to chaos and terror, even as the body remained alert, its reflexes intact—heavy-limbed but still powerful. To others, this looked like the obeying of some will, bent on a definite goal.

They could see the flames now, could hear the dog, whose pitiful yelping said that the fire had already spread to the kennel. Diverted by the spectacle, they were all the more amazed when he sprang up, all mussed and disheveled and fierce, his hand still clutching the fence post. He cocked his arm in self-defense. He hadn't expected them, these people advancing like a mobile stone wall radiant with a multitude of faces.

At the head stood old Wackonis. When he saw Balthazar bring up the arm with the post, he shielded himself with his ax. Balthazar's body, registering the danger, did what it had to do. With all the strength bestowed by his arm and shoulder, he lowered the post on Wackonis's skull, felling him.

"He killed 'im!"

"*Killed* 'im!"

And then another cry, one to summon the communal spirit: "*Ei virai!* Forward, men!"

It was in a clearing of cut stumps interspersed with young oak, the green cover being here and there pocked by the dark craters of former grubbings. A dozen or so people in clamorous pursuit, leaping over the craters with shirt-tails flapping. Balthazar was seeking the safety of the tall forest. Knowing, without thinking, that it was a matter of life and death, he was entirely at the command of his self-protecting body and the destination dictated by it: the sawed-off carbine stashed in the oak.

They tried to cut him off, knowing they stood to lose him as soon as he hit the forest; he swung to the left; again they cut him off, forcing him to backtrack around and take to the alder grove. On one side of the grove was pasture-land; on the other, farmland—crop fields separating the grove from the timberline.

As Balthazar's feet sank in the mud, his boots chewed up clods of black peat. He was too winded to keep running; tried to keep on the move, but not having the breath for it, he dropped down on all fours and crawled, his heart banging, his voice wailing. The others took time off from the chase to hold council. Only one way to catch him: surround the grove and track him down hunter-style. They took up their assigned stations. Balthazar, hearing them, searched the ground for a club—he had discarded the fence post while fleeing—grabbed a branch of debris so moldy it fell apart in his hand, and finally had to settle for a rock.

The people of Pogirai had many scores to settle with Balthazar, with this criminal who had jumped them with his murderous intent, and all because they had tried to lend him a neighborly hand. Naturally, they had in mind a killing. But they knew his strength, knew they would have

to gang up on him, and they spurred one another on with their foul imprecations.

Clock hands twitching spasmodically forward; gestures, glances, and motions performed simultaneously the world over; a comb touching long sleek hair; scintillating mirrors; reverberating tunnels; ship screws lashing seawater . . . Balthazar's heart was ticking off time; saliva drooled from his mouth. No, not yet! Let me live, no matter where, anywhere, just let me live! Seeking cover, he hugged the marshy floor, pawed at it as if to burrow a hole, to hollow out a hiding place. Because the present—his being there, trapped—was like the confirmation of some voice or dream, of that which must be, inexorably. But there was nowhere for him to hide. The alder grove, thick-shrubbed at the rim, was starker where he was, too dark for any bushes to grow, and the ground bulged with rugged roots laced with cow tracks and the flattened mushrooms of manure. An easy target. The carbine. To have the carbine now. But there was no carbine.

Balthazar probably should have gone to meet them with hands held high. But that presumed an ability to distinguish between the fire and the phantoms, and the people of Pogirai, but for Balthazar the people were a part of it, were in a way its executioners. His eyes bulging, loosening from their sockets, he squeezed the rock in his fist.

The men paddled the tree trunks like regular brush-breakers. Balthazar's strategy must be attributed to what little remained of his sentience. Rather than wait to be taken, he went on the attack, charging at those closing in from the side of the crop field. Surprise, he had figured, was his best chance of escape. But he was too heavy, kept getting mired in the mud, couldn't get up the momentum.

A young man, acclaimed by the girls as the best dancer at all the village reels, was the first to be met. They came within two feet of colliding. Balthazar aimed for the face. Now, to be a good dancer is to be endowed with a

certain grace; the lad ducked—not a quarter of a second too soon—and the rock creased the side of his head. Only a tree behind which he had jumped saved Balthazar from an ax blade. A yell went up.

"Over here! Over here! Over here!"

Again on the run, Balthazar wrapped both hands around a sapling and pulled it up by the roots. How he uprooted the tree, a feat surpassing human strength, was a mystery. Brandishing the sapling like a giant cudgel, muddied, he stood his ground against his attackers.

"Over here! Over here! Over here!"

Some sheep were raising a cloud of crop dust in the sun. A hedgehog rustled among the leaves of an apple tree. A ferry barge was moving away from the shore; on it was a man who held his horses by the bridle, steadying them as they inhaled through snorting nostrils. From high above the forest's moss-like expanses came the calls of cranes in passage: *kruuu-kruuu*.

They came together in a clearing. The air swished as Balthazar swung, at the same time a pole landed on his shoulder, loosening his grip and forcing him to drop the sapling. A long, iron-hooked staff, the kind used for putting out roof fires, its thick ashwood shaft held by Wackonis's son with both hands, rose up into the air.

If only a moment of everything's happening could be arrested, fixed, examined in a glass jar; if only it could be peeled away from the moment before and the moment after, and the tissue of time stretched into an ocean of space! But no.

The gaff came down on Balthazar's skull. He reeled, fell with his whole length. Silence except for the breathing of tired men, reverberations of the phrase "Over here!" and the tramping footsteps of the others, coming on the run.

Balthazar's house, stable, cow barn, and pigsty were

turned to ash. Of his farm in the forest, all that survived was the hayrick.

"He had it coming."

"The son of a devil."

64

OLD WACKONIS died, but Balthazar lived. He was carted to his father-in-law's place in Gine. Surkont sent for the doctor at once. Thomas had never seen his grandfather so irritable. Always an even-tempered man, he now snarled when he spoke, turning abruptly on his heels, his gray, close-cropped mustache bristling, his lips holding back some unutterable phrase. Balthazar still lay in a coma, so Grandfather went down to the village to keep a bedside vigil.

A large kerosene lamp burned brightly on the bench. Balthazar lay in bed, his head propped up by a single pillow. He had already been washed clean, leaving no trace of the caked mud and blood, and his livid face stood out against the white bandage of thick homespun. He was given Extreme Unction, but later, contrary to all expectations, he opened his eyes. His gaze bespoke puzzlement, peace. He seemed unsure of where he was, confused by all the fuss.

The priest, bound by the seal of confession, divulged nothing of what he was told, declaring only that Balthazar was in full possession of his faculties. (It may have been the shock that delivered him from the web of his entanglement.) He was alone with the priest for a long time. Of their conversation nothing is known, although later, with

the passage of time, Father Monkiewicz began alluding to it, at first discreetly but then more boldly, justifying these indiscretions by the use he made of them. For it was his habit, when taking up the evils that lay in wait for man's soul, to illustrate his sermons with examples; thus did many facts in the Balthazar case become public knowledge.

Despite all his experiences as a confessor, despite all he had heard in the confessional, Father Monkiewicz was shaken. Not by the gravity of Balthazar's sins—sins never before confessed until now, as if the realization of their sinfulness had just been borne in on him—as by the man's stubborn, even resigned insistence on his own damnation. The priest said he had no right to speak that way, that God's mercy was infinite, that repentance was all that was needed to obtain forgiveness. And Balthazar did repent his sins, so fervently, so sincerely, that he repented all he had ever been, sparing nothing. He listened closely to the priest but at a given moment butted in: "Nothing can save me. *He's* around."

The clarity with which the past was revealed figured in Balthazar's imagination as a bright circle rimmed by shadow, from which he had come and into which he would return. He had learned to anticipate those subterfuges, perpetually new, by which he had laid on him the same suffering burden. And his words "He's around" rang with such surety that Father Monkiewicz had tossed a nervous glance about the room.

A hopeless dilemma. How to grant absolution and the last rites to someone guilty of so grievous a sin. The priest, obedient to his conscience, tried to wring from Balthazar at least a semblance of hope. What he got was a dying man's acquiescence, as the man was visibly too weak to protest. The hours spent in Balthazar's company left the priest feeling edgy, as if the affliction he had been called upon to cure was contagious; as if, being powerless against Evil, he had been called upon to act merely as a witness.

When the others entered the room, Balthazar, whether deliberately or from delirium, gave no sign of acknowledging their presence. Transfixed by some point in space, he muttered: "The oak."

This may have been a reference to the carbine in the oak tree, a normal deathbed reflex, that of retrospection, or it may have been an allusion to something else. He fell into a coma again.

Dr. Kohn arrived late that same night. He said that maybe, if he could be operated on . . . but that it would mean a long haul by wagon and then a train ride to a big hospital—which, in effect, meant keeping vigil and letting nature take its course. Balthazar did not live to see the sunrise. The darkly pitted shields of the sunflowers were just emerging from the mist; chickens, clucking somnolently, were shaking the dew from their feathers when Balthazar, wearing the same puzzled expression, took one last look at the roof beams overhead and the faces of the people.

"All together now, fellas."

Those were his last, inscrutable words, and a few minutes later he was dead.

By morning there was nothing more to see. The image of the live Balthazar thus remained for Thomas what it had always been, unaltered by the mask of deathly repose: the slightly upturned, somehow virginal upper lip; the rounded, boyish-looking face with its fugitive shadows and traces of a smile. So be it always.

"Didn't I tell you? Drank himself to death, the skunk!" Grandmother Misia made the sign of the cross, then added: "Lord, shed light upon his soul."

Antonina breathed a deep sigh and lamented man's fate: "Alive today, rot tomorrow." Helen had lost all recollection of her plan to resettle Balthazar and to move into the forester's cottage herself. She only regretted that so much property had gone up in smoke, her regret springing

less from selfishness than from solicitude for the fruits of human labor.

The whole manor turned out for the funeral. Rain fell during the burial, and Thomas clung to his grandmother's side, holding the umbrella over her. As the priest shook the aspergillum, drops of holy water merged with the downpour rioting in the oak leaves.

The more he brooded over the Balthazar affair, the more confounded the priest became. Whatever conclusions he drew acquired for him the force of personal conviction only after he was used to proclaiming them out loud, to fortifying his belief through constant iteration. He talked of those who denied entry to the Holy Spirit; of man's free will, so fashioned as to accept or reject the gift. He likened the will to a spring on a mountain peak—rushing forth, spilling aimlessly, looking for a way until, guided by the force of its own momentum, it ran down this side or that.

After Balthazar's passing, Father Monkiewicz, though not a particularly skilled preacher or theologian, suddenly became adept at moving his audience, his success owing not least to a tacit understanding: they could always see the man behind the example. From then on, Balthazar occupied a prominent place in the memory of the parish. Women would invoke him to reform their husbands of their intemperate ways.

Thomas's grandfather had several Masses said for the repose of the forester's soul. The priest humbly accepted the money, at the same time rankling over this unnecessary —but incurable—display of humility before his masters. Privately, he had his own thoughts. At times he was even a little tempted to see Balthazar as a victim of the manor— only a little, but tempted he was.

Balthazar was now departed, the word "departed" being hard to imagine when pronounced by lips that some minutes or years hence would also find themselves among the departed. But the vats belonging to Balthazar's distil-

lery were imaginable, all too tangibly. The people of Pogirai moved them closer to the village and made profitable use of them, and in time they became the cause of much bickering and even accusations of theft, these coming from the family of the deceased. The wild pigs, meanwhile, made good use of Balthazar's garden.

65

BIRCH GROVES in May are light green; framed by dark spruce forests, they give off a light more befitting the planet Venus. In autumn their bright-yellow leaves become shimmering flakes of sun, and the aspen blazes red in the crowns of its chandeliers. Swollen rowan-berries, buff plant hides, and matted leaves on the trails add further color to October in the forests.

They were hunting the place where the hills ran down to the marshland and saw before them slopes heaped up in a multitiered beauty. The morning air was cool, limpid. Romuald curled his hand into a trumpet and called in the dogs: *"Ha lee, toh lee! Ha lee, toh lee!"*

"Ohhhleee"—came the echo.

Thomas stood at his side, relieved of all his doubts and self-torment. They had lost their reality the moment Barbarka had come up to him after Mass and told him that Romuald would be waiting for him a week from that Sunday because that was the day he was planning to take out the hounds. Barbarka. The news of their wedding had been received at home with a shrug of the shoulders and some unflattering remarks, and Thomas, now more than ever, felt uncomfortable around her. Still, Romuald had sent word—nothing else mattered. So there were no bad feel-

ings, it was all his imagination. Romuald's welcome—
"Long time no see! What you been up to?"—was the
clincher.

Thomas was happy. He took in the sharp smells and
his lungs swelled him with a sense of his own power. He
flung back his shoulders, certain that if he jumped, his
resilience would carry him a hundred or two hundred
meters.

He cupped his mouth in imitation of Romuald. *"Ha
lee, toh lee!"*

"Ger gacktracking," Victor stuttered. His finger was
pointing to a glade down below.

The dogs were running in a pack. Lutnia in the lead,
followed by Dunay and Zagray. With no scent to follow,
they were running wild; time to call them off and move on
to other stands.

The world rose up luminous, simple; the chain bind-
ing him to the Thomas obsessed with his own thoughts
severed. Forward, march. He could feel the gunlock on his
Berdan grazing his back, and he reveled in its coolness.
Whatever was meant to happen today was bound to be
good.

To Thomas the future was always a storehouse of
things already prepared, waiting to be fulfilled. It was
gained through premonition, was somehow present in the
body. It even had its own emissaries in certain animals—
the cat, for one, if it happened to cross your path. Above
all, one had to have an ear for that inner voice, to be able
to tell the bright sounds from the dull sounds. But if the
future was already given, if it didn't shape itself as it went
along, free to become whatever it willed, then what was
left to our own willing and endeavoring? That was some-
thing for which Thomas had no answer, knowing only that
he would have to submit to the decrees being ordained
through him and that every step he took was both his and
not his.

Today he was submitting. The voice was full of brightness; it had the ring of crystal. The feet sank into a carpet of moldering leaf, his gun clanked against a ring on his belt; a hush among the pine; a nutcracker, dapple-necked, on the wing; anthills without motion, the movement now shifted to the interior, to kingdoms already giving way to their hibernal sleep. Thomas could have wandered like this for hours—if Romuald hadn't pulled up and, rubbing his jaw, pondered the best route for them to take. Three trails came together; they settled on the one skirting a cliff with a steep drop. In places they had a bird's-eye view of the spruce tops tapering to a point just below their feet; elsewhere the forest, ribbed with ravines trimmed by half-naked hazel shrubs and bright green at the bottom, arched gently down. Romuald stationed Thomas near the edge of one of these ravines and told him to keep a close lookout for any movement on the trail and in the narrow crossing below. As he watched the backs of Romuald and Victor grow smaller, he felt somehow cheated: those who get to keep going always seem to have the best of it.

He stood leaning against a pine trunk. Then he sat down on the ground, balancing his Berdan across his thighs. A crinkling noise—opposite him. He turned in the direction of the rustling and saw a mouse, its tiny nose poking out from its hole under a bedding of roots. With snout comically tilted, it sniffed the air, decided the coast was clear, and took off on the run, blending so well with the buff-colored matting that Thomas soon lost track of it. Another rustle, this one more like a brittle flaking, coming from a neighboring branch, snapped his head back. He rose to his feet and craned his neck: it was a giant spruce, from which a sprinkling of scales fell. Small birds were fluttering in the crown, but except for the fluttering and the flash of a sun-pierced wing he could make out nothing. He circled the tree but without improving his view. It gnawed at him not to know their names; the small ones, just because

they were so hard to identify from a distance, always gave
him the most trouble. Romuald, when asked to name their
species, would brush it aside with a "Aw, who the heck
cares."

He was jolted by the pack, by a sudden surge of
yelping from the interior that rose up like the blast of a
pipe organ in church. Not the voices themselves but a
chorale that launches from the opening bars into its soaring,
swooping pattern made even mightier by the echo. Thomas
gripped his gunstock and kept shifting his gaze from the
russet path to the bottom of the ravine, then back again to
the path. There was no reading any direction in it, in the
baying, in that constant rising and falling, the blending of
which, the accreting of which into a steady, deep-throated
rumble, was so impressive that he gave up trying to locate
it. With Romuald beside him he would have had the mean-
ing of that music, would have had the thrill of it, but on his
own he distinguished nothing, an incomprehensible lan-
guage.

Then it seemed to fade. And with the dwindling of
prospect came the sort of apathy one gets when the figures
all tally and the prospect of a recount palls, when things
are such as to rule out the accidental. The green at the
bottom, the footpath, by their sheer presence, were a de-
nial of some unexpected intrusion. And Thomas was not
mistaken: unsure of the boy's aim, Romuald had posted him
in a spot where there was little likelihood of a killing (he
knew it to be a crossing seldom used by the hare).

Relieved of having to answer to the call of the forest,
Thomas fell to daydreaming. Idle, freed from his hunter's
duty, even gladdened by his leisure, he cleared a hole
among the needles and began carving little furrows in the
ground with the edge of his boot. It was one of those games
of make-believe not altogether compatible with his years:
let this one be a canal, let that one be the river, now an-
other canal over here . . . Meanwhile, the pack continued

its discourse with space, and high above the howling, the wind whistled through the crowns of the tall-timbered forest.

How could he have detected the unfamiliar in their baying, the warning contained in their voices: Beware, beware! No; lost in his daydreams, distracted by his frivolous pastimes, he could not suspect that the verdict had been passed and that a tragedy was in store.

Everything was calculated to make sure the blow struck with maximum cruelty. A hero's confidence. The fear he had long nurtured, the overcoming of that fear, then the acceding to the weakness, to the loving and desiring, without which man would not be vulnerable to fate's wrath; the illusory rejoicing, and the promise that what was suffered once would never be repeated. Without ignorance, there can be no tragedy. But there it was, heading his way—the beaming light of illumination, in whose folds he was now playing idly under the vigilant scrutiny of speechless spectators: a fool, a madman, suspecting nothing, seduced by the magic of sound, furrowing the little trenches of his undoing.

The dogs had jumped a buck. Following the scent, they had described a huge arc, so that the baying now reached Thomas from the valley. He raised his head and fixed absently on the source, too distant as yet to be a warning. Then a bolt of lightning; not that he was jolted by the seeing of it; rather, with his whole body he felt the composition of the ravine suddenly rearrange itself into something new and unknown. Everything came at once: the wonder, the shouldering of the gun, the shot, and the realization: "A buck!"—but in a frenzy, in despair of the outcome, when even as the finger is bearing down on the trigger the mind has thrust upon it the certainty of a miss.

Thomas stood open-mouthed. He had yet to fathom it, the sense of what had happened. A groan wrenched itself from his mouth, the gun angrily hit the ground, every-

thing emptied, and heaving, run through by the cruelty of fate, he dropped down on his haunches.

A breeze rocked the pine's fluffy paws. No more sound came from the dogs. So the idle daydreaming had been a trap. Why, why, when his inner voice had made him so confident? How would he ever bear the humiliation? Only now, under the fingers pressing his eyelids, did the buck—its forelegs tucked, its neck bent back—become a reality. Just one second earlier, just one single second. But it had been denied him.

There was a rustling nearby; out of the scrub came Lutnia, whimpering, her eyes searching his, followed by the other two, bewildered. Their disillusionment—a man had shot and brought discredit to the man—only made it worse. He sat still on the stump, cradling his burning cheeks. A twig snapped under a boot: his judges were coming.

Romuald pulled up in front of him. "Where's the buck, Tommy?"

Not a gesture, not even to look up. "I missed."

"But he was heading straight into your sights. I coulda dropped him myself, but I said, 'Let Tommy have 'im.'"

To Victor, who was coming up the trail, he said: "Tommy let 'im get away."

Every word—a cold blade—stabbed. No escape. He did not dare to look them in the eye. Forced to retreat, to go back into his prison, into the body that had betrayed him and which he could not renounce, he clenched his teeth.

Not a word on the return trip. The trail, its twists and forks so magical a while back, was now a dismal skeleton. What had he done to deserve this? Even worse than the shame was the rancor he bore himself—or God—for having believed in the promise.

When they reached the fork in the meadow, Thomas

said they were expecting him at home, and went his own
way.

"Thomas! The gun!" they shouted after him.

The Berdan had been left leaning against an alder.
Without turning his head, he stuck his hands into his
pockets and tried to whistle.

66

THOMAS WAS going on fourteen when he
made a discovery: after every great disappointment comes
usually a great joy, one to make us forget what the world
was like when there was not that joy.

Asters white with frost. A titmouse takes wing, and
the slender branch, knobbed with minuscule white globes,
rocks. He stands under a pear tree, facing the window of
the room once occupied by Grandmother Dilbin, and in-
hales the tawny, shriveled-up pears on the ground, the
effluvium of the garden's fading. His attention is on the
closed shutters. Too early yet. Or could she be awake? He
slips up to the shutters, carefully undoes the hook, but at
the last moment withdraws his hand.

His latest worry was that, deep down, he was really
unworthy of her. Whenever they sat with the fruit basket
between them, he would deliberately choose the most
bruised apple. In setting the table, he took pains to see that
she got the best plates—there was hardly a dish in the
house that wasn't chipped or cracked; laying out the cut-
lery, he would hesitate, decide his own fork was nicer, and
promptly switch.

Did he feel like waking her? Of course he did, but he
also knew that it would have been selfish of him.

The thresher's fitful grinding echoed from across the pond. He circled around the manor house, bounded up onto the porch, sidestepping the nasturtium seeds laid out to dry, and bumped into Antonina on his way through the kitchen. Years of traipsing back and forth had left shallow depressions in the hallway's plank flooring. He peeked inside the "cloakroom." What about weighing a bundle of cotton to kill time? He took the steelyard down from the wall, knotted the four corners of the sheet on the hook, and slid the brass weight back and forth. The machine managed to distract him, but not for long; he abruptly chucked it and put his ear to the door. Unable to restrain the urge, he pressed down gently on the latch, straining, without allowing any creaking, to open the door a crack for a peek inside. But it creaked, and then came a voice—hers: "Thomas!"

After the last hunt Thomas had taken sick, starting with shivers on the way back. His teeth chattering, he hurriedly undressed and slipped between the cold sheets. To make him sweat, Misia gave him a sudorific of dried raspberries. There was no telling how long he had been nurturing it—perhaps the other morning's false delirium had signaled a fever coming on—or whether it didn't answer to some need. Doubled up, with his chin grazing his knees, he was stricken with one desire: to burrow under the covers, to feel the weight of the quilt and sheepskin on top of him. That was several weeks ago, though it seemed a lot longer.

His mother sat before the mirror, her head tilted to one side, braiding the chestnut hair that had lain on the pillow as Thomas approached in the dark. Earlier he had touched her cheek with his lips and sat down on the edge of the bed, on its side frame. A brooch—or something else that defied closer definition—gleamed mysteriously on her nightstand. Later the shutters were opened, and Thomas stared at her from behind: at the eyes visible in the mirror, slightly slanted, gray, their shading made deceptive by the

light reflected in them; the thick eyebrows that collapsed whenever she laughed and caused the eyes to disappear in the slits between brow and cheekbone.

From his early childhood, he knew of only two incidents involving his mother, and then only secondhand. He had gone over them so often in his mind that certain details had taken on the force of memory, though actual recollection was impossible, since he was much too young at the time.

The "bath" was an open stretch of shaded shoreline along the Issa, access to which was by a footpath dropping down from the fields. His mother had set him down next to the path, was already in the water when she saw a dog, its tongue out and its tail between its legs (rabies was quite common in the district), running straight in their direction. She jumped out of the water and, stark naked, dashed uphill to the park. The hand towel she had snatched up on the run and that had fluttered behind her, the way her panic was transmitted to him, the mouth gasping for air, the wildly pounding heart . . . Did he only imagine these things? He could even see the dog—reddish-brown, with hollow flanks—and hear it panting at their heels. Or were they from a dream?—he was haunted by such fleeing nightmares. Paralyzed, entirely at the mercy of her running, he had been scared stiff that her legs would give out, that she would collapse from exhaustion. This "she" was no more than a sign, bearing no resemblance to the woman in the photograph or to the real person he could now touch any time he liked.

In his talks with her, he kept returning to this childhood incident, and after she had repeated it from the beginning, he would ask: "But the towel. What about the towel?"

"What towel, Tommy?"

The other incident was one he never broached in her presence. He was one and a half at the time and deathly

ill with diphtheria. So close was he to dying that, according to Antonina, his mother had butted the wall and crawled about the room on her knees, wailing and imploring God's mercy. With hands prayerfully raised, she had vowed that if her son recovered she would make a pilgrimage on foot to Vilno, to the shrine of Our Lady of Ostrabrama. Recovery came quickly. But when he later pestered the grownups about her vow, they became evasive. "Well, you see, Tommy, times were rough then, there was a war on . . ." Thus was born the recognition: no pilgrimage. He was reminded of it during her talks, held usually in her room, with Helen and Misia. And what thrilling stories she could tell about her wartime adventures near the front: of how she made it across the border—out in the wilderness, at night, alone with the smuggler who had showed her the route, of how it was so dark she lost the trail, and how, terrified of running into a border patrol, she had hid in the bushes until daybreak— "Really? Honestly, Tekla?" Helen would cut in. But left alone with Misia, she would begin with some condescending remark like "Well, well, that's Tekla for you . . ." implying that she was flighty, whimsical, had wonderful adventures but never any money, and so on. Misia, from her perch by the oven, loved to incite her to more of these prissy complaints, but the woman was too dull-witted to see that Misia was simply having fun at her expense. Thomas, who had never forgotten his mother's broken vow, was deeply wounded by his aunt's insinuations. Maybe she really was the flighty type . . . And then it surfaced, the resentment, born deep down, at having been left behind, alone. The one time he caught himself thinking such thoughts, he immediately confessed to his guilt. To punish himself, he chose the most severe penance—for three straight days he neglected to go into her room to say good morning—most severe because it was bound to create the wrong impression. The next time

he was tempted to sit in judgment of her, he shut his eyes and forced himself to think of how beautiful and courageous she was.

Leaves turned a dark red, the Issa steaming amid patches of rusted sweet flag. From time to time they would harness a horse and drive out to the villages to visit some of his mother's girlhood friends. Pitchers of beer on the table, the puffing of long-stemmed pipes, and the toasting, the children, the hounds, and the flowery green chests, the cheese smells in the vestibule, the buttermilk, the apples, the chickens fluttering in their roosts; the leisure of the village hut at that time of year when the fields have been worked and the farm retreats to the four-cornered sanctuary of the yard; when the mud on the roads spills over the rims and whistles in the spokes; when the tiled stove is fired and to sit at dusk staring at the fire and thinking of nothing is a fine thing; and then the pink turns to rose and you wish it could last and the fire slowly dies and it's not what it was and with the darkness comes a slackening of the will.

The wick of a globe lamp, green on the outside and white on the inside, has to be specially trimmed to keep it from leaving black whiskers on the chimney. Thomas sits doing his lessons; his mother puts aside the sweater on her needles and licks the pencil's lead tip. Her chair next to his, shoulder leaning against shoulder, a ring of lamplight, together, here, while from outside comes the hooting of owls in the orchard.

Still, what has already been cannot be so easily dismissed. One day she asked him what he would like to be. He blushed and lowered his head. "I . . . might become a priest."

She gave him a quizzical look. "Why a priest, of all things?"

"Be-because . . . "

He was swallowing his tears; he couldn't help it. He

was unable to come right out and say, "Because I missed a buck and it makes me sad that you forgot your vow." Besides, that would have been only partly true.

"Because . . . I'm bad."

A priest's surplice gave the one who wore it the right to be different; things expected of others were not expected of him. That was what he had meant to say.

His mother made a face.

"I am."

"What a perfectly silly thing to say."

He turned away and, clenching his teeth, said: "I don't ever want to be alone."

The door opens only once like this: the face above the high-necked gray sweater, the face of a stranger, radiant, beckons, waits, summons; and he, stock-still, confused, suddenly lets out a cry, jumps, and arms enfold—it's *her*. Never again.

Sleep brings peace. She tucks him in and her kiss softly accompanies him into the brushwood of night. Her footsteps fade as, burying his nose in his pillow, he thinks of what he might give her as a present. The bird book? No, that was something of a different order.

"But I do love her, don't I?"

67

IT WAS St. Andrew's Eve, and when the wax was poured, his mother's augury was a garland—flowers or thorns, no telling—and his a leaf that, magnified by the shadow, loomed like the African continent with a cross on top. And then the snows, when people came in blowing clouds of vapor, stamping their feet to shed the glassy stuff,

all the while the Issa's noisy mobile ferment was turning to ice. Christmas that year was celebrated in the traditional way, except that the empty plate which custom dictated be set out for the wayfarer on Christmas Eve was now really intended for a stranger, and not, as in years past, in the secret hope that his mother would show up. Now it was she and not Antonina who, assisted by Thomas, took care of the holiday festivities. It was she who cooked the borscht with mushroom pasties; she who made *slizyki*—sheets of dough rolled up cylinder-fashion and baked until stone-hard. The *slizyki* were served with syrup—a crock of which stood on the table—whose ingredients were water, honey, and ground poppyseed. The dishes served between the borscht and dessert were nothing compared to Thomas's favorite, cranberry pudding, which he ate by the heaping bowlful; and when the feasting finally caught up with him, the hay stuffed under the linen tablecloth in memory of the Christ child's manger made a comfortable little mattress for his elbow. Later, under the Christmas tree, he and his mother joined the others in caroling—she even taught him a few he had never heard. The stable lantern lit, they would set out for Midnight Mass, wading the whole distance through the powdery snow.

Thomas's mother, being a practical-minded woman, decided to sit out the winter in Gine. Crossing the border in the dead of winter was strenuous enough, but there were other reasons for postponing it. Thomas's father, who had been having his ups and downs, mostly downs—the fault of his peregrine, itinerant life—was now living hand to mouth as a municipal clerk. Since Helen had already been given her share in land, Tekla was entitled to something, too. But to raise a cash crop meant waiting for the threshing season and for the market price to rise. Then his mother hit on an idea, one that drew a loud "You're crazy!" from his Aunt Helen: why not smuggle a couple of ponies across the border—the short, stocky Lithuanian

breed was much prized abroad—and make a present of them to her husband. But how, if she barely had made it across by herself, would she ever manage it with *horses*? Rubbish, it would *have* to work.

The border—open only to smugglers, wolves, and foxes for the reason that the Poles thought of the city of Vilno as theirs, while the Lithuanians claimed it as their historic capital illegally seized by the Poles—was a nuisance for many. His mother picked out a pair of horses, four-year-olds, both sorrels with a dark stripe down the back. She was relying on them for the journey home, on luck, and, if they were caught, on the leniency of the border guards (as long as no officers were around).

Window recesses powdered white, a hush except for the steady twitter of bullfinches husking lilac seeds. The prospect of a journey abroad awakened in Thomas an interest in geography. A German atlas, published in 1852, served as his textbook. Because it was so old, his mother had to pencil in the boundaries of certain states, many of which now bore different names. Although the atlas showed neither Ginc nor any of the surrounding localities, something it could easily be forgiven, Thomas became fascinated by maps—by the way the finger went down, and under it were born forests, land tracts, roads, villages, and vast multitudes of people in motion, each distinct, each somehow distinguishable from the other; but how, the moment it was lifted—*poof!* And just as he had hungered for flight, for a higher perspective on those kneeling in church, so now he ached for a magical magnifying glass powerful enough to bring out all that was hidden beneath the paper's surface. The more we devote ourselves to that realm of contours, zones, and lines, the greater our enthrallment. The thrall is as great as when the mind tries to imagine what lies between two numbers. Now, if a map could be drawn to include every house and human, sta-

tionary or in motion, that would still leave all the horses, cows, cats, plant species, fish in the Issa—not to mention fleas on dogs, shimmering beetles in the grass, and ants and many other things. That meant a map was always approximate. Another discovery gained through his map explorations: Seated up here in the chair is one me, but down there under the finger being held on the blank spot that ought to have been Gine is another. I am pointing at myself, at the shrunken me. The second me is not the same as the one up here; down there, it is merely one among many.

The days were getting longer. Grandfather came back from one of his "business trips," flushed with success: he was told that the property division would be approved. In the end, money had spoken louder than Joseph's accusations. The Juchniewiczes were to move in after St. George's Day; as feared, their property was to be parceled.

It was a cold and snowy Palm Sunday—spring was late that year—without a catkin in sight. Blue crowfoots were already pushing up through the rot of last year's debris when it dawned on Thomas that this was to be his last spring in Gine. He took his time scouting the park, finally found the right spot—a rectangular clearing on a slope—dug up a young chestnut, bore it back, and planted it. If he ever came back to Gine, he would run down first thing, locate the clearing, and gauge the tree's growth.

The Issa was still iced, its surface a mirror reflecting cloud banks, but the shoreline was already giving up the first cornet-shaped leaves of a pale green. One day, on the brush-lined trail overlooking the river, he ran into Onutè, companion of his childhood games. He had laid eyes on her several times in the past, but never at such close range and never like this. Stopping in her tracks, she stared at him quizzically, even bewilderedly. She was grown-up. Ducking his head down, with a burning in his cheeks and behind his collar, he passed her with a stern, hard look.

The sternness was a mask, but Onutè could easily have mistaken it for the arrogance of a *pan*, which he nearly was. All this occurred to Thomas much later, long after the danger had passed, and it touched him with sadness.

68

SIX MONTHS after the wedding, a baby son was born to Romuald and Barbarka. The thawing fields already bulged with naked black hummocks when an early April freeze forced them to take the sleigh to church. The baby was christened Witold.

The sky was cloudy, crows cawed in the sallows, and Romuald's red-tasseled parade whip lazily flicked the horse's spine. Barbarka folded back the corners of the plaid shawl: the baby was asleep. They were traveling, naturally, in complete obliviousness of that time designated not only by the return of spring and winter, the waving of ripening grain fields, and the migrations of birds. The earth under their green-lacquered sleigh was not volcanic, did not belch fire, nor was there any cause to think of those floods and conflagrations by which the history of mankind was made.

They had not reached the porch when Witold started wailing. Barbarka laid him in the cradle and, with one hand on the rocker, fixed her gaze on the table already laid out for the reception. Happiness was being the mistress of one's house. Now, when she opened the cupboard doors, she was filled with a sweetness equal to that of the pungent, freshly baked rolls inside. My rolls. My husband. My son. And, let us also note, my floor—whose planks squeaked in

concert with the squeaking of laced-up shoes. Hence the woman's beaming face as the guests began to arrive, as Romuald, wringing his hands, said: "Well, Barbarka, time to serve up, bring on the feast!"

Old lady Bukowski took one look at her grandson and declared a resemblance to her son. This was her way of consoling herself—another was by emptying glass after glass. Night thickened; a thaw wind whistled in the branches. Someone drawn there by the light would have looked in on people laughing, reclining on chairs, and, out in the middle, on dogs—allowed into the house because of the winter cold—scratching their hides. The one scratching his neck with his hind paw, he's thumping the floor—but the sound is muffled by the window.

A wolf on the outskirts of the forest lifts its head in the direction of the well-lighted window and attends to the inscrutable habitat of humans, those creatures forever segregated from what the wolf is trained to understand. Others more cunning than it may also be enticed by the lighted square. But woe if there are any frock-coated devils among them; their interest in what goes on inside human dwellings will not go unpunished. By attaching too much importance to such trivialities, they will never survive an age demanding a sense of proportion. Soon no one along the Issa will testify to having seen one swinging its legs from a mill rafter, to having heard them dancing their jigs. And even if someone were to spread such tales, no one need assent to them.

The thaw wind came from the west, from the sea. Out there were ships, pitching and sounding their horns as they plied the waters between the shores of Sweden and Finland, between the Hanseatic city of Riga and Hanseatic Danzig. But here was Barbarka, changing her son's diapers, holding him by the ankles and lightly tilting the little fanny that always roused her to such tenderness. Such sentiments, like those she had when she offered her son her blue-

veined breast, were not to be transposed beyond the realm of experience proper to them. We are given to live on the border of the human and the bestial, and it is good so.

69

It was around this time that Romuald hired a new farmhand: Dominic Malinowski. Whatever had caused him to leave his native Gine, the reason must have been serious.

They were in the barn, flailing—Dominic and the farmer in whose service he was that winter. The fight might have been avoided, even though it had been building since morning. Dominic was a master of self-control. His mouth was always clamped shut, drawn tight by the holding back of things he would have liked but never was able to say. The more he approached young manhood, the more he resembled a scrawny predatory bird. Many times he had been on the verge of taking this bully of a man by the throat, knowing at the same time the danger of surrendering to his impulses. "Wham!" echoed the old man's flail. "Whack!" answered Dominic's, and so it went, duet-fashion, with the threshing that afternoon. They broke only once, when the old man took out his bad temper on someone in the house. That's how it started.

That someone was a servant girl, the same age as Dominic, whom Dominic thought stupid for letting herself be bullied so easily. That he had taken a liking to her is beside the point; the fact is, he spoke up in her defense. The old man's stubborn, sclerotic pride then got a taste of Dominic's muscle. He held him up by the throat, felt his Adam's apple under his fingers, and hurled him to the

ground, where he lay, groaning. Dominic was already beyond the gate when he heard the outcry.

A moment of triumph. "You won't boss *me* around." He was not yet back at his hut by the ferry when he began to consider all the possible consequences. And consequences there were. His former boss managed to incite the other farmers, including the wealthiest, against him; they made common cause and for a long time Dominic went unhired. Until Borkuny, that is.

Meanwhile, he stayed at home, carving spoons, kneading troughs, clogs—enough to bring in a few pennies every day. His mother would often sit on the bench opposite and follow the agile movements of his hands. "Land," she would say, and her son would raise his eyes to that face scored with wrinkles, to that mouth caught in the cramp iron of deeply engraved folds. It was the same every day: her petition for land under the Reform. "But Joseph said . . ." And: "They're parceling it out everywhere . . ." Dominic hung his head in silence and dug his knife into the limewood with greater intensity than usual. Lost in thought, he brought the knife back toward him slowly, plowing a long groove with the blade.

70

THEY PUT off leaving until June. Thomas's mother had the wagon fitted with a canopy—a hazel bowframe, spread with a tarpaulin—similar to the one on a gypsy's. With a hundred kilometers to go before reaching the border, and another forty on the other side, it would be a shelter from both rain and night. She also got up a good supply of provisions: dried cheeses with caraway, cured

sausage, and black-smoked hams, a favorite of Thomas's father.

The day before, Grandfather showed him into his room, shut the door behind him, sat down, and took to hemming and hawing. He talked of how city people were corrupt, of how one should avoid falling into bad company . . . but when asked how one could tell good from bad company, he broke off with a nasal *pff! pff!*—as if too ashamed to answer: "Well, you know, vodka, cards . . ." —and pulled him to him, and Thomas felt a powerful wrenching as he kissed his bristly cheeks, and then, just as abruptly, his grandfather freed himself and began fumbling in his pockets for a handkerchief.

At breakfast the next morning he blistered his lips while gulping down his tea and left the table without finishing it. He saw the wagon's white tarpaulin framed in the window, overheard the last-minute conversations, and raced outside, across the porch and down the sloping lawn, past the row of blooming peonies. Through a gap in the park trees, the valley rim lay in mist, a sunny day was coming up pink and clear above the dew, birds were singing. He wanted to hold it in his memory. "You'll forget us, oy, you'll forget us," said Antonina when all were huddled on the porch steps and she held his face in her hands, sadly. Misia's cheek smelled of wet rennets. Luke was his usual squeezing, slobbery, bear-hugging self. Then came the blessings, signs of the cross traced in the air. "All right, Thomas," said his mother gravely. Thomas gripped the hardened leather of the reins. Now, at all such partings there comes a moment when someone must do the breaking—and the more abrupt it is, the better. Thomas cracked the whip, wheels clacked, cries went up; looking back over the canopy's canvas cover, they saw, in the shrinking aperture of the lane's green tunnel, a flurry of handkerchiefs and hands in the air.

With reins taut, they eased their way down the rutty,

rain-washed road, and soon a brooding Christ flashed among the dense foliage. Back up the way loomed the granary's outer white wall. Thomas let the horses break into a trot, and without changing stride, they passed the cemetery oaks, under which lay Magdalena, Grandmother, and Balthazar, forever left behind. Gine vanished around the next bend; before them, the unknown.

Later, as the horses began pulling for the uphill climb, the Issa, twining in and out of meadows, shone for the last time. The water of one's native river is sweet in recollection. Muscles rippled under horsehide, and they took the incline, but down on the flats it started up again, the whipping and the cajoling: "Hey, Birnik, you're gonna get it!"

The horses, destined for a new home abroad, far from their native grounds, were named Smilga and Birnik in commemoration of their former owners. Smilga had a reputation for being honest, hardworking—a horse that pulled for all it was worth and never got fat. Birnik was just the opposite: immune to the whip, round as a cucumber, a faker and a shirker. But when it came to climbing, Birnik went at it with a fury: a hill was an obstacle, an offense to his lazy nature, and had to be quickly overcome.

His mother had on a flowery kerchief, the hay seat shaped itself to the sitting, and no sooner were they out on the road than the horses' drinking pail, though well secured, began to clank and something went wrong with the whiffletree. They crossed forest meadows, tails flailing against flies, and steered for the big-lake country, traveling the same route as the one taken by Magdalena in the coffin. An afternoon meal in the shade of an oak, a clean tablecloth spread on the grass. Just before nightfall, they looked down from a high elevation on a new terrain, where as far as one could see there was more water than earth, where lake adjoined lake, peninsulas blurred with isthmuses, and the eye beheld a green archipelago. Then it was downhill,

through foothills and between boulders, some so tall and erect they resembled petrified animals. The haymakers were already at work in the meadows—row upon row of tiny human figures, rocking in unison to a common rhythm. Night lodgings in a fishing village; silence, boats reeking of pitch, and the crunching of oats in feedbags.

The time has come, Thomas, to wish you luck. Your future can only be guessed, for no one can predict how you will be shaped by the world that awaits you. The devils along the Issa have fashioned you as best they could; the rest does not belong to them. But keep an eye on Birnik. He's falling asleep again, slacking off, not knowing that thanks to you his name will one day be worthy of mention. You raise your whip—and here our tale is ended.